Introducing James H. Cone

Introducing James H. Cone

A Personal Exploration

Anthony Reddie

scm press

© Anthony Reddie 2022

Published in 2022 by SCM Press
Editorial office
3rd Floor, Invicta House,
108–114 Golden Lane,
London EC1Y 0TG, UK

www.scmpress.co.uk

SCM Press is an imprint of Hymns Ancient & Modern Ltd
(a registered charity)

Hymns Ancient & Modern® is a registered trademark of
Hymns Ancient & Modern Ltd
13A Hellesdon Park Road, Norwich,
Norfolk NR6 5DR, UK

All rights reserved. No part of this publication may be reproduced,
stored in a retrieval system, or transmitted,
in any form or by any means, electronic, mechanical,
photocopying or otherwise, without the prior permission of
the publisher, SCM Press.

Anthony Reddie has asserted his right under the Copyright, Designs and
Patents Act 1988 to be identified as the Author of this Work

Scripture quotations unless otherwise indicated are from the New
Revised Standard Version of the Bible, copyright © 1989 by the
Division of Christian Education of the National Council of the
Churches of Christ in the USA. Used by permission. All rights reserved.

British Library Cataloguing in Publication data
A catalogue record for this book is available
from the British Library

978-0-334-06108-3

Typeset by Regent Typesetting
Printed and bound by
CPI Group (UK) Ltd

Contents

About the author	vii
Acknowledgements	ix
Introducing James Hal Cone	1

Part 1: James Cone in Context

1	The Theological Persona of James Cone	15
2	The God of Black Theology	36
3	Jesus Christ in Black Theology	57
4	The Church in Black Theology	80
5	Black Theology, Black People and Black Power	97

Part 2: Perspectives on Key Texts

6	*Black Theology and Black Power* and *A Black Theology of Liberation*	121
7	*God of the Oppressed*	139
8	*Martin & Malcolm & America*	157
9	*The Cross and the Lynching Tree*	175
10	*Said I Wasn't Gonna Tell Nobody*	192

Index	209

About the Author

Anthony G. Reddie is Director of the Oxford Centre for Religion and Culture, Regent's Park College, University of Oxford. He is also an Extraordinary Professor of Theological Ethics at the University of South Africa and is editor of *Black Theology: An International Journal*. He is a recipient of the Archbishop of Canterbury's 2020 Lambeth, Lanfranc Award for Education and Scholarship, given for 'exceptional and sustained contribution to Black Theology in Britain and Beyond'.

Acknowledgements

My initial thanks are reserved for Professor James Hal Cone who has been my main inspiration as a Black theologian. This book is about him and is written for him. Of all the books I have written over the years, this has been the most enjoyable to work on. Some of that is the subject matter of course. Writing about one's hero is an unusual but deeply satisfying task. The other reason it has been enjoyable is because it has been written against the backdrop of being part of an extraordinarily gracious and stimulating community of people that is Regent's Park College. I am thrilled to be the Director of the Oxford Centre for Religion and Culture. Since commencing this role, I have enjoyed the fellowship and collegiality of Regent's Park College, a permanent private hall of the University of Oxford. I have loved the intellectual stimulation of colleagues in the college and the wider context of Oxford, with all the many amazing opportunities it affords. I offer this book as a modest contribution to the quest for a more diverse and inclusive world of scholarship. In addition, my thanks go to my good friend and colleague, Carol Troupe, whose wise counsel over the years has kept me focused and on track. I would like to thank my family, particularly my deceased mother, Lucille Reddie, who has always been my inspiration. Thanks also to my father, Noel Reddie, but not forgetting my siblings, Richard, Christopher and Sandra, plus my deceased Uncle Mervin and his widow, my Auntie Lynette, and best of all, my nephew Noah and niece Sasha; the next generation of my family. You are all special people in my life, and without you I would be a lesser human being. Finally, of course, there is God, through whom all things are possible; often making a way out of no way. My gratitude knows no bounds and cannot be expressed in words. Thank you all.

Introducing James Hal Cone

In being commissioned by SCM Press to write this introductory text to James H. Cone, I am deeply aware that this is a peculiar task I am undertaking. At one level, this task is somewhat similar to the other scholarly tasks I have been asked to undertake over the past 20 or so years. So, in one sense, this is another writing task like many others. And yet, it is a task like none other.

This is an introduction to arguably the greatest theologian of the twentieth century, and one of the greatest of all time. Yes, I do believe that James Cone is both of these things. But James Hal Cone is so much more than that for me. He is the sole reason I became interested in academic theology. James Cone is my all-time hero.

I remember Friday 1 June 2018 like it was yesterday. I was in a fairly forlorn mood at the time for a variety of reasons that need not detain us at this juncture, but my mood was changed dramatically when I received an email from Wesley House, Cambridge, where I am a College Fellow. The email stated that I had a letter from the publishers Maryknoll, in the US, that had arrived in the college. Giving the college administrators permission to open the letter, scan it and then email its contents to me, I was overwhelmed to receive news from Maryknoll that I was being requested to endorse James Cone's posthumous final book *Said I Wasn't Gonna to Tell Nobody*.[1]

The fact that this request had come directly from James Cone himself in the final months as he orchestrated the final publication of his long and illustrious career, knowing that he would not live to see this book in print, was, emotionally, too much for me to hold in and I was overcome. To be asked by the great James Cone, via his publisher, to endorse his final book was a rare and special honour. The fact that among the thousands of fans and colleagues whom James Cone could have asked, I was one of the blessed chosen few (approximately 14 people have written endorsements present in the final publication) was a startling realization. I was definitely affected by this moment and the request that preceded it.

In readiness to write my endorsement I was sent an advance copy of the final proofs. As I read the book on train journeys across the country, I found it difficult to contain my emotions as I learned of the hinterland and the 'backstory' to the life of a searing prophet and a theological legend in the making. Make no mistake, there has never been a theologian of the likes of James Hal Cone and it is my hope that through the pages of this book, you will come to see just what a unique theological voice and vision he exerted on the second half of the twentieth century and into the first part of the twenty-first.

We will look in more detail at James Cone's final book *Said I Wasn't Gonna Tell Nobody* in the final chapter of this text. As I read the final proofs of it in the summer of 2018, I can genuinely report that I found the whole process a revelatory one. To read of his early life, his cultural, spiritual and intellectual formation (issues we will address in the first chapter of this book) was to have a private window seat at the human development of greatness.

Black people have done theology before James Cone, but none were like him. Black people have challenged racism, segregation and the corruption of Christianity before James Cone, but no one outlined the desecration of the very nature of Christian theology by the sin of White supremacy as well as he did. Cone effectively created a whole new genre of academic theology. Not many people can lay claim to being the progenitor of a theological movement. There are many who have asserted that the true 'Father' or 'Grand Patriarch' of Black Theology is the Revd Albert Cleage[2] and not James Cone. It is undoubtedly the case that Albert Cleage's first book *Black Messiah*[3] pre-dates James Cone's *Black Theology and Black Power*[4] by a year, and so many consider it to be the first ever Black theology book. Cleage's legacy is not to be dismissed, and his early formulation for a radically pro-Black hermeneutical approach to the Christian faith is one that can claim to be an important forerunner to the later developments in Black theology.

The critical difference between the two, aside from their respective theological abilities (Cleage was a visionary church and community leader, but it cannot honestly be said that he possessed James Cone's intellectual brilliance as a scholar), lies in the trajectory that followed their initial works. Having published *Black Theology and Black Power* in 1969, within a year James Cone had followed it up with *A Black Theology of Liberation*, arguably the first self-articulated, systematic theological text in Black theology.

Unlike Cleage,[5] whose scholarly work largely consisted of popular essays and sermons,[6] James Cone was committed until the very end of his life to the singular trajectory of seeking to deepen and sharpen his intellectual commitment to a freeing notion of the Gospel of Jesus Christ, namely, Black liberation theology. Although some will argue for Cleage as being the founder of Black theology, I am clear, as are most experts in the field, that James Hal Cone is the creator of the academic, systematic structuring of the discipline named Black liberation theology, Black theology for short. This book seeks to explore the theological significance of James Cone and the development of Black theology that emerged from his brilliantly incisive work from 1969 through to his death in 2018.

Restating the Identity of Black Theology

As I stated previously, there were notable Black people who undertook Black theological work before James Cone. Most particularly, one can cite Benjamin E. Mays[7] and Howard

Thurman,[8] as two distinguished, Black, ordained church figures, scholars and thinkers who wrote significant work in defence of Black people. James Cone, like these two great luminaries, along with Martin Luther King (who represents the bridge between the former two and Cone) all emerge from a Black church tradition that has produced great Black church leaders. The Black church tradition in the United States is a particular theological, philosophical and ideological tradition that finds its roots in the epoch of slavery. The existence of racism within American Christianity led to the development of a separate Black church tradition that began in the late eighteenth century.[9]

It is important to understand that while James Cone is an heir of that tradition and emerges from it – growing up in the pre-civil rights, Jim Crow (terms I will explain in Chapter 1) American South, of Bearden, Arkansas – he also revolutionizes it. James Cone is a revolutionary theologian and the emergence and development of Black liberation theology is a theological movement that has revolutionary intent.

I make the distinction between the Black theology that James Cone assists in creating and the earlier Black church tradition because, as we will see, the existing rules and norms of what constitutes 'proper' theology are set aside by Cone. At the time of writing, one is witnessing examples of people purporting to be engaged in Black theology, but what they are exhibiting is an interest in Black church studies. There are aspects of these formative experiences that sow the seeds for my later development as a Black theologian, but to be clear, the Black theology I now espouse is not the same as being a Baptist or a Methodist. James Cone was brought up within the African Methodist Episcopal (AME) church tradition. Clearly, his formation within this historic Black church tradition provides some of the roots of Cone's later theological development but being within the AME church does not make a person a de facto practitioner of Black theology. Similarly, in the British context, traditionally Black-led church traditions such as Black Pentecostalism in Britain are no more synonymous with Black theology than being a Methodist, an Anglican, a Baptist or indeed, any specific or particular church tradition.

In a similar vein, Black Christians who are committed to anti-racist activism do not have to be Black theologians to do so. There is a long tradition of Black Christians being involved in racial justice work, as seen in groups such as 'Evangelical Christians for Racial Justice' and 'Claiming The Inheritance', both based in Birmingham. There is no doubting the importance of these organizations, but this work was not based on the principles of Black theology. As I have written elsewhere, not all theology done by Black people is Black theology, any more than all theology done by women is feminist theology.[10]

As we will see, the Black theology that emerges from the iconoclastic vision of James Cone is a radical and revolutionary understanding of Christian theology that is grounded in and based on the lived experiences of and the existential realities facing Black people in the world. Cone's theological vision is something more than the various Black Christian traditions that exist in the Baptist, Methodist, Anglican (Episcopalian – US Anglicans), Reformed and Pentecostal forms of ecclesiology. Attempts to reduce Black theology to the latter is often a cynical or misguided effort to water down the abrasive prophetic challenge of the discipline for the purposes of rendering it acceptable to church authorities.

In 2020, I was invited by the national coordinator for the Inclusive Church movement[11] to identify five key people whom I think have played an important role in the contemporary development of Black theology, in the UK and across the world. The second of the five was the great Dwight Hopkins, arguably the most important scholar who has followed in the generation behind Cone. In what is a compelling interview Hopkins makes it clear that in the fuller title of 'Black liberation theology', the operative word is not 'Black', but rather, 'Liberation'.[12]

What Hopkins is making clear in this statement is the crucial and critical difference between a contextual theology that represents the religious and cultural experience of a group of peoples, and a theology of liberation that may commence with the latter, but then goes way beyond it in order to critique and transform that experience.[13] That is to say, while all theologies of liberation can be identified as a specific form of contextual theology, not all contextual theologies are liberative. This latter assertion can be seen in the work of Jarel Robinson-Brown, whose 2021 book details the nature of the heteronormativity and homophobia present in aspects of the Black church tradition in the UK, from various sides of the religious spectrum, be it from Black Methodists or Black Pentecostals.[14] The idea that either of the latter represents Black theology without a radical, liberative critique of the existing traditions of either movement, is simply to misunderstand that the operative, orienting word is 'liberation' and not simply 'Black'. To restate, not all theologies done by Black people can be said to be Black theology. Theology by Black people is not Black theology if it does not commit itself to a radical, liberationist critique of existing theological tropes and frameworks that have limited and continue to limit and oppress the Black self, such as heteronormativity and homophobia, as experienced by the likes of Robinson-Brown.

The basic intent of this book lies in the lifelong commitment of James Cone to develop a no-holds-barred, liberationist approach to Christian theology that sought to speak to the continued challenges facing Black people in their daily attempts to be full human beings in a world overshadowed by White supremacy. This was Cone's life work and was something from which he never wavered, irrespective of whether his theological project was in fashion or not.

This book is not a theological biography of James Cone. While I had the pleasure of meeting him several times and even had the privilege of a few private one-to-one conversations with him (he called me Anthony, I called him Professor Cone), I cannot say that we were close friends or that I knew him very well. Rather, this text is an introduction to his theological legacy and the canon of brilliant thinking and ideas he bequeathed us.

James Cone announced himself on the theological scene with his iconic *Black Theology and Black Power* first published in

1969. He left the scene and this mortal coil 49 years later with *Said I Wasn't Gonna Tell Nobody*, published a few months after his death in 2018. This book has been constructed in two parts. Part 1 consists of five chapters and these outline the major theological themes that James Cone explored across the near 50 years of his life as the pre-eminent Black theologian. Chapter 1 starts with an appraisal of the man himself. James Cone was possessed of a particular theological persona. His theological vision never wavered. The fire of his rhetoric was as undiminished and uncowed at the end of his life as it had been in his prime, in the early to mid-1970s, when arguably his greatest work was developed. There are not many people who can attend a reception in their honour and then turn and abrasively critique, even verbally attack their host for his or her failings in the quest for racial justice. Most of us will censor ourselves when in the company of gracious hosts, irrespective of how hypocritical we may think they are. Yet, Cone's predilection for speaking 'Black Truth to White Power' remained undiminished and unaffected by all the bourgeois conventions of being nice to hosts because that is the so-called done thing.

Chapter 2 looks at Cone's understanding of the 'Doctrine' of God. As theology is human speech about God (Cone was always clear that theology was a human enterprise because 'God does not do theology'), it seems right that we begin with Cone's conception of God. The roots of Black theology do not lie in Critical Race Theory or Marxism, although both have offered helpful forms of analysis to the development of the discipline. Rather, Black theology's *raison d'être* lies in the righteousness of God, as a God of liberation. If this latter assertion is not true, then Black theology ceases to exist as a form of Christian theology.

Chapter 3 focuses on Cone's Christology. Although Cone was, in many respects, a conventional Trinitarian Christian, there is no doubting the fact that his work has a strong focus on Jesus Christ. Cone's theology drew a great deal of its power from his focus on Jesus and the model he exemplifies as one who draws alongside those on the margins. All that we are, can and should be, as human beings, is encapsulated in the life, death and resurrection of Jesus the Christ.

Chapter 4 focuses on the nature and the role of the church as the incubator for and the practical expression of liberation in the world. Cone's ecclesiology is the natural expression of his doctrine of God and his identification with the Jesus of history, whose presence continues in the world and within the church, as the Christ of faith. Black theology emerged from Black Christianity in the Americas, which itself was distilled within the collectivism of the Black church tradition, of which Cone was a part.

Chapter 5 concludes Part 1, looking at Cone's understanding of Black people, those who have been racialized as such, and especially the ones who are the descendants of enslaved Africans. What is their relationship to God in Christ and in what ways is their suffering in the world an important conduit for God's revelation in the world? What always struck me, every time I met James Cone, was how his love of God in Christ was never an abstraction or a purely theoretical idea or even a metaphor. Cone loved Black people. Period! He was brought up by, shaped by them, and sought to serve them. Even when not all Black people were loyal to or loved James Cone, he was indefatigably loyal to and loved them, all Black people. Not just the ones who were saved, or the ones who belonged to his ecclesiological branch, but all Black people.

Chapter 6 begins Part 2. This chapter is the first to look at what I consider are the key texts of Cone's theological oeuvre focusing on his first two books, *Black Theology and Black Power* (1969) and *A Black Theology of Liberation* (1970). This is a personal choice and I dare say another of Cone's great fans writing this book may have chosen other texts on which to focus. Given the limitations of words in this book and given that it is an accessible introduction to Cone's work, I have chosen the books that have been key to my own theological development. I hope that my reflections on these books will resonate with the reader, encouraging further exploration into Cone's work across his 49 years as a published writer in the public domain. I believe *Black Theology and Black Power* and *A Black Theology of Liberation* are companion pieces. The first is an explosive statement of intent that acts as an incendiary device against the moribund and desiccated theological and academic scene that confronted James Cone in late 1967/early 1968. This is followed within 18 months by the second work that seeks to put flesh on the bones of the framework he has put in place with the first text. Cone's second book marks the theological maturation of his vision for the academic or scholarly conceptualization of Black theology. These two books are different sides of the one coin.

Chapter 7 focuses on *God of the Oppressed* (1975). I have heard Noel Erskine, one of the pioneers of Black theology in the Caribbean describe this book as Cone's greatest and I am inclined to agree with him. I believe that *God of the Oppressed* is Cone's magnum opus. If one could buy only one Black theology book that contained the very essence of the discipline, then this is that book. Cone went on write other great works, but I do not believe he ever surpassed the brilliance found here.

Chapter 8 focuses on *Martin & Malcolm & America: A Dream or a Nightmare?* (1992), which emerged as a bold restatement of the earlier developments that gave rise to his first book in 1969. *Martin & Malcolm & America* looks at two of the triumvirate of generative figures who helped shape the theological identity of Black theology (the other being the great African American novelist and essayist, James Baldwin). In looking at Martin Luther King and Malcolm X, Cone explores the theological anthropology of Black theology, offering more specific and amplified thoughts on the existential dilemmas facing Black people, in a manner similar to the points outlined in Chapter 5.

Chapter 9 focuses on *The Cross and the Lynching Tree* (2011). This was Cone's last great work, and it occupies the place of the mature flowering of an old master, who summons up one last, herculean effort to distil their greatness. This book had a long gestation. I first met James Cone in 1996, when he came to the UK on a lecture tour in Birmingham focused on The

Queen's Foundation for Ecumenical Theological Education. In the public lecture he gave at Queen's, he spoke about the relationship between the lynching of Black bodies and the crucifixion of Jesus, the latter providing the theological import of the former. Given the visceral nature of the subject matter, it is as if Cone needed to summon all his emotional and intellectual energies across the following 15 years in order to bring this iconic text to life.

Chapter 10, the last of the book, explores Cone's final text, *Said I Wasn't Gonna Tell Nobody* (2018). I have to confess that I thought long and hard as to whether I should choose this text and not, say, *The Spirituals and the Blues* (1972) or his insightful theological biography, *My Soul Looks Back* (1984). Given that *Said I Wasn't Gonna Tell Nobody* is a rushed book, for obvious reasons, and that the latter part of it seems a hurried and less vivid account of his theological development and life than the first part, this text to many will be a controversial choice. I accept that.

My reasons for choosing it lie in the first chapter, the theological identity of the man called James Hal Cone. As I have said previously, James Cone was a particular sort of theologian. We will not see his like again. But Cone was in many ways a very private man. His life was lived through this scholarship and his erudition and not necessarily through personal, reflective material that is more commonly found among practical theologians, for example. So, when Cone opens the doors to his inner thoughts and feelings, there is a sense in which he is offering the reader a final and authoritative glimpse into the back story that gives rise to the legend we witnessed across the latter part of the twentieth century and into the first section of the twenty-first. I have chosen to reflect on *Said I Wasn't Gonna Tell Nobody* because it completes the James Hal Cone story. The book is the best final summation of his life and career, written by the man himself. What better way to end a book than to let the great man narrate his own ending!

I have resisted the temptation to offer book reviews of each of these texts. Rather, I have provided my subjective insights into why I think each respective book matters and why I think people should read it. My choice of texts is personal and not everyone will agree with me. And that is fine!

I trust you will enjoy this introduction to James H. Cone. For those of you who are Cone afficionados, you will find much of what is written in this book unenlightening. You probably know all that is written already. Even if it tells you nothing new, I hope it does remind you of what attracted you to the work of James Cone in the first instance and will propel you to go back to his original works and to reread his unparalleled genius. For those who are not familiar with Cone's work (the primary audience for this book), I hope that it will give you an insight into the greatest theologian of the twentieth century, certainly the most evocative and radical in the last decades of that compelling epoch.

I would not be writing this book or indeed any of my previous books were it not for the inspiration and later, the kind words and tentative mentorship of James Cone. I trust this book does justice to one of my seminal heroes and the primary reason I wanted to become a Black theologian, way back in 1994!

Notes

1 James H. Cone, *Said I Wasn't Gonna Tell Nobody* (Maryknoll, NY: Orbis Books, 2018).

2 See Jawanza Eric Clark, *Indigenous Black Theology: Toward An African-Centered Theology of the African-American Religious Experience* (New York: Palgrave Macmillan, 2012) and Jawanza Eric Clark (ed.), *Albert Cleage Jr. And The Black Madonna and Child* (New York: Palgrave Macmillan, 2016). See also Earle J. Fisher, 'Brother Malcolm, Dr. King, and Black Power – A Close and Complementary Reading', *Black Theology: An International Journal*, vol. 18, no. 3, 2020, pp. 263–87.

3 See Albert Cleage Jr, *Black Messiah: On Black Consciousness And Black Power* (New York: Africa World Press, 2017).

4 See James Cone, *Black Theology and Black Power* (Maryknoll, NY: Orbis Books, 2009).

5 For those wishing to know more about Albert Cleage, see the aforementioned text by Jawanza Eric Clark, *Albert Cleage Jr. And The Black Madonna and Child*. Brief details can also be found –on the associated Wikipedia page, see https://en.wikipedia.org/wiki/Albert_Cleage.

6 See also Albert Cleage Jr, *Black Christian Nationalism: New Directions for the Black Church* (New York: Africa World Press, 1987).

7 See Benjamin E. Mays, *The Negro's God: As Reflected in His Literature* (Eugene, OR: Wipf and Stock, 2010).

8 See Howard Thurman, *Jesus and the Disinherited* (New York: Beacon Press, 1996).

9 See Ann H. Pinn and Anthony B. Pinn, *Fortress Introduction to Black Church History* (Minneapolis, MN: Fortress Press, 2002). See also Alton B. Pollard and Carol B. Duncan (eds), *The Black Church Studies Reader: An Introduction* (New York: Palgrave Macmillan, 2016).

10 Anthony G. Reddie, *Working Against the Grain: Reimaging Black Theology in the 21st Century* (London: Routledge, 2008), pp. 9–28.

11 Inclusive Church describes itself as 'a network of churches, groups and individuals uniting together around a shared vision'. Further details on the movement can be found in the following link: www.inclusive-church.org.

12 One can view Dwight Hopkins' interview and other talks conducted under the banner of 'Inclusive Church' by going to their YouTube channel: www.youtube.com/user/inclusivechurch/videos.

13 For a helpful outline on the development of contextual theologies, see Angie Pears, *Doing Contextual Theology* (Oxford: Routledge, 2009).

14 See Jarel Robinson-Brown, *Black, Gay, British, Christian, Queer: The Church and the Famine of Grace* (London: SCM Press, 2021).

PART I

James Cone in Context

I

The Theological Persona of James Cone

Anyone who had the pleasure of meeting James Cone will not forget that moment. In this chapter I want to illustrate that what made James Cone unique as a theologian in the latter half of the twentieth century and the first quarter of the twenty-first was the way in which he undertook his theology.

On many occasions, especially in the first iterations of what became Black liberation theology, Cone was at pains to state that Black theology was a practical theology. In making this claim, Cone was not meaning to suggest that Black theology adhered to the basic tenets of practical theology as a form or discipline. The latter, although varied in conception and in the way it is expressed, is often perceived as the interplay between theological tradition and the context and the lived experience of religious practitioners.[1] As we will see in the following chapters, James Cone was not a practical theologian in the formal sense. He was trained as a systematic theologian and saw the discipline in very systematic, formal academic terms.

If Cone, therefore, was a theologian whose work focused on the intellectual probing of the formal categories, ideas and theories governing the Christian faith, then what did he mean by asserting that Black theology was a practical theology? A clue can be found in his first book, *Black Theology and Black Power*, as he outlines the social and political context that gave rise to the development of Black theology. Cone writes:

> On the American scene today, as yesterday, one problem stands out: the enslavement of black Americans. But as we examine what contemporary theologians are saying, we find that they are silent about the enslaved condition of black people. Evidently, they see no relationship between black slavery and the Christian gospel. Consequently, there has been no sharp confrontation of the gospel with white racism. There is, then, a desperate need for a *black theology*, a theology whose sole purpose is to apply the freeing power of the gospel to black people under white oppression.[2]

In this quotation, Cone is establishing a clear methodological criterion for Black theology, namely, its relationship to the experience of oppression of Black people in the world. That is to say the starting point or point of departure, if you will, for Black theology is not abstract theory, or developing new and intriguing forms of intellectual thought for their own sake; the essential first step in creating Black theology is existential need. In suggesting that Black theology is a practical form of theology, Cone meant to indicate something of the nature and character of the discipline. The emphasis, for Cone, was always on the need for Black theology to be of practical service to ordinary Black people trying to make sense of the absurdity and often futility of Black life lived in a world run and defined by White supremacy.

Once we understand this basic premise, then we can understand the pressing urgency and impatience often expressed by the man himself when he discussed and debated the necessity for Black theology in contemporary Black life, first in the US, and then in his later work, across the world.

Be careful what you say to Professor Cone!

In order to demonstrate what I mean by the above phrase, let me share with you a true story, from the first occasion at which I met James Cone. This was the spring of 1996 and Cone came to the UK for a lecture. He was invited to Birmingham and the Queen's College (now the Queen's Foundation for Ecumenical Theological Education) by Robert Beckford, at the time Britain's first tutor and lecturer in Black theology. The highlight of the brief visit was a public lecture in the cleared dining hall of Queen's. This was the only room that could house the 200 or so people wishing to see the great man in person.

I was a first-year doctoral student at the University of Birmingham. I had initially come across Cone and his challenging and dazzling intellectual thought four years earlier, when in 1992 I had undertaken a course in Black Christian Studies taught by Beckford on a Tuesday afternoon at Queen's. I had devoured the reading on that course and had ordered his books via the only Afrocentric Black bookshop in Birmingham at the time, Harambee books, on Grove Lane, in Handsworth. There is a generation of scholars outside the US, who through not having direct, first-hand access to the great man, gained our first awareness of James Cone via his books, and his early 1970s picture complete with beard and impressive afro.

I mention the seemingly ephemeral nature of 'his look' because that was very much in keeping with the persona of the man for many of us. James Cone very much looked the part of anti-establishment, radical, revolutionary, Black theologian. This was how a Black theologian *was meant to look*. Nothing prepared us for the older looking, balding man who took to the podium complete with a light, high-pitched voice with the southern African American lilt to it that never faded despite having lived and worked in Manhattan for most of his adult life. The voice seemed at odds with his persona as a 'take no nonsense' Black liberation theologian.

In this public lecture, Cone spoke about the nature of the cross and its connection with Black bodies, the latter often dislocated, dismembered and demonized under the guise of White supremacy. What we did not know, way back in 1996, was that this lecture marked the early seeds of what was to become, arguably, Cone's last great intellectual triumph, *The Cross and the Lynching Tree* published in 2011. Cone outlined the theological significance of the cross and how its symbolic importance, like much else in mainstream, White theological scholarship, had been distorted and disregarded by White people with power.

In one arresting section, Cone gave vivid descriptions of the nature of lynching in the American South in the early twentieth century, juxtaposing that with the analysis of Church historians and biblical scholars on the nature of crucifixion and its impact on the body politic of colonial regimes in the ancient Near East. The point Cone was making was that these two grisly forms of torture were synonymous. Both were not about simply killing people. Human nature has sadly accrued efficient means of simply disposing of 'undesirables'. A spear through the heart would have sufficed in first-century Judea as efficiently as a bullet to the brain in twentieth-century America. Rather, as Cone demonstrates, the cross and the lynching tree are joined by means of their symbolic association with the machinations of White supremacy. In both cases, the apparatus of torture and humiliation was meant to break the spirit and the will of a subjugated people to resist and rebel. The crucial difference between the two is that the cross, unlike the lynching tree, has a paradoxical symbolic power for Black people. Cone explains it thus:

> African Americans embraced the story of Jesus, the crucified Christ, whose death they claimed paradoxically gave them life, just as God resurrected him in the life of the earliest Christian community. While the lynching tree symbolized white power and 'black death', the cross symbolized divine power and 'black life' – God overcoming the power of sin and death.[3]

As Cone detailed the complex theological, symbolic relationship between the cross and the lynching tree, many of us, including myself, sat entranced. However, the visceral moment that most captured my imagination, and which explains the revolutionary brilliance of James Cone, lay not solely in what he said in his scripted remarks, but emerged in his radical response to 'non-legitimate questions' designed to make Black speakers look foolish and inadequate. If there is one salient point of learning I took from that evening, which has remained an undiminished and vibrant part of Cone's theological mythology, it was his abrasive and towering refusal to be humiliated by the blandishments of conventional, White hypocritical civility. This will take some explaining, so please be patient with me as I attempt to tease out the iconoclastic brilliance of the unrelenting desire of Cone to maintain Black self-determination and self-respect when caught in the glare of White normality.

One of the factors all Black academics have to face is the seeming anomaly of our presence as sentient beings who can be considered intellectuals, scholars and thinkers. As Emmanuel Eze has shown, even in the rarefied guild of Enlightenment thinkers, such as Hume and Rousseau, the notion that Black people of African descent could be considered full human beings and worthy of consideration of equality, was at the very least, seriously in doubt.[4]

One of the first lessons I had to learn soon after I had been awarded my PhD in 2000, was that reactions to my scholarly work would always be shrouded within the enveloping gloom of White normality, even by fellow Black people in the audience. On varied occasions, one would be greeted by the classic non-legitimate question. Such questions were often asked by White people, but occasionally Black people and other minority ethnic people also, in which the intent was not to seek elucidation, but rather to instil a measure of humiliation on the Black speaker.

Non-legitimate questions usually commence with an insincere and fatuous attempt to 'butter-up' the Black speaker, then, after a somewhat tortuous detour affirming their agreement with the thrust of what he or she has said, comes the 'sucker punch'. What then emerges is the *real intent of the question.* The real question starts with what I am calling the 'magic but'. Namely, after the flattery, comes the 'but' after which, the real point of the intervention is revealed. A very pointed question designed to accomplish two things: 1. The superiority of the questioner, as they seek to remind the audience that they are every bit as clever as the Black speaker and 2. To remind the audience of the anomaly, indeed the very contradiction, of the Black speaker being equated with the status of an expert.

I have had my fair share of non-legitimate questions from White and Black questioners. These questions take many forms, from the 'I don't believe you know what you are talking about, so I will question the very premise of your talk', to the 'You mentioned points, a, b and c, but to my mind, you completely missed the point, and should have said points x, y and z.' In either case, the Black speaker has to find a way of navigating the intellectual challenge thrown at them. Do you seek to answer such questions, knowing that they are simply clever tactical approaches seeking to undermine you? Or do you ignore them? Or maybe, you try to reinterpret the question in order to remind the audience of *what you actually said and why*.

No one trains you for such moments. You soon quickly learn that being a walking contradiction, namely, a Black intellectual, is such that your presence brings out the worst in your audience. Some responses are more visceral and emotional than they are rational and intellectual. As Willie James Jennings has shown in his brilliant *After Whiteness*, one of the corrosive aspects of the phenomenon of Whiteness is that of mastery and control.[5] The phenomenon of Whiteness that is more than the colour of the skin of those who are racialized as 'White', was an invention of the era of discovery by Europeans as they traversed the world. In their encounter with 'others' who were not White they had to account for the differences between themselves and these new peoples and cultures they were meeting, particularly within the context of colonial expansion and the subsequent growth of empires.[6]

In the more practical theology-oriented work I have undertaken, I have sought to demonstrate how Whiteness can only function fully when it seeks to control those who are deemed as 'the other' (that is, not one of them), by attempting to determine what is acceptable, normal and true.[7]

Subliminally, for many people listening to a Black expert speak is to evoke the sense of 'something not being quite right'. For some Black questioners this means trying to undermine Black speakers, as they attempt to show the predominantly White audience that they are siding with them and not with the person up front, especially if the latter is deemed to be transgressive or subversive. For the majority White questioners (which is often common for theological events whether in church or academy), the subliminal sense of 'how can this Black person possibly be an expert and know more than me' is often evoked. In either case, the Black speaker is subject to forms of linguistic entrapment that are rarely thrown at White speakers.[8]

So, what has all this got to do with James Cone? Well, it was from James Cone that I learned the importance of how one occupies the space in which scholarly and intellectual work is taking place. That it is not sufficient to write as an iconoclast radical, and then offer up the posture of a passive and apologetic respondent when confronted with the self-evidently arrogant persona of Whiteness. Rather, how one did theology as an embodied person was as significant as what one was doing in that theological work. Cone's persona as a Black person with whom liberties could not be taken was central to this theological brilliance. I believe he offered a dramatic template for all Black theologians who followed in his wake, plus those from other academic disciplines.

So, back to the story: James Cone has concluded his lecture. Now it is time for the Q&A. A range of questions come from the large audience. One of the worst is from a Black pastor who is doing his postgraduate studies at the nearby University of Birmingham. He is an enthusiastic and aspiring scholar, but he is up against one of the greatest theologians of the twentieth century. I am convinced that if he were asking the question of a White man of Cone's ilk, his question would have been a more genuine one than the barely coded non-legitimate version he subsequently asked. The question was couched in the form of 'I've studied White academic theology for the first time and in order to show myself correct and acceptable to the many White people in the audience, I am going to remind them of how unorthodox and incorrect you are compared to the White people I have been studying in class.' The question is then posed. The respondent asks why Cone made no mention of St Anselm, Peter Abelard or Thomas Aquinas in his reflections on Christian atonement and didn't this demonstrate an unhelpful approach to Christian theology in ignoring such important sources?

A written text like this cannot hope to do justice to the nature of this encounter. The question itself was not an aberrant or incorrect one. Anselm, Abelard and Aquinas are indeed central figures in the development of Christian thinking on atonement theologies. The issue was not so much the nature of the question but the sly accusatory way in which it was posed. That is, it was done in such a way as to demonstrate the competence of a fledgling student and to expose the illegitimate position of a Black intellectual. I have no doubt that this question would have been framed in a more respectful manner if the speaker had been a White man or woman, especially the former.

Cone's response was a case study in the slow, enveloping discharge of prophetic rhetoric. It began with an acknowledgement that he was aware of these figures – this was, after all, the Charles A. Briggs Distinguished Professor of Systematic Theology at the prestigious Union Theological Seminary in New York City. Warming to his task, he threw back a rhetorical question to the respondent, asking why it was that his initial question was one that seemed to ignore the realities of Black suffering? Why would a Black pastor, a fellow descendant of enslaved Africans, feel the need to refer to White scholars whose writings had nothing at all to do with Black suffering? The audience was aghast, and the respondent was silent.

At this juncture, having made his point so tellingly, to the extent that the respondent was silenced in embarrassment (something many a speaker dreams of doing to one's supposed adversaries), many of us would call a halt to any further rhetoric. The point has been made, the mastery and credentials of the Black speaker have been maintained. But not Cone. It seems to me that the issue for Cone was not simply the need to stake a claim as to the authenticity and legitimacy of being an expert in a Black body – the issues at stake were deeper. The crucial question was one of dignity for *our people*. As I will discuss shortly, for Cone, the vocation of being a Black theologian was a multifaceted one. I recall a conversation we had over ten years ago when he took the time to mentor me over a cup of coffee at the American Academy of Religion.

The question of dignity and respect are ones that are central in the reflections and faith-based activism of Black people over several centuries. If one reads Cone's final book, his theological biography *Said I Wasn't Gonna Tell Nobody*, one will see that the whole book is replete with statements pertaining to the need for Black theologians to proclaim their sense of self respect and dignity. Central to Cone's intellectual development was the need to establish the status of Black theology as a legitimate scholarly discipline and the Black theologian as a purveyor of scholarly truth, every bit as legitimate as one's White counterparts.

So, in turning on this respondent, in what became an avalanche of scorching rhetoric, Cone was seeking to describe and declaim every aspect of what it meant to be a public intellectual in a world that has assumed such roles as the sole preserve of White people, especially privately educated ones. Cone continued his intellectual attack. Why was this Black man so concerned about what White people thought? White people, in a largely White tradition, defined by White standards that cared nothing for Black people. Why was he so concerned to seek answers to questions that no Black person had ever asked? At what point in Christian history had any oppressed Black person ever thought about the writings of St Anselm or Thomas Aquinas as they sought to make sense of their suffering?

Many, who like me have had the pleasure of watching James Cone in full flight, throttle open and his foot firmly on the gas, will know that it is a sight to behold. Undoubtedly, there was a sense of playing to the gallery here, but one could not doubt the sincerity of his words or the forceful intent with which he made his point. To quote Cone from *Said I Wasn't Gonna Tell Nobody*, speaking of his early writing between c.1968 and 1971:

> I wasn't writing for rational reasons based on library research; I was writing out of my experience, speaking for the dignity of Black people in a white supremacist world. I was on a mission to transform the self-loathing Negro-Christians into black-loving revolutionary disciples of the Black Christ.[9]

I think the force of Cone's rhetoric was, in part, inspired by the indignities of a Black respondent seeking to embarrass a Black speaker for the sake of wanting to look acceptable in the eyes of White supremacy. I suspect that Cone saw this Black respondent as a 'self-loathing Negro-Christian'. The fire of Cone's attack was spectacular and, if truth be told, a little hyperbolic. This questioner was clearly no match for Cone and yet Cone pummelled him intellectually into the ground.

Afterwards, a number of us fledgling, young Black scholars continued to discuss the lecture long after Cone and many others had left. We stood huddled in the Queen's College car park discussing the events of the evening. Opinion was mixed, not on the brilliance of Cone's ideas, but on his response to the Black pastor who had unfortunately ignited Cone's indignation. I thought Cone's response, if a little harsh, was nonetheless acceptable, given the unremitting Whiteness of the room. We all loved his combative response to another non-legitimate question from the Principal of the college who wondered if Black power was no better than White power, and whether Cone was guilty of exaggeration in his claims that 'White Christianity was in league with the anti-Christ'. Cone gave short shrift to such thoughts. His response was a foreshadow of the words and sentiments that emerged later in *Said I Wasn't Gonna Tell Nobody*.

> White Supremacy ... is the AntiChrist in America because it has killed and crippled tens of millions of black bodies and

minds in the modern world. It has also committed genocide against the indigenous people of this land. If that isn't demonic, I don't know what it is. White supremacy is America's original sin. It is found in every aspect of American life, especially churches, seminaries, and theology.[10]

In a follow-up riposte, Cone challenged the Principal to identify one part of the world that would not now be better off if White people had not travelled there and interfered in their affairs. The defiant tone in which the question was asked, alongside the withering response to the earlier Black respondent, convinced the Principal that discretion was the better part of valour, and so he wisely declined to respond to Cone's challenge.

The divide among the group regarding Cone's posture to the Black respondent in many respects said more about us than it did about him. The more critical voices against Cone thought his response was 'unworthy' of a respected Black academic. Why did he have to be so harsh and seemingly cruel to this Black pastor? Why did he not offer a more emollient response and then chastise him in private? Such protestations owe more to the 'respectability politics' of middle-class aspirational Mission Christianity, into which most Black people of African descent living in the UK have been socialized. Mission Christianity is the model of Christian faith that was exported across the British empire by White missionaries, and deep within it is the embedded belief that becoming a disciple of Jesus Christ is about Black people conforming to the cultural, genteel norms of White British people. It is the religion that seeks to 'civilise the native and the heathen',[11] converting them not only to Jesus but to the values of Whiteness and Britishness. Respectability politics is the outworking of this historic feature of Mission Christianity, in which Black Christians are acutely concerned with looking respectable in the eyes of White people and being acceptable to the broader social mores and cultures that define White normality, whether in Britain, or North America, or many other places where Whiteness prevails.

I remember making a spirited defence of Cone at the time,

stating that he didn't care about being respectable. His was a revolutionary form of scholarship and persona that was intent on tearing up the rules of White respectability. Cone, in his earliest work, *Black Theology and Black Power*, makes it clear that he has no interest in adhering to the hypocritical strictures of White cultural norms and notions of acceptable behaviour. When White people can be silent for so long in the face of Black suffering (it took the visceral sight of George Floyd being murdered before our very eyes for many White people to be awakened to the existence of structural racism), it begs the question as to why and how they get to dictate what is or is not acceptable.[12]

Given that Cone was never interested in what White people thought about him, it seems incongruous, therefore, to subject his theological works and life to the skewed normative frameworks of a White tradition that has shown scant regard for Black bodies. I remember at a subsequent meeting of the national Black Theology forum that met at the Queen's Foundation,[13] a leading Pentecostal scholar who purports to be a Black theologian posed the question 'Is James Cone saved?' I was aghast at the question. Of all the things one could ask James Cone, pondering how we would equate his immortal soul with the divine within the dictates of White evangelicalism would not be one of them. My withering retort was 'saved from what and for what and by whom? A White Jesus?'

To understand the radicalism of James Cone one has to appreciate the revolutionary nature of both his work, but also his personal credo as a Black liberation theologian.

How to position oneself as a Black theologian

One of the most poignant moments in my scholarly development was the occasion of the American Academy of Religion in 2006 in Washington DC. I was sat near the back of a Black Theology group meeting at which papers were being discussed and I was conversing with a doctoral student. I was speaking

THE THEOLOGICAL PERSONA OF JAMES CONE

about having been asked to lead a workshop at an ecumenical theological conference back in the UK in the New Year. Little did I know that the great man was sat behind me listening casually to our conversation. At the end of the meeting, as we got ready to depart, James Cone asked if he might have a word in private. The two of us went for coffee and the great man gave me a one-to-one mentoring session encouraging me as a still relatively fledgling Black theologian in the UK.

The two pieces of invaluable advice he shared with me were:

1. Do not get deflected from your vocation as a scholar in Black theology. This advice was amplified when I told him that one could count on one hand the number of authentic Black theologians committed to liberation in the UK. He was fierce in his insistence that I build on the promise I had shown thus far in my early published work. His argument was that I should 'only do those things that *literally* needed me to do them, because if I didn't then they would not get done!' That meant my resignation from the plethora of Connexional (National for want of a better word) committees in the Methodist Church (of Great Britain) on which I sat. It wasn't that this committee work lacked importance, but as Cone accurately surmised, the collective enterprise of governing the Methodist Church didn't need me to be there for it to happen. Yes, my presence might help the process, but my absence would not prevent that work from taking place. Yet, with the exception of a handful of people, my writings in Black theology in Britain are often the only texts of their kind. Cone was absolutely correct about not dissipating my energies. I am not aware of Cone sitting on many academic committees or undertaking other forms of representative work. For him, his energies were focused purely on the scholarly task of producing scholars and communicating his passion for Christian theology and the task of the theologian in aiding the church to be a prophetic sign of God's righteousness and justice.

2. Of equal importance were his strictures on how I should engage with White theologians and the White academy in the UK. He spoke directly to my being asked to lead a workshop at this major ecumenical event the following year in 2007 in the UK. He asked who were the keynote speakers. I gave their names. He enquired if they had shown any expertise in radical liberative work critiquing issues of 'race' and White supremacy. I said absolutely not. Cone admonished me for considering accepting a subordinate position within a theological event at which all the keynote speakers were White and among whom there was no semblance of any commitment to radical justice issues, certainly as they pertained to Black people. I was advised not to attend an event as a guest if I were not guaranteed parity with my White colleagues, given the nature of my scholarly achievements to date. Cone reminded me of the not-so-subtle ways in which White people and White institutions will invariably see Black people as inferior to themselves.[14]

The character of James Cone matches that of Black theology

I want now to illustrate how James Cone's persona and how he thought about himself as a Black theologian has had an important influence on the development of the discipline itself. As Andre Johnson has demonstrated, James Cone's persona is not an anomaly. It emerges from a long African American prophetic tradition that finds its moorings in the epoch of slavery.[15] While there is a long lineage of both prominent and invisible Black women and men within the African American prophetic tradition that exemplify the radical approach to the Christian faith, seeking to speak Black truth to the often corrupt and vicious nature of White power, Cone himself would often cite the example of his own parents as his primary teachers. In his 1999 theological reminiscences entitled *My Soul Looks Back*,[16] Cone reflects on the significant developments in his social, political and religious consciousness growing up in Bearden, Arkansas. There is no doubting the influence of his parents, but especially his father Charles (Charlie), on the young Cone, in terms of his righteous courage in standing up to the absurdities of White supremacy in the American South.[17] Speaking of his father, Cone states:

> My father prided himself on being able to out-think white people, to beat them at their own game. His sixth-grade education was no measure of his quick, substantial intelligence. That was why he walked and talked with such confidence, and also why he managed to avoid much of the dehumanizing climate of the black–white social arrangements. For example, he refused to work at the sawmills and other factories in and around Bearden because he contended that a black person could not keep his or her dignity and also work for white people.[18]

The influence of Charlie Cone exerted a strong lasting impact on the social, political and theological development of James Cone. Emerging from such radical roots, James Cone represents the critical role of the prophet. His is the challenge of speaking into existence those aspects of the faith that have yet to be concretely realized within the collective life of a people, be it within the church or within the wider society. As I will demonstrate in a later chapter, the nomenclature of *liberation* and the belief in the central identity of the gospel of Jesus as being defined by liberation, is one that owes more to James Cone than any other theologian. Prior to Gustavo Guttierez publishing his iconic *A Theology of Liberation*,[19] James Cone had written (to my mind) his first great book, *A Black Theology of Liberation* (1970),[20] which outlined a defiantly radical conception of the Christian faith through the lens of the wretchedness of Black suffering that made a no-holds-barred case for the liberating nature of the gospel of Jesus Christ. In the previous year, Cone had boldly stated that the Black Power movement of angry, militant, sometimes armed young Black activists was analogous to the gospel and indeed was more in keeping with Jesus Christ's message of liberation and justice than the pietistic and passive hypocrisy of the White church in America.[21] Indeed, such was the prophetic and inflammatory nature of Cone's assertions that fellow Black theologians such as J. Deotis Roberts rejected it, on the grounds that the Black Power movement was un-Christian.[22]

Yet, as Andre Johnson explains, Cone's scholarship was a blatant challenge to the existing status quo, shaming the church into meaningful existence with the horrid realities of the world, in which White supremacy was the ultimate scourge for Black and all peoples of colour. Johnson writes:

> However, Cone does not only offer prophetic recall to the White church—he does so of the Black church as well. Cone reminds his audience the Black church was born out of slavery and many saw the church as a place where community developed and where people shaped their identities. Also by not accepting the 'white man's interpretations of Christianity,' Black people gave birth to the spirituals and other coping mechanisms that helped them sustain life on this side of eternity.[23]

As the grand architect of Black theology, Cone's indefatigable love for Black people and his complementary love of Jesus and the prophetic tradition that emerges from his life, death and resurrection (more of which in the following chapter), helps to shape the identity and trajectory of the discipline. Black theology *is a theology of liberation*. As Dwight Hopkins has demonstrated, no liberation theology of whatever kind is worthy of the name without a commitment to the liberation of the poor and oppressed.[24] In short, Black theology without a commitment to the human liberation of all persons condemned to the margins as non-beings, is an oxymoron. Church theology, be it of the historic kind found in White majority Christian denominations in the UK or in Black Pentecostalism, is not to be equated with Black theology. Church founders,

THE THEOLOGICAL PERSONA OF JAMES CONE

be they John Wesley or Selwyn Arnold, are not liberation theologians.

James Cone's genius was to help create a mode of Christian theology that broke the mould of conventional theological production in the US and across the world. Cone's own persona and character underpin the radical expression of his theological work that remains as biting and challenging today as it did when it first surfaced over 50 years ago.

Those of us who had the privilege of meeting him (many of my friends and colleagues had the added gift of studying with him), in addition to reading his many books, will testify that the man and the work were very much synonymous. Cone's priceless ability to speak Black truth to White power is the essential quality that has defined the very best of Black theology, whether it is undertaken in North America, the Caribbean, Latin America, South Africa, Great Britain or in the Pacific. Indeed, wherever 'darker people'[25] are marginalized and oppressed, the legacy of James Cone and the radical style of his work will be in evidence.

The genius and courage of James Cone was to continue calling out the complacency of White people for their serial failures to deal with White supremacy. His work, like his persona, remained edgy, irascible but always compelling and to the mark, in terms of calling people to account for their commitment, or lack of, to the radical challenge of the cross of Jesus Christ.

I want to conclude this first chapter with some further words from Cone. Writing on the continued evasions of White theologians to engage seriously with the issue of 'race' and racism, Cone writes:

> White North American and European male theologians hardly ever mentioned the sin of racism in their public lectures and writings during the 1960s and 70s. They wrote mostly about the 'death of God' controversy and the secular spirit that created it. It was as if they were intellectually blind and could not see that White supremacy was America's central

theological problem. They engaged Latin Americans on class contradictions, talked to feminists about gender issues, and dialogued with Jews about Christianity and anti-Semitism. However, when the time came to talk about theology and racism, they initially could not believe that we had the audacity to engage them in a serious intellectual discussion about theology and its task. What could Blacks possibly know about theology? When we refused to be intimidated by their intellectual arrogance, they tried to convince us that 'race' was of secondary importance to class and would be automatically eliminated when justice is achieved in the political economy. When we rejected that view as faulty and racist, they walked away as if we were too emotional and insufficiently intelligent to understand their sophisticated, theoretical analysis.[26]

I would imagine that nearly every Black and womanist theologian has encountered the dynamic James Cone lays out here. That is, most White Christians and theologians will talk about anything but 'race' and the nature of their Whiteness and the privileges accrued by the latter, even the most basic privilege of not having to talk about it.[27] In countless places and spaces, I have seen attempts to talk about race, racism and Whiteness morph into hitherto unexpected concern of inter-faith dialogue, class analysis, the needs of poor White people, the sexism of James Cone (the latter was a comment by a leading White feminist on Facebook on the death of James Cone), disability issues and concerns around modern slavery. Now, to be clear, all these areas are valid ones for debate and action, but much like the parasitical nature of the 'All Lives Matter' movement, none of these issues seem to warrant any extensive conversation *until the issue of race, racism and Whiteness is mentioned.*

James Cone's own persona alongside the brilliance of his thought and writing has helped to shape the nature and identity of Black theology. In the next chapter I will look at Cone's understanding of God and how this formed the central basis for the articulation of a God of the oppressed.

Notes

1 There are many texts detailing the nature and intent of practical theology. A helpful introduction is Kathleen A. Cahalan and Gordon S. Mikoski (eds), *Opening The Field of Practical Theology: An Introduction* (Lanham, MD: Rowan and Littlefield, 2014).

2 James H. Cone, *Black Theology and Black Power* (Maryknoll, NY: Orbis Books, 1989), p. 30.

3 James H. Cone, *The Cross and the Lynching Tree* (Maryknoll, NY: Orbis Books, 2011), p. 18.

4 See Emmanuel C. Eze (ed.), *Race and the Enlightenment: A Reader* (Oxford: Blackwell, 1997).

5 See Willie James Jennings, *After Whiteness: An Education in Belonging* (Grand Rapids, MI: Wm. B. Eerdmans, 2020), pp. 23–156.

6 See Willie James Jennings, *The Christian Imagination: Theology and the Origins of Race* (New Haven, CT: Yale University Press, 2010), pp. 1–10.

7 See Anthony G. Reddie, *Theologising Brexit: A Liberationist and Postcolonial Critique* (Abingdon: Routledge, 2019), pp. 13–37.

8 I will concede that because of the presence of patriarchy and sexism, there is a sense in which White women will face some aspects of this kind of questioning of their authority, but I would counter this with the observation that their experiences are not analogous to those of Black women. Plus, there have been many occasions when White women have also been the source of non-legitimate questions. As Jacquelyn Grant, one of the architects of womanist theology, has shown, historically White women are more 'White' than they are 'women' when placed within the hierarchy of power and acceptability in many White-majority contexts like North America. See Jacquelyn Grant, *White Women's Christ and Black Women's Jesus: Feminist Christology and Womanist Response* (Atlanta, GA: Scholar's Press, 1989).

9 James H. Cone, *Said I Wasn't Gonna Tell Nobody* (Maryknoll, NY: Orbis Books, 2018), p. 92.

10 Cone, *Said I Wasn't Gonna Tell Nobody*, pp. 53–4.

11 See Carol Troupe, 'Engagement with Mission Magazine Archives: A Black Laywoman's Perspective', in *Black Theology: An International Journal*, vol. 19, no. 2, 2021, pp. 101–21.

12 Cone, *Black Theology and Black Power*, pp. 23–30.

13 Crucial in the development of Black theology in Britain has been the role of the monthly Black Theology in Britain Forum, which began in 1992. The forum has met on the last Wednesday or Thursday of the month since that time. The early leaders of the group were Emmanuel Lartey, George Mulrain and Robert Beckford. The format

of the monthly forum in Birmingham has changed very little since its inception in the early 1990s. While the venues have changed over the years, moving from The Centre For Black and White Christian Partnership to the Graduate Centre for Theology and Religion in the University of Birmingham, and now to the Queen's Foundation (for Ecumenical Theological Education), the Forum remains committed to the articulation of Black theological conversation. I chaired the Forum from 2004 to 2012. The current chair is Dr Dulcie Dixon McKenzie. For further details on the work of the Black Theology Forum see Anthony G. Reddie, *Black Theology in Transatlantic Dialogue* (New York: Palgrave Macmillan, 2006), pp. 160–5.

14 In February 2010, the Methodist Church discontinued my funded research fellowship at the Queen's Foundation without any warning, or transparent process of evaluation or appeal at the decision. In August 2012, the Queen's Foundation made me redundant, despite the fact that the Methodist Church was committed to pouring millions of pounds into the site and intended to expand the staff – but there was no place for me. Over the next two years I applied for several academic jobs in British universities and on several occasions, despite being the author of over 15 books and editing the only academic journal in Black theology, I was overlooked in favour of White scholars, some of whom had only just been awarded their PhDs. It was during these lean and dispiriting years that the indefatigable energy and example of James Cone kept me going.

15 See Andre Johnson, 'The Prophetic Persona of James Cone and the Rhetorical Theology of Black Theology', in *Black Theology: An International Journal*, vol. 8, no. 3, 2010, pp. 266–85.

16 See James H. Cone, *My Soul Looks Back* (Maryknoll, NY: Orbis Books, 1999), pp. 17–40.

17 Cone, *My Soul Looks Back*, pp. 19–24.

18 Cone, *My Soul Looks Back*, p. 19.

19 See Gustavo Gutiérrez, *A Theology of Liberation: History, Politics and Salvation* (London: SCM Press, 2001 [first published in 1973]).

20 See James H. Cone, *A Black Theology of Liberation* (Maryknoll: Orbis Books, 1970/1990).

21 See Cone, *Black Theology and Black Power*, pp. 62–90.

22 Cone, *Said I Wasn't Gonna Tell Nobody*, p. 90.

23 Andre Johnson, 'The Prophetic Persona of James Cone', p. 277.

24 Dwight N. Hopkins, *Head and Heart: Black Theology, Past, Present and Future* (New York: Palgrave Macmillan, 2002), pp. 53–74.

25 See the co-edited work of Dwight N. Hopkins and Marjorie Lewis, *Another World is Possible: Spiritualities and Religions of Global Darker Peoples* (London and New York: Routledge, 2014).

26 See James H. Cone, 'Theology's Great Sin: Silence in the Face of White Supremacy', in *Black Theology: An International Journal*, vol. 2, no. 2, 2004, pp. 139–52 (143).

27 I make this point in one of my previous books. See Anthony G. Reddie, *Is God Colour Blind?: Insights from Black Theology for Christian Faith and Ministry* (London: SPCK, 2010/2020), pp. 37–51.

2

The God of Black Theology

God is real

In his second book, *A Black Theology of Liberation*,[1] James Cone says this about God: 'The reality of God is presupposed in black theology.'[2] The important thing to say about this statement is that James Cone was in some ways quite orthodox or conventional in his theological outlook. Whereas 'aspects' of liberal theology have questioned whether God exists, or if God is merely an extension of human consciousness with no independent life or existence beyond human thought, James Cone was in no doubt that God was real. The presupposed nature of God did not lead to anti-intellectualism or to lazy or sloppy thinking. On the contrary, Cone goes on to say:

> Black theology is an attempt to analyze the nature of reality, asking what we can say about the nature of God in view of God's self-disclosure in biblical history and the oppressed condition of black Americans. If we take the question seriously, it becomes evident that there is no simple answer to it. To speak of God and God's participation in the liberation of the oppressed of the land is a risky venture in any society. But if the society is racist and also uses God-language as an instrument to further the cause of human humiliation, then the task of authentic theological speech is even more dangerous and difficult.[3]

There is much to unpack in this statement because, in many respects, this quotation contains many, if not all, of the essential ingredients to be found in Cone's recipe for talking about God and God's nature as it applies to Black theology.

For Cone to say that God is *real* is to presuppose the existence of God as an active participant in the world and most crucially, in human history. For Cone, the God of the Bible (and we shall say more about this later in this chapter) is also the God of history, in that the actions of the former are consistent with those of the latter. As we will see, the key characteristic of God for James Cone and Black theology is that of 'liberation'.

A God of liberation is seen to be active in the Hebrew scriptures (often traditionally known as the Old Testament) and the Christian New Testament. God who is the same yesterday, today and forever, can be known by the deeds this God has undertaken.[4] For Cone, God is not merely a good idea. A good idea might well inspire people to fight for change, but a good idea is not necessarily real and whether a good idea possesses the resources to empower and transform people to fight sacrificially, for radical change, is open to doubt.

The God of Black theology is not a metaphor or an organizing principle. When exploring the social context out of which Black theologians undertake their theological work, Cone is clear that all theology is done within particular context and social reality. The depth of Black suffering and oppression means that a God who is not in the business of liberating those who are socially marginalized and oppressed is no God at all.[5] Not only is God real but this God is not disinterested or oblivious to the suffering of God's people. Once again, the biblical witness to God's saving acts is clear as to the character of God. Cone writes, 'The God in Black theology is the God of and for the oppressed, the God who comes into view in their liberation. Any other approach is a denial of biblical revelation.'[6]

Cone's assertion that God is real finds expression in his own faith formation as a child of one of the historically Black denominations, the African Methodist Episcopal Church (AME). Cone's formation within this Black church tradition was one that provided him with the resources of faith that would be later supplemented by his acute theological thinking.[7]

Cone held to the famous dictum of St Anselm that theology was 'faith seeking understanding'.

A God that is real is not so much a philosophical treatise for Cone as an experiential and visceral reality. Namely, that the lived experience of the suffering of Black people testified to the nearness and the realness of God. In one of my early books, I outline how, for the Black working class communities of the Windrush Generation of post-World War Two Caribbean migrants to Britain, the realness of God and the experience of God's mercy and support, expressed in the person of Jesus and the witness of the Holy Spirit, is what kept many of them going.[8]

The fact that Cone's doctrine of God assumed God's involvement within human history did, of course, present many problems. One advantage of holding to a view that God is a metaphor, or simply an idea that generates action by human beings, is that one cannot expect such a God to be active in terms of overturning evil that leads to human suffering. But, if one believes in a God who is actively on the side of the oppressed, then the ultimate theological challenge arises when one has to account for the existence of evil and suffering in the world.

One of James Cone's most trenchant critics was William R. Jones who, in his masterful book *Is God A White Racist?*,[9] critiques Cone's presumed theism. Jones argues that Black theologians have 'compounded the confusion of an already inscrutable mystery' by assuming uncritically classical, Western constructions of 'God' for their proclamations concerning God's political allegiances.[10] Jones' challenge to Cone to evidence the nature of God's allegiance to Black people as the God of the oppressed still represents one of the continuing seemingly insoluble problems facing many Black theologians who have followed in his footsteps, including this author.[11]

Jamall Calloway provides an excellent summary of the ongoing challenge presented by William R. Jones to James Cone's continued belief in God's divine identification with Black suffering and oppression.[12] In summary, to argue for the existence of a God who possesses the characteristics of being sovereign, with the power to act in human history, one has to account for why Black people (and other marginalized and oppressed peoples) still suffer. Either an active and real God can change things but chooses not to (hence, Jones' memorable phrase 'Is God a White Racist?') or God has no intent to identify with a particular experience of humanity (meaning that he is not a God of oppressed people) or, even more startling, possesses no power to intervene in human history. As Calloway demonstrates, Cone spent the best part of 50 years trying to wrestle with this theological conundrum.[13] Calloway emphasizes that the faith of the Black Christian is the only relatable response Cone can make to the criticism outlined by Jones. He states:

> Jones is an internal critic whose rational critique led him to a Black humanist perspective, a perspective that is inherently a part of Black liberation theology. Nevertheless, for Cone, suffering is defeated through an acceptance of an understanding of Biblical Christology. Jesus' death and resurrection functions as the decisive event for which Jones was searching. Cone slightly rectifies this argument in his first memoir but completely rectifies it in his second and final memoir. Cone reduces his Christological defense of suffering in *My Soul Looks Back* by focusing on the faith of the people who believe in both God and liberation.[14]

Being the consummate theologian he was, Cone was always ready to debate his critics and to understand that there was no such thing as a foolproof theological system that did not carry anomalies and blind spots. For Cone, there was no intellectual proof for the belief that God is on the side of the oppressed. At one level, for all the sophistry of arguments and conceptual thinking deployed by Cone, one finally ends up falling back on the resources of faith.

Biblical revelation

In the wake of the Church of England's 2021 Racism Task Force report, 'From Lament to Action',[15] a number of conservative Anglican commentators used social media to argue that the report was the latest in an unfortunate trend of so-called 'woke theology', being adversely impacted by the existence of Critical Race Theory (CRT). As CRT is a comprehensive and diverse intellectual movement, any attempt to summarize it here would not do it justice. And indeed, this book is not concerned with CRT. As I responded in an angry and frustrated response, the Black theology that is cited in the report (some of which was indeed my work) owes nothing to CRT (not that I am in opposition to it) but has everything to do with the Judeo-Christian God that is revealed in the Bible.

James Cone's doctrine of God is one grounded in Christian tradition. Cone asserts that the Christian understanding of God arises from the biblical view of revelation, a revelation of God that takes place in the liberation of oppressed Israel and is completed in the incarnation, in Jesus Christ. This means that whatever is said about the nature of God and God's being-in-the-world must be based on the biblical account of God's revelatory activity.[16]

In *God of the Oppressed*, Cone goes to some length in outlining the biblical evidence for the liberative characteristics of a God whose existence is deeply concerned with a people whom God has identified as God's own.[17] Cone makes it clear that the biblical God is not a disinterested bystander of human history, rather like the Deist view of God in Greek philosophy. Rather, 'The God of the Bible is involved in history, and God's revelation is inseparable from the social and political affairs of Israel.'[18] As Cone narrates the activity of God throughout the Hebrew scriptures, he is not so much 'proof-texting' (taking random verses out of context in order to prove a point) as seeking to show the consistent quality of a God who is not indifferent to human suffering and seeks to liberate a small nation that is often at the mercy of larger, more aggressive powers.

THE GOD OF BLACK THEOLOGY

As we will see shortly, it is this quality of God, seeking to side with those who are oppressed and at the mercy of the exploitation of others, that provides the interpretive or hermeneutical grounds for asserting that 'God is Black'. God's identification with diasporan Black people, the descendants of enslaved Africans, is premised on the grounds that this God does not side with the powerful and those who are oppressive. In the Exodus narrative, when God denounces the oppressive actions of Pharaoh and, through Moses, declares that Pharaoh should set free the oppressed Israelites, Cone is in no doubt that this facet of God's character is the consistent relational quality that supports the Black Power movement in 1960s America and is denouncing the modern-day pharaohs who represent White supremacy.[19]

Although we will look in more detail at the person of Jesus and the role of Christology in the following chapter, there is no doubting the importance of the aforementioned as the key revelation in Cone's doctrine of God. I believe it is no coincidence that Cone's doctoral thesis was on Barth, as there are significant remnants of the latter's thought in Cone's developing model of Black theology. Like Barth, Cone believes that the fullest expression of God's revelation can be found in Jesus Christ. Therefore, the activity of Jesus as detailed in the gospels present us with the clearest rationale for asserting that the God of the Bible is most concerned with the liberation of those whose humanity is imperilled by oppressive forces. In *A Black Theology of Liberation*, Cone writes:

> Special revelation has always occupied the central role in Christian theology. It means that there has been a self-revelation of God in biblical history and decisively in Jesus Christ. It is this conviction that Karl Barth takes seriously by using Christology as the point of departure of his *Church Dogmatics*. God has been fully revealed in the man Jesus so that the norm of all existence is determined exclusively by him.[20]

Cone's extensive reflections on Christology demonstrate its central importance in Black theology, which although orthodox in terms of its 'Trinitarian' character, is nonetheless, very much a Christocentric or Christ-centred movement, in which a very human Jesus, who is in solidarity with those who are marginalized, remains its central theological motif. Jacquelyn Grant, one of Cone's many successful doctoral students at Union Theological Seminary in Manhattan, New York, describes the significant divide in how advantaged White people have traditionally seen Jesus and how those who are disadvantaged and Black have viewed him. In her now classic *White Women's Christ and Black Women's Jesus*, Grant pushes Cone's Christological work further than he did initially, through identifying the 'Jesus of history' not only with disenfranchised Black people, but with Black women in particular.[21]

The biblical basis of Cone's ideological attack on all manifestations of Whiteness, including privilege, supremacy, normativity and benign indifference to suffering, finds its most powerful anchoring in Jesus Christ. Any cursory glance at Cone's impressive and highly influential canon of work will see a plethora of biblical themes and scriptural references and no formal mention of Critical Race Theory. Cone's doctrine of God is not oblivious to the usefulness of other disciplines such as sociology, anthropology, psychology or cultural studies, and these are used to help illuminate the social context in which Christian theology is undertaken.[22]

The critics of the Church of England's attempt to commit itself to racial justice often pillory and caricature this work on the mistaken presumption that Black theology is biased and racist, but the 'White theology' they espouse is neutral, objective and without any bias. Cone's use of Marxist analysis, for example, was to enable Black theologians to better critique and deconstruct the false neutrality of White Christianity and the ways in which this phenomenon has given the world territorial conquest, chattel slavery, colonialism, genocide, apartheid, Jim and Jane Crow, segregation, and reservations. As the radical White American theologian James Perkinson has shown, there is nothing benign or harmless about White theology and Christian missions that helped to give rise to it.[23]

God of the oppressed

One of the central themes of Cone's doctrine of God is that the biblical God of Jesus Christ is one committed to liberation of the oppressed. As outlined in what I have asserted is Cone's greatest piece of work, this phrase is one that has become iconic to the very self-understanding of Black theology as a theology of liberation. Liberation is the theological norm that runs through the very heart of Christian theology – Cone asserts this when he says, 'In view of the biblical emphasis on liberation, it seems not only appropriate but necessary to define the Christian community as the community of the oppressed which joins Jesus Christ in his fight for the liberation of humankind.'[24] For Cone, Christian theology without a commitment to liberation is a dangerous oxymoron. If God is committed to liberation, then as a corollary, it presupposes that God is seeking to liberate something or someone.

As we have seen, Cone's conception of God is as one who is engaged with humankind and cares for those who are oppressed and marginalized. This care for those who are oppressed finds expression in God's identification with such communities. For Cone, God's identification with humankind is not some vague, abstract, non-specific form of neutrality, much like a referee who controls a game by ensuring that the various protagonists are adhering to the rules. The latter analogy is one I remember hearing a Sunday school teacher invoke as a means of explaining God's relationship to human beings. Even as a gauche young child it struck me that if God were a neutral referee that was not going to be of much help to the underdogs in the game, especially if the dominant team were also in the business of cheating and using underhand tactics to make an unfair and biased game even more loaded in their favour. In a previous piece of work, I have critiqued the notion of the 'fair race' and the 'even game' as being illusory constructs because, metaphorically, what they tend to mask is the inherent bias and systemic advantage some people (invariably White) hold over those who are continually disadvantaged (invariably Black people or people of colour).[25] Quoting Cone in this previous essay I state:

> In a racist society, God is never color-blind. To say God is color-blind is analogous to saying that God is blind to justice, to right and wrong, to good and evil. Certainly this is not the picture of God revealed in the Old and New Testaments. Yahweh takes sides.[26]

A God of the oppressed is one who has decisively taken sides in the continual struggle between the powerful and those who are being oppressed. Like traditional, White, evangelical Christianity, Cone believes that one of God's core characteristics is 'righteousness', but whereas the former will see human adherence to this demonstrated in terms of doctrinal faithfulness to the belief in the saving actions of Jesus on the cross, Cone sees this in radically different terms. God's righteousness demands not fidelity to the abstractions of a cross that has been shorn of its bloody connotations with systemic evil and colonial power leading to suffering and mutilation, but solidarity with all those who continue to be lynched and sacrificed daily on crosses made from the evils of White supremacy.

The seismic, revolutionary turn that James Cone helps to bring about lies in his understanding of what makes for authentic Christian discipleship. At the outset of Cone's intellectual maturing as an academic theologian, the United States was engulfed in the ferment of the Civil Rights and the Black Power movements as they sought to bring down the dying remnants of the Jim/Jane Crow system. For the majority of White people, worshipping God and adhering to White privilege and power continued to go hand-in-hand. There was little dissent from the notion that White supremacy was of God, mainly because the very creation of White supremacy owed a great deal to the distortions of the Judeo-Christian system invoked by White Euro-American expansion.

Namely, European expansion and the usurping of the lands, labour and the liberty of Black and Brown people went hand in hand with notions of the civilizing mission of White people across the world.[27] White Christianity, as demonstrated by James Cone, is not a benign phenomenon. In my own work, I have described it as a violent religion, whose impulses are taken from the Great Commission in chapter 28 of Matthew's Gospel. This, in turn, is informed by a military, expansionist reading of the Exodus narrative and the genocide inflicted on the indigenous peoples of the so-called Promised Land.[28]

Cone is identifying God with a particular set of people – the oppressed; for Cone the oppressed are primarily African Americans in his early work, but in later work, such as *Speaking The Truth* and *My Soul Looks Back*, Cone expands this category globally, to include all subjugated and oppressed peoples from the global South.[29] One of the common complaints one hears from more traditional Christians, is that Cone's particularization of God's focus and care is problematic because it takes us away from the universalizing qualities of God, in terms of God's love and identification with the whole of humankind.

Cone's position on this, built upon his exegesis of the God of the Bible, is unwavering. In the life, death and resurrection of Jesus, we see the focus of God's liberating activity expressed in Jesus' mission to be alongside a dehumanized and dispirited colonized community of people, living under the yoke of imperial power.[30] When we look at Christology in the next chapter, we will see in much more vivid terms Cone's identification of God's liberating activity on behalf of the oppressed, focused on the person and work of Jesus Christ.

What often upsets some of Cone's critics when they read of his particularizing of God's focus and activity is that they feel condemned and challenged because they are identified as those who are outside God's immediate favour. The issue is not that they are opposed to God taking sides and choosing some over others, it is the fact that in Cone's radical, liberationist schema, it is comfortable, White, middle-class believers who will feel the cold wind of exclusion and judgement and not those upon whom they were happy to impose such distinctions. For example, growing up in a conservative evangelical central Methodist mission, the bulk of the membership were largely content in their belief that God's judgement was directed at non-believers who were not 'washed in the blood of Lamb' and saved by grace, through faith in Jesus Christ. I do not remember much anguish as to the apparent 'unfairness' that God might save some and not others, so long as they were confident that *they* were in the 'Lamb's Book of Life' and were a part of those to be saved from the fires of hell.

This form of discrimination was all the more pointed in a city (Bradford, in West Yorkshire) where there existed vast social disparities in terms of class and ethnicity. In a city that had pronounced ethnic enclaves and one of the largest Muslim communities in the United Kingdom, I never sensed any difficulties in the predominantly White middle-class membership determining that non-White, non-Christian believers were in error and would be judged for their aberrant beliefs. The doctrinal heart of Methodism, in which all people can be saved, was nonetheless balanced with a clear sense that not all *would* be saved. Salvation was a gift of God but understood firmly in terms of faith in Jesus Christ as Lord and Saviour.

Cone shifts the focus of God's identification from questions of faith adherence based on doctrine to one of praxis based on actual solidarity with those who are oppressed. In making this shift, Cone is still working with a notion of a God who is making divine judgements on humanity, but no longer in the ways that were acceptable to White norms and perspectives. As Cone narrates, in the crucial moment when he realizes the extent to which his theological training in White systematic theology had conditioned him to become a stranger to his own lived realities and experiences, White Euro-American Christianity has managed to convince many of us that God is indifferent to human suffering if the latter is located in Black colonized bodies.[31]

Cone points out the failure of White Christianity in the ways it has been happy to talk in abstractions about the love of God, while allowing racism, colonialism and empire to flourish, all the while remaining silent to the existence of the latter.[32]

In a particularly damning section from *Black Theology and Black Power*, Cone says this about the White church in America:

> If the real Church is the people of God, whose primary task is that of being Christ (Kerygma), by rendering services of liberation (diakonia), and by being itself a manifestation of the nature of the new society Koinonia), then the empirical institutionalized white church has failed on all counts.[33]

In order for God to be a being grounded in love, righteousness and justice and for the church to be an expression of the very nature of God, then the liberation of those who are oppressed must be a core component in the saving activity of God. Cone puts it this way in *God of the Oppressed*:

> The historical character of liberation as an essential ingredient in salvation is also found in the New Testament. Jesus' message centered on the proclamation of liberation for the poor, and his exorcisms clearly illustrated that he viewed his ministry as an engagement in battle with the powers of evil that hold people in captivity. The healing of the sick, feeding the hungry, and giving sight to the blind mean that Jesus did not regard salvation as an abstract, spiritual idea or a feeling in the heart. Salvation is the granting of physical wholeness in the concreteness of pain and suffering.[34]

Cone's doctrine of God is one that connects God to the realities of human suffering and social contexts in which Christian faith is lived. In doing so, he rightly identifies the ways in which Christianity has been turned into an abstract concept that allows faith to be reduced to semantic word play (are you saved or not), empty ritual, skewed morality (obsessions with sexual practice but little appetite to challenge racism and White supremacy) and silence in the face of systemic injustice heaped on the poor of the global South. This focus on the partiality of God in siding with those who are oppressed and marginalized, leads to perhaps the most startling aspect of Cone's doctrine of God – namely, God is Black.

God is Black

In the quarter of a century in which I have been teaching Black theology, perhaps the most challenging and arresting of all the statements coming from James Cone's work has been the assertion that God is Black. What has always intrigued me when receiving opposition to this idea from Cone, is that most of the respondents, whether White or Black or people of colour, are more than happy to work with the unstated notion that God is White.

Witnessing the rise of global anti-racist consciousness following the murder of George Floyd in May 2020, has seen a number of more recent texts seeking to challenge some of the normative workings of Whiteness in the world. One such text is Chine McDonald's *God is Not a White Man*.[35] In what is a helpful, introductory text for people who have not thought about issues pertaining to 'race' and racism, McDonald highlights the bloody and dangerous implications for human history in how we have thought and conceived of God. Assuming that God is a 'White man' or is analogous to this figure, has been to sanction a long litany of chattel slavery, imperialism, economic exploitation and human displacement, all emerging from the altar of White supremacy.[36]

Cone doesn't only refute any notion that God is subliminally or substantively White, he argues for a radical counter assertion, namely that God is Black. Now to be clear, Cone was not the first person to argue that God is Black. In 1898, Henry McNeal Turner, a prominent Black Methodist and one of the leaders of the African Methodist Episcopal Church, asserted that 'God is a Negro'.[37] In 1924, Marcus Garvey, a

Jamaican-born, Black nationalist-oriented community leader and preacher, also stated the view that God was Black.[38]

The genius of Cone, however, was to build on these earlier protestations, but to add a thick layer of theological skill to the rhetoric of his forefathers in the wider Black liberation movement. For Cone, the Blackness of God lies right at the very heart of the Black theology project. Cone describes its significance in this way:

> The blackness of God, and everything implied by it in a racist society, is the heart of the black theology doctrine of God. There is no place in black theology for a colorless God in a society where human beings suffer precisely because of their color. The Black theologian must reject any conception of God which stifles self-determination by picturing God as a God of all peoples. Either God is identified with the oppressed to the point that their experience becomes God's experience, or God is a God of racism.[39]

This is perhaps the most difficult doctrine for many people (both White and Black) to understand because it runs contrary to most of what we have been told to believe about what God is like. If God is not a White man, then God is certainly not Black. Rather, many of us have been encouraged to think of God as having no visible image. To understand the thrust of Cone's argument one must quickly move beyond the purely aesthetic to the deeply symbolic. This is not to say that as a proud Black man, having lived with centuries of negative imagery directed at Black people, Cone was not aware of the importance of aesthetics. What God looks like matters if you have been taught to hate yourself and to assume that you are an inferior being, largely because of the colour of your skin.

In a previous piece of work, I demonstrated that such is the internalized racism and self-hatred and lack of regard engendered by White supremacy, many Black people continue to harbour negative thoughts about themselves, even when one had hoped that such restrictions and negative traits had been overcome.⁴⁰ But the essential power of Cone's understanding of God goes way beyond the merely visual. If God is Black but retains the essential qualities of the so-called White God, then God remains a problematic being that cannot save those who are oppressed on the grounds of their seemingly problematic Blackness.

Rather, the profound basis of Cone's assertion that God is Black is to be found in the very nature of God's being. For God to be in actual solidarity with those who are oppressed and for that God to be able to save them, then God needs to take on their identity to become one like them. In one respect, this in itself is not wholly controversial. Traditional Christianity has long argued that one of the ways in which God effects salvation for humankind is by taking on our identity, so that as God becomes like us, so then we can become like God. The fundamental switch that Cone makes is to add specificity and a particular identity to the notion of 'becoming like us'.

Whereas traditional Christianity has seen this in largely abstract terms, Cone sees the 'us' not as generic humanity, but as those who are condemned to the margins as the 'least of these' (Matt. 25.31–46). Cone limits the content of Christian theology to the oppressed community and not to a more generic understanding of humanity.⁴¹ His grounds for doing this have been discussed previously. The key point is that God's fundamental being is one that is identified with those who have been humiliated because of their Blackness. Quite recently, I found myself walking the streets of London and recalling with a colleague that it had been a year since the murder of George Floyd. We reflected on how a Black person could die because of an innocuous offence in a shop. A few days later I gave a remote presentation to a group of Christian activists related to the Council for World Mission's 'Unmasking Empire' strategy,⁴² in which I outlined the litany of Black deaths in police custody in Britain over the past 50 years. It made for sombre viewing and the palpable silence at the end of my presentation was revealing.

THE GOD OF BLACK THEOLOGY

It is in this and so many contexts that Cone's assertion that God is Black is such a powerful and dynamic theological truth. Cone states:

> The blackness of God means that God has made the oppressed condition, God's own condition. This is the essence of the biblical revelation. By electing Israelite slaves as the people of God and by becoming the Oppressed One in Jesus Christ, the human race is made to understand that God is known where human beings experience humiliation and suffering.[43]

This, then, leads to another amazing and dramatic theological turn. Namely, that salvation for White people lies in them becoming Black! Now, constraints of space prevent me explaining this in all its complexity, largely because James Cone's ideas on how this could be achieved were never explained fully; that is, what this might mean in terms of practical demonstrable Christian discipleship.

A clue to this provocative challenge is found in his reflections on the activism of the great German pastor and theologian Dietrich Bonhoeffer. In *The Cross and the Lynching Tree*, Cone outlines the sacrificial activism of Bonhoeffer who gives up his privileged position as a White German professor and pastor in order to enter into the struggle against the evils of the Nazi regime in Germany.[44] His martyrdom in 1945 is a sharp reminder of the cost of carrying the cross and following in Jesus' example as exercising costly grace. And yet, as African American ethicist Reggie Williams has shown in his remarkable book *Bonhoeffer's Black Jesus*,[45] the inspiration for Bonhoeffer's conversion to the authentic way of Christ was through his exposure to the radicalism of Black Christianity in the form of the Abyssinian Baptist church, under the leadership of Adam Clayton Powell Jr, in Harlem, New York, while he was staying in the city and studying at Union Theological Seminary (where Cone himself worked for almost 50 years). It can be argued that in identifying with the sufferings of oppressed peoples (in this case the struggles of Jewish people in Nazi Germany),

Bonhoeffer was offering a practical, lived response to the challenge set out by Cone, in his creative and radical doctrine of God. Namely, that for White people to be saved, they need to identify with and enter the struggle for racial justice to the point where the cost for doing so is a demonstrable example of their commitment to follow Christ and to be in solidarity with God through their solidarity with Blackness.

By participating in the struggle for liberation through the lens of Blackness, participants are enabled to experience the power of God's revelation, because God is revealed through Blackness. Cone puts it like this, 'To receive God's revelation is to become black with God by joining God in the work of liberation.'[46]

There is much more that can be said about James Cone's understanding of God. Sadly, a short introductory text like this cannot do justice to the wide-ranging brilliance of Cone's work, but I hope that this chapter has whetted your appetite to delve into Cone's work in greater depth in order to understand the power of his intellectual challenge to systematic theology in particular, and academic theology and Christian practice and discipleship more generally.

Conclusion

As I have reread Cone's work in preparation for writing this book, I have been reminded of the skilful way in which his rigorous training in systematic theology and his love of God that is revealed in the scriptures and the Black church tradition enabled him to create a revolution of thought that is also built on relatively orthodox lines. Yes, his assertion that God is Black and that liberation is the core component of the gospel of Jesus Christ may well be shocking to many people's ears, and yet, as we have seen, these trenchant assertions emerge from a deep engagement with the Christian tradition. In some respects, while being a revolutionary theologian, Cone is in some ways quite a constrained and intellectually restrained

THE GOD OF BLACK THEOLOGY

one. For example, Cone's identification of God with Blackness is built on solid theological grounds and not Black cultural or nationalistic terms. Cone's Black theology, unlike that of his immediate contemporary, Albert B. Cleage Jr, is not a Black nationalistic project.[47] In making this point, I am not seeking to make any judgements on either figure. But I do note Earle Fisher's critique of Cone, in which he compares his Black liberationist rhetoric to that of Cleage's, asserting that the latter provides a more consistent Black radical form of praxis than the former.[48] Part of this assessment is, to my mind, based on their respective training and trajectory for their parallel activism in support of Black liberation. Whereas Cleage chose to confine his Black activism within pastoral ministry and community engagement, Cone chose the route of the scholar, working from Union Theological Seminary. For Cone, the precision of intellectual argument took precedence over the captivating rhetoric of preaching and the more practical aspects of the Black liberation struggle. It is beyond the scope of this book to make any assessment as to which of the two approaches yielded more fruit.

Cone's theological work – through his many books, but also in terms of his teaching at Union, and the plethora of PhD students he ushered into the world – make him for me, the most eminent Black theologian the world has ever seen.

In the next chapter, we will explore what is, perhaps, Cone's greatest area of theological reflection, namely his love for Jesus and the singular example he sets for us as the beacon for God's liberative activity in human history.

Notes

1 See James H. Cone, *A Black Theology of Liberation* (Maryknoll, NY: Orbis Books, 1970/1990).
2 Cone, *A Black Theology of Liberation*, p. 55.
3 Cone, *A Black Theology of Liberation*, p. 55.
4 Probably the most eloquent section in which this theme is

explored can be found in Cone's *God of the Oppressed* (San Francisco: Harper and Row, 1975), pp. 57–76.

5 Cone, *God of the Oppressed*, pp. 36–56.

6 Cone, *A Black Theology of Liberation*, p. 61.

7 See James H. Cone, *My Soul Looks Back* (Maryknoll, NY: Orbis Books, 1999), pp. 64–72.

8 See Anthony G. Reddie, *Faith, Stories and the Experience of Black Elders: Singing the Lord's Song in a Strange Land* (London: Jessica Kingsley, 2001), pp. 37–46.

9 William R. Jones, *Is God A White Racist?: A Preamble to Black Theology* (New York: Beacon Press, 1973/1997).

10 Jones, *Is God A White Racist?*, p. ix.

11 See the chapter entitled, 'What is the Point of This? A Practical Black Theology Exploration of Suffering and Theodicy', in Anthony G. Reddie, *Working Against the Grain: Reimaging Black Theology in the 21st Century* (London: Equinox, 2008), pp. 172–87.

12 Jamall A. Calloway, '"To Struggle Up a Never-Ending Stair": Theodicy and the Failure It Gifts to Black Liberation Theology', *Black Theology: An International Journal*, vol. 18, no. 3, 2020, pp. 223–45.

13 Calloway, '"To Struggle Up a Never-Ending Stair"', pp. 239–43.

14 Calloway, '"To Struggle Up a Never-Ending Stair"', pp. 239–40.

15 See The Church of England's Report 'From Lament to Action', www.churchofengland.org/sites/default/files/2021-04/FromLamentTo Action-report.pdf (accessed 28.09.2021).

16 Cone, *A Black Theology of Liberation*, p. 60.

17 Cone, *God of the Oppressed*, pp. 57–76.

18 Cone, *God of the Oppressed*, p. 57.

19 Cone, *Black Theology and Black Power*, pp. 43–6.

20 Cone, *A Black Theology of Liberation*, p. 51.

21 See Jacquelyn Grant, *White Women's Christ and Black Women's Jesus: Feminist Christology and Womanist Response* (Atlanta, GA: Scholar's Press, 1989), Pp. 195–230.

22 Cone, *God of the Oppressed*, pp. 36–40.

23 See James W. Perkinson, *White Theology: Outing Supremacy in Modernity* (New York: Palgrave Macmillan, 2004).

24 Cone, *A Black Theology of Liberation*, p. 3.

25 See Anthony G. Reddie, 'Participative Black Theology as a Pedagogy of Praxis', in Dale P. Andrews and Robert London Smith Jr (eds), *Black Practical Theology* (Waco, TX: Baylor University Press, 2015), pp. 59–72.

26 Cone, *A Black Theology of Liberation*, p. 6.

27 See Stephen Ray, 'Contending for the Cross: Black Theology and

the Ghosts of Modernity', in *Black Theology: An International Journal*, vol. 8, no. 1, 2010, pp. 53–68.

28 See Anthony G. Reddie, 'Reassessing the Inculcation of an Anti-Racist Ethic for Christian Ministry: From Racism Awareness to Deconstructing Whiteness', *Religions*, vol. 11, no. 497, 2020.

29 See James H. Cone, *Speaking The Truth: Ecumenism, Liberation, and Black Theology* (Maryknoll, NY: Orbis Books, 1986). See also *My Soul Looks Back*, pp. 93–113.

30 Cone, *God of the Oppressed*, pp. 74–98.

31 Cone, *Said I Wasn't Gonna Tell Nobody*, pp. 1–30.

32 James H. Cone, 'Theology's Great Sin: Silence in the face of White Supremacy', *Black Theology: An International Journal*, vol. 2, no. 2, 2004, pp. 139–52.

33 Cone, *Black Theology and Black Power*, p. 71.

34 Cone, *God of the Oppressed*, p. 140.

35 Chine McDonald, *God is Not a White Man: And Other Revelations* (London: Hodder and Stoughton, 2021).

36 McDonald, *God is Not a White Man*, pp. 16–39.

37 For further details, see 'Before Garvey! Henry McNeal Turner and the Fight for Reparations, Emigration and Black Rights. Bishop Turner and Black Theology', *Colored Conventions Project*, https://coloredconventions.org/before-garvey-mcneal-turner/ame-church/black-theology/ (accessed 29.09.2021). For more information on the ministry and activism of Henry McNeal Turner, see the work of Andre Johnson, e.g., *The Forgotten Prophet: Bishop Henry McNeal Turner and the African American Prophetic Tradition* (Washington DC: Lexington Books, 2014).

38 For details on Marcus Garvey's radical statement, see 'Garvey Preaches Faith in Black God', *The New York Times*, 4 August 1924, www.nytimes.com/1924/08/04/archives/garvey-preaches-faith-in-black-god-negro-leader-makes-plea-for-free.html (accessed 29.09.2021). For the context of Garvey's activism within Black theology, see Charles Lattimore Howard, *Black Theology As Mass Movement* (New York: Palgrave Macmillan, 2014).

39 Cone, *God of the Oppressed*, p. 63.

40 See Reddie, *Working Against the Grain*, pp. 75–9.

41 Cone, *Speaking The Truth*, p. 9.

42 For more details on this strategy and the more specific 'Legacies of Slavery' project within CWM, see Revd Dr Collin Cowan, 'Unmasking Empire', *Council For World Mission*, www.cwmission.org/resources/members-library/publications/unmasking-empire/ (accessed 29.09.2021).

43 Cone, *A Black Theology of Liberation*, pp. 63–4.

44 James H. Cone, *The Cross and the Lynching Tree* (Maryknoll, NY: Orbis Books, 2011), pp. 41–2.

45 See Reggie L. Williams, *Bonhoeffer's Black Jesus: Harlem Renaissance Theology and an Ethic of Resistance* (Waco, TX: Baylor University Press, 2014).

46 Cone, *A Black Theology of Liberation*, p. 66.

47 There has been a recent upsurge in interest in the ministry and activism of Albert Cleage. See Jawanza Eric Clark (ed.), *Albert Cleage Jr. and the Black Madonna and Child* (New York: Palgrave Macmillan, 2016). See also Earle J. Fisher, *The Reverend Albert Cleage Jr. and the Black Prophetic Tradition: A Reintroduction of the Black Messiah* (Washington DC: Lexington Books, 2021).

48 See Earle J. Fisher, 'Brother Malcolm, Dr. King, and Black Power – A Close and Complementary Reading', in *Black Theology: An International Journal*, vol. 18, no. 3, 2020, pp. 263–87.

3

Jesus Christ in Black Theology

As I stated previously, Black theology for the most part is relatively orthodox in terms of being a Trinitarian, Christian theological discipline. I think it is fair to say that, certainly within the auspices of James Cone's theological method, Christology remained his foundational point of departure in how he constructed the initial development of Black theology.

In his first book, *Black Theology and Black Power*, Cone writes, 'Christianity begins and ends with the man Jesus – his life, death and resurrection. He is the Revelation, the special disclosure of God to man, revealing who God is and what his purpose for man is.'[1]

For Cone, the centrality of Christology and Jesus in Black theology arises from two sources. In the first instance, there is Cone's historic formation within the wider African American Black church tradition. Cone was raised in the south of the United States in a Christian household. His parents were part of the African Methodist Episcopal Church (AME), one of the historic Black denominations founded by African Americans breaking away from the hypocrisies of White Euro-American Christianity.[2]

In this crucible of cultural and religious formation, James Cone would have been introduced to a form of Christianity that was steeped in the traditions of his ancestors, enslaved African peoples.[3] This model and mould of Christianity was founded on the recontextualization of the Christian faith from within the prism of Black experience. The roots of Black theology, as we shall demonstrate in a later chapter looking at Cone's connection to Black people, emerges from the existential realities of being born into a Black body in a context in which Christianity was used as a justification for enslavement when coerced by the dictates of White supremacy.[4]

In the first chapter of *Said I Wasn't Gonna Tell Nobody*, Cone outlines the ways in which the Christianity of his parents and ancestors shaped him to deal with the hypocrisy of the White world of America. This formation was a dialectic of defiant resistance and accommodationist pragmatism.[5] Namely, this mode of Black Christianity sought to challenge the seemingly normative assumptions of White superiority while accepting that one had to be covert in the ways in which one sought to resist, often disguising intent and strategizing beneath a veneer of acquiescence. Fundamental to this form of Christianity was the centrality of a contextualized understanding of Jesus who sat alongside Black people in the midst of their struggles and suffering. Howard Thurman, the famed African American mystic and, in many respects, a progenitor of Cone in terms of Black theological scholarship, identified Jesus as having a symbiotic relationship with those he deemed the 'disinherited'.[6] As a forerunner of Cone in the Black theological tradition, Thurman constructs a hermeneutical approach to critiquing the wicked machinations of White, Euro-American Christianity by focusing initially on Jesus.[7] He identifies Jesus' life and the social context in which he lived as analogous to the disenfranchisement of Black people in America, more so than having anything to do the seeming normativity of White, Euro-American Christianity. Thurman says 'We begin with the simple historical fact that Jesus was a Jew.'[8] He continues, 'The striking similarity between the social position of Jesus in Palestine and that of the vast majority of American Negroes is obvious to anyone who tarries long over the facts.'[9] Here, Thurman is outlining not only some of the essential markers that would later characterize Cone's own development of Black theology but, of equal import, he is offering a summation of what would have been the basic template of the African American Black church tradition, namely, that the 'Jesus of history' identified with the suffering and struggles of Black folk, more so than he did with those with power, who claimed to be his followers, while oppressing others in Jesus' name. This was the truth of Jacquelyn Grant's towering work on womanist theology in the late 1980s, when she juxtaposed the 'White Women's Christ', who supported the status quo of White supremacy, with the 'Black Women's Jesus' who identified with the struggles and suffering of poor, Black women.[10]

The roots of Black theology emerge from a Black church tradition that had already grown accustomed to critiquing the skewed ethics and problematic practices of White Christianity.

The second source for Cone's strong adherence to Christology as the point of departure in Christian theology in general and Black theology in particular, lies in his own training in Barthian anthropology in his doctoral studies at Garrett-Evangelical Theological Seminary. I stated, previously, that Cone's focus on Barth for his doctoral studies resulted in Cone and Barth sharing this focus on Jesus as the starting point for engaging in constructive Christian theology. Cone states, 'As Christians we know God only as he has been revealed in and through Jesus. All other talk about God can have, at most, provisional significance.'[11]

The focus on Jesus also derives from the practical nature of Cone's Black theology, which echoes his own formation in the African American Black church tradition. In the midst of existential despair, when Black bodies were being crushed and literally dismembered through the cruelty of lynching, Black people sought in God an immediate form of amelioration for their suffering. There was little appetite or indeed time for abstract theological musings when faced with the reality of oppression and the threat of non-being, that is, of ceasing to exist due to the imposition of powerful others.[12]

The practical, experiential nature of Black Christianity across the African diaspora (one finds echoes of this in African, Caribbean and Latin American theologies)[13] has often seen a focus on the visible, manifest example of Jesus' life, death and resurrection, as the basis for a faith that is trying to make sense of seemingly insoluble senselessness. While the concept of God as a being can be construed in very vague and abstract terms, the life of Jesus, especially his identification with the poor and marginalized of Judea, offers an immediate point of focus for those whose lives are besmirched by the realities of human suffering, marginalization and oppression. To quote my late mother, 'Only Jesus knows the struggles Black people have faced.'

The Jesus of history was a colonized Jew

The central point of departure in James Cone's theological understanding of Jesus lies in his identity as a colonized Jewish man in Roman-occupied Judea. This is non-negotiable for Cone. He writes:

> The historical Jesus emphasizes the social context of Christology and thereby establishes the importance of Jesus' racial identity. *Jesus was a Jew!* The particularity of Jesus' person as disclosed in his Jewishness is indispensable for Christological analysis.[14]

For Cone, the fact that Jesus was not an 'Aryan' White man is hugely significant. The God of the oppressed is disclosed in Jesus' identity not only as a Jewish man, but as a colonized Jew at that. In more recent reflections on Black theology in Britain, after the murder of George Floyd, I have used Jesus' encounter with Pontius Pilate in John's account of the lead up to Jesus' crucifixion, as a means of engaging White British people with the paradox of their Christological gaze. In John 18 we see Jesus in conversation with Pontius Pilate, the Roman governor of Judea. Jesus is before Pilate because he has been handed over by the Jewish authorities to be tried for crimes against the state. The fact that Jesus is here in front of Pilate is because, as the text states in verses 31 and 32, only Pilate can put him to death and because it underscores the type of death Jesus would die – at the hands of an invading, imperial power.

JESUS CHRIST IN BLACK THEOLOGY

In my recent talks about the roots of Black theology, I have pointed to this encounter in order to demonstrate the salient truth of Cone's Christological point of departure. In identifying Jesus as a colonized Jewish man, his encounter with Pilate, the representative of Caesar, the Godlike power that exerts control of life and death over all colonial subjects, Cone is exposing the death-dealing hypocrisy and theological sleight-of-hand of White Christianity. For White Christianity, while wanting to believe that their mendacious praxis and idolatrous surrender to White supremacy is of Christ, they are actually a manifestation of Pontius Pilate and not Jesus. I have challenged White Christians since May 2020 on what they are seeing when they look at this encounter between Jesus, a colonized and oppressed Jewish man, alongside an imperial apparatchik, a colonial governor of an occupied state. They need to recognize that White Euro-American Christianity (in my case the British Christianity that exported missionary faith across its empire), is more synonymous with Pontius Pilate and not with a colonized Jewish man. White British, European and American Christianity represents Pontius Pilate and not Jesus. As my friend and colleague in the Council for World Mission 'Legacies of Slavery' project, Revd Dr Peter Cruchley has suggested, 'Pontius Pilate is the first White man in the Bible.' Whether he is ethnically White in terms of phenotypes is open to question. What is not in question is that Pilate, as a colonial representative of an imperial regime, not unlike the British empire Governors-General who often ruled in the name of the Crown, is certainly ontologically White, namely, he in essence is a White person by dint of the role he has as the arbiter of life and death over colonized peoples.

Cone is clear when he identifies Jesus as a part of an oppressed community from the moment he was born. Cone states, 'The appearance of Jesus as the Oppressed One whose existence is identified exclusively with the oppressed of the land is symbolically characterized in his birth.'[15] In identifying Jesus as a Galilean Jew, Cone wants to establish the critical 'otherness' of his identity in order to ensure that the domestication of Jesus as 'one of us' can be seriously challenged. Cone writes: 'The historical Jesus must be taken seriously if we intend to avoid making Jesus into our own images.'[16]

The irony is, of course, that White Christianity has proved more than adept at creating a White Christ in its own image in order to justify enslavement, colonization and the conscription of Black bodies. In his reflections on the Council for World Mission Christian education-mission picture 'The Healer'[17] (in which a White Jesus is pictured standing alongside a White British doctor as the latter attends to the needs of Black natives in Southern Africa), Peter Cruchley notes the ways in which a White Jesus is so clearly located with the British missionaries and not with the Black Africans. The Jesus in this picture has a kindly countenance and is no doubt meant to represent a benign, and non-contentious Christological figure, and yet his demonstrable Whiteness clearly puts him at odds with the colonized peoples with whom he is depicted in the picture. Once again, as is the case with the powerful dictates of White supremacy, a White Jesus who is more akin to Pontius Pilate is offered up as the template for the Christ of faith, rather than a colonized Black person, whose life is more analogous to the Jesus of history than this White man, no matter how benign he appears.

I will reflect more specifically on the idolatrous nature of a White Jesus Christ later in this chapter. But for now, suffice it to say that Cone's emphasis on the Jewish identity of Jesus accords with the latter's relationship to disenfranchised Black bodies in a world of White supremacy.

Jesus is Black

At the core of James Cone's conception of Black theology is a Jesus who, in his total identification with the suffering realities of Black people, is himself Black. The Blackness of Jesus, like that of God, is understood in two primary dimensions. We shall explore these two differing dimensions in a moment.

JESUS CHRIST IN BLACK THEOLOGY

In the first instance, Jesus is Black because for him to be the expression of God's righteousness, he can be no other. In *God of the Oppressed*, Cone writes:

> Without the certainty that Christ is with us as the historical Jesus was present with the humiliated and weak in Palestine, how can black people account for the power and courage to struggle against slave masters and overseers in the nineteenth century and the Ku Klux Klan and the policemen in the twentieth?[18]

Jesus cannot be who he is (a phrase Cone uses in *God of the Oppressed*[19]) if he is not in total solidarity with those who are not only oppressed but in danger of being rendered as non-beings without any material or metaphysical worth (look at the casual way in which George Floyd was murdered, for example). The Blackness of Jesus arises out of the contextual nature in which Christianity seeks to connect the Jesus of history, a colonized Jewish man in first-century Palestine, with the Christ of faith, who continues to witness to the suffering and humiliation of oppressed peoples throughout the world. In a world in which we see the continued manipulation of White supremacy to distort human relations, God in Christ has to be Black (note how the former president Donald Trump could equate White fascists and nationalists with Black anti-racists claiming after the riots of Charlottesville that there was 'wrong on both sides').

In this British context we have witnessed a right-wing Conservative government led by Boris Johnson denouncing anti-racist strategies as 'woke'[20] and producing a government report into systemic racism that claimed that there was no such phenomenon.[21] Given the current climate in which we are seeing attempts to reduce racism to a form of moral relativism, can we seriously question whether Jesus Christ is Black? Certainly, a White Jesus who identifies with the status quo and supports White entitlement and privilege is not a salvific figure Black people can waste any time following or worshipping. In this regard, Black theology would side with the Black Nationalist Marcus Garvey who asserted that it was a form of genocide for Black people to worship a God who looked like their oppressors and not like themselves. I will speak more on the notion of a Black Messiah shortly. To reiterate the theological grounds of asserting that Jesus is Black, Cone says:

> In a society that defines blackness as evil and whiteness as good, the theological significance of Jesus is found in the possibility of human liberation through blackness. Jesus is the black Christ![22]

Like Cone's doctrine of God, Jesus' Blackness is understood not solely in ethnic or cultural terms, around the aesthetics of his appearance, but more so on ontological grounds, in terms of the essence and being of God that identifies with Black suffering. As I have stated elsewhere, Jesus in Black theology is 'One of Us'.[23] Being one of us is central to the ways in which the Judeo-Christian God of the oppressed of the Bible seeks to be in solidarity with the demonized nature of Blackness in a world that continues to echo to the strain of White supremacy. A Black Jesus speaks to the skewed effects of White supremacy where rich countries like Britain prepare to offer top-up booster vaccine jabs to counter Covid-19, while only 1 per cent of the whole of Africa is presently vaccinated.[24] The huge disparities in vaccination provision between the White global minority and the Black global majority and the lack of sharing between the former with the latter, is a reminder of the exploitative greed of White supremacy. Even though the logics of sharing are such that we all know that so-called normality will not happen unless there is equity in vaccination coverage, we are reminded yet again that 'logic' and 'White supremacy' have rarely belonged in the same sentence. The construct of 'race' has never had any intellectual basis to it and yet White people have continued to believe it because it suited their purposes to do so.

Central to the work of a Black Jesus Christ is the sense of empowerment Black people gain from the knowledge that not only is God's anointed identifying with them, but he is also supporting them in their daily struggles to surmount the continued travails of systemic racism that face them. Cone makes this clear when he writes:

> The black Christ is he who threatens the structure of evil as seen in white society, rebelling against it, thereby becoming the embodiment of what the black community knows that it must become. Because he has become black as we are, we now know what black empowerment is. It is blacks determining the way they are going to behave in the world. It is refusing to allow white society to place strictures on black existence as if their having guns means that blacks are supposed to cool it.[25]

In Cone's early Christological work, he demonstrates how Jesus' identity and his work and message are all intertwined. The identity as an oppressed, colonized Jewish man gives rise to his message and mission, from which the inevitable consequences of his death arise[26] (more of which later in this chapter and in the penultimate chapter, when I reflect on Cone's book *The Cross and the Lynching Tree*). As I have stated previously, Cone's conception of a Black Jesus is anchored in Black existential experience and doctrinal certitude. The latter he gleaned from the scriptures and his theological articulation of a radical Jesus whose message of love and forgiveness is filtered through the defining norm of the thrust for liberation and freedom of all those who are marginalized and oppressed. The former was learned from generations of his ancestors, many of whom had come to know a personal Jesus whose presence rejected the racist Christ that was ensconced within White, Euro-American norms of slavery, segregation and Jim Crow. The latter is summed up in the pithy response of Cone to his formative years growing up in segregated Arkansas, 'How could both black and white churches be Christian if they took opposite stands and both claimed Christ and the Bible as the basis of their views?'[27]

The answer for Cone and Black theology is simple – White

Christianity of the sort that Cone evokes is a lie and the White Christ is the 'anti-Christ'. I will speak more on the antithesis of the Black Christ and the White Christ shortly. Of critical import is the way in which Cone moves interchangeably between the Jesus of history and the Christ of faith, arguing that the existence and identity of the former is the key to understanding the presence of the latter in the world today as one who is in solidarity with Blackness and the cause of Black liberation. While not wanting to impose the 'Christian tag' on the Black Lives Matter movement, I have no doubt that the liberating God found in Jesus Christ is being revealed in this radical grassroots coalition of brave, indefatigable agitators for truth. This view will be controversial for many White people to realize, but then so was the case when God's righteousness was being revealed through the aegis of the Black Power movement in the 1960s.[28]

The theological adroitness of Cone sees him skilfully moving between differing modes of understanding Jesus' identity, both as the Jesus of history and the Christ of faith, but also as the Black Jesus who identities with us, and the Black Messiah, who is indeed one of us. The latter does not feature across all of Cone's writings, but as I have stated previously, as a Black man who grew up in the segregated American South, he knew the significance of Jesus' Blackness as one who was also a part of us, not just symbolically, but also literally by dint of his birth and ancestry. This view owes a great deal to Cone's contemporary Albert Cleage, a noted Black Christian nationalist of whom mention was made in the previous chapter. Cleage argues for a more literal, Black-phenotype Jesus who is 'The Black Messiah'.[29]

In *A Black Theology of Liberation*, Cone reflects briefly on the relationship between the Black Jesus of Black theology and the popular conception of the Black Messiah found in Black religious and cultural forms of nationalism, espoused by Albert Cleage.[30] Cone sees the two as analogous, which, given his desire to point to the concreteness of Jesus' existence as a real person of history, means that he is willing to concede that the notion that Jesus was literally Black is not far-fetched or without merit.[31]

However, writing later Cone states, 'Does Black theology believe that Jesus was *really* black? It seems to me that the *literal* color of Jesus is irrelevant, as there are the different shades of blackness in America.'[32] The latter comment is slightly ambiguous because Cone seems to be saying that what is irrelevant is not whether Jesus was 'Black' but how Black he might have been, given the internalized racism that still exists in many Black communities around what people sometimes term as 'Colorism'. Colorism is where lighter-skinned Black people are viewed more favourably than darker-skinned people. Kelly Brown Douglas, one of the most famed womanist theologians, has critiqued this facet of Black religious and cultural life as being a damaging facet of the internalized racism imposed on the psyche of Black people by the values of White supremacy.[33] The weight of Cone's writings, however, are anchored in the theological articulation of a Black Christ as opposed to a more popular, cultural depiction. Cone is determined to show that the connection between the Jesus of history and the Christ of faith lies in the theological truth that God's being is bound up with God's identification with those who were oppressed throughout history, whether in first-century Palestine or twentieth-century North America. Cone writes 'Can we really believe that Christ is the Suffering Servant par excellence if he is not black?'[34]

The White Christ is the Antichrist

If Cone asserts that Jesus Christ is Black, then there can be no doubting the damning verdict he gives to the notion of the 'White Christ'. If the Black Christ is known by his liberating deeds, being in solidarity with those who are suffering, then the White Christ is condemned by his association with slavery, colonialism and empire and the ravenous nature of White supremacist greed. I wonder if there has been any greater theological sacrilege than that of a slave ship being called 'Jesus' which transported African men and women to the so-called new world, under the rubric of a religious faith that saw such actions as a part of God's providence?[35] The work of great Black historians such as Albert Raboteau, for example, in the magisterial *Slave Religion*[36] outlines the development of Black Christianity that emerges from the visceral experience of the suffering of Black people, as the clear riposte to the corruptions of White slave-holding Christianity.

Cone outlines the corruption of Christianity when viewed through the lens of White supremacy as being inimical to the authentic expression of the Christian faith.[37] He writes:

> If there is any contemporary meaning of the AntiChrist (or 'the principalities and powers?') then the White church seems to be a manifestation of it. It is the enemy of Christ. It was the white 'Christian' church which took the lead in establishing slavery as an institution and segregation as a pattern in society by sanctioning all-white congregations.[38]

In the British context, we witnessed early in 2021 the 'electronic lynching' of Revd Jarel Robinson-Brown.[39] Following the death of Captain Tom Moore, Jarel Robinson-Brown posted a tweet critiquing the ways in which the death of this courageous and generous man was being cynically used to represent the forces of White nationalism. In the 'witch hunt' that followed, wholly disproportionate to the nature of an innocuous tweet, one saw at first hand the continued existence of a White Christ, a warped Christological figure of empire that is used to justify White privilege and supremacy. I remember entering into dialogue with one of Robinson-Brown's detractors, a Church of England person engaged in church planting, endeavouring to see if we could find common ground in the midst of this contentious moment. Suffice it to say that White privilege and patrician arrogance has not disappeared. Black people may not get physically lynched any more to the same extent as was once the case but we can still be on the receiving end of nasty racists who, imbued with the cover provided by a White imperial Jesus that continues to support and sanction White supremacy, could confidently denounce me and Jarel Robinson-Brown as racists. If anyone doubted the continued relevance of Cone's strictures against the false claims made by White Christianity one only needs to look at the 'culture wars' being stoked by the right-wing media in the UK, into which a plethora of, particularly, Church of England reactionaries, are prepared to delve, all the while convincing themselves that their opposition to the cause of racial justice and anti-racist praxis is the way of Christ. It may well be the way of the White Christ, but it remains anathema to the Jesus of history, who was a victim of the violence of 'ontological Whiteness' in the form of Pontius Pilate, the first White man in the Bible. The wretched lie of Whiteness finds expression in White right-wing advocates more than happy to support the status quo of White supremacy and Black marginalization, while denouncing Black anti-racist activists as *actual racists*. These individuals continue in the distorted belief that White Christianity, represented by the White Christ, is benign, generous and without negative consequences. As Cone and most Black people know, if we are honest to the realities of experience, White Christianity is nothing of the sort!

Jesus died like a Black person

One of the central aspects of James Cone's focus on the historical Jesus is the manner of his death. Of course, it should be noted that Cone is indeed not alone nor is he unique in his focus on the significance and symbolic power and importance of Jesus' death. One could argue that this is a central point of departure for Christian theology. If Jesus is one with God and Jesus is executed on the cross, then what does it mean for God to be all powerful and sovereign, and what can such a death mean when related to the corporate life of human beings? The key hermeneutical tool for Cone lies once again in God's identification with oppressed people and the belief that Jesus lived his earthly life in solidarity with such people, as 'one of us'.

If Jesus is one of us, a member of the category of human beings who are oppressed, whose lives are stunted by injustice, misery and pain, the pain of systemic racism, of colonization and marginalization in one's own land, then it stands to reason that according to Cone, Jesus' death also exemplifies this commitment and character. Namely, if Jesus is ontologically Black, sharing in our struggles to make sense of our demonized Blackness, then it must be clearly the case that when it comes to his death, Jesus died like a Black person.

In Cone's late classic *The Cross and the Lynching Tree* he juxtaposes the nature of the cross as an instrument of state sanctioned terror and the precarious nature of Black existence in a White supremacist world. Cone writes:

> The paradox of a crucified savior lies at the heart of the Christian story. That paradox was particularly evident in the first century when crucifixion was recognised as the particular form of execution reserved by the Roman Empire for insurrectionists and rebels. It was a public spectacle accompanied by torture and shame – one of the most humiliating and painful deaths ever devised by human beings.[40]

Cone outlines the grim similarities between the 'spectacle' of lynching in the US, between particularly the peak years 1880 and 1940, and the 'spectacle' of Jesus' crucifixion at the heart of the occupying Roman forces. Both entities are about brutal colonial power imposing its vicious and evil will on those who are the colonized and oppressed, seeking to ensure complete subservience and compliance from the latter. The fact that, in both cases, death comes as a merciful relief after days of unremitting terror and unimagined pain *is entirely the point*. As I have often said in many classrooms, if one wants to kill someone, human beings are remarkably adept at doing this with great efficiency. In Jesus' day, a spear thrust into the chest of an opponent or enemy would pretty much ensure instant death for that recipient and in the peak years of lynching, a gunshot to the head would achieve the same result. If death is the *sole point*, then crucifixion and lynching are slow and convoluted machinery for killing people. As Cone demonstrates, however, in this amazingly brutal and brilliant book, the essential point of both modes of killing *is not simply to kill the body, but more importantly, to crush the spirit and the soul.*[41]

Cone was not the first to explore the gruesome legacy of lynching and its impact on the Black psyche. In *Terror and Triumph*, Anthony Pinn outlines the contested and troubled relationship between White slave-holding Christianity and Black bodies, explicating the levels of demonization and virulent denigration that provided the essential backdrop to transatlantic chattel slavery.[42]

Pinn's influential *Why Lord?*[43] goes further than William R. Jones' thesis that rests on a form of 'Humanocentric theism', in which the latter adopts a 'Deist' position concerning the Divine. For Pinn, full blown humanism is the logical position for a radical, human-centred position that prioritizes human agency as the primary hermeneutical perspective on understanding Black suffering and evil in the world. Anthony Pinn's work seeks to move beyond the formal category of theodicy, arguing that to work within this framework is to continue to centre God and God's attributes as the critical point of departure.[44] Conversely, moving beyond traditional theological sources and their concomitant sense of 'authority' such as the Bible, Pinn creates a mode of religio-cultural reflection he terms 'Nitty-Gritty Hermeneutics'. Pinn describes 'Nitty-Gritty hermeneutics' thus:

> Defined by its nitty-gritty character, nitty-gritty hermeneutics exhibits a sense of nonconformity. It ridicules interpretations and interpreters who seek to inhibit or restrict liberative movement and hard inquiries into the problems of life.[45]

Anthony Pinn's solution to the vexed question of Black suffering and evil is to move beyond the parameters of conventional theistic informed theologizing and to mine the resources of Black expressive culture, in order to find human meaning-making in the production of music and art, as means of addressing the deepest of existential challenges.

If Pinn has constructed a humanist informed approach to Black theology and how it addresses the vexed conundrum of evil and suffering in a world in which God is alleged to be sovereign, then Cone, conversely, continues to work with the mechanics of Christian faith and metaphysics. To Cone, the key to understanding Black suffering is to appeal to the mystery of the cross and the subversion of White supremacist power by a God who effected the resurrection of Jesus in order to demonstrate that evil can never have the final word. For Cone, however, we must never sacralize or spiritualize the cross to the point where the evil that underpins its realities disappears into the ether. It is this spiritualizing of the cross, he believes, that permits White American Christians to fail to see the connections between the humiliation wrought on victims in the first century and the nineteenth and twentieth.[46]

The importance of Cone's searing analysis lies not solely in his identification with the literal lynching of Black bodies in White supremacist America, but in all the incidences of futile Black deaths in police custody or at the hands of police officers in the UK. A British Nigerian man who was 'hounded to his death' by police in Leeds was finally remembered 50 years after his death. David Oluwale was last seen fleeing two police officers on 18 April 1969 and was later found drowned in the River Aire. On one of the charge sheets, when asked for his nationality the police had simply written the word 'Wog'.[47]

I want to recall also the death of Clinton McCurbin, an African Caribbean man who died of asphyxia at the hands of the police in Wolverhampton on 20 February 1987, having been arrested for using a stolen credit card. Eyewitness accounts spoke of seeing McCurbin gasping for breath as White officers pinned him to the floor and crushed the air out of his body, regardless of the fact that his body had lain limp for several minutes as he lost consciousness. Later that year, despite the cautionary words from my very law abiding and hyper religious and respectable parents to focus on my studies (I was in the last year of my degree course in Church history at Birmingham University), I nevertheless travelled to Wolverhampton along with thousands of others to protest the death of Clinton McCurbin. That was my very first march. No officers were ever charged with his death. The coroner ruled it death by misadventure. Black people across the Midlands protested and sang songs of defiance, we railed with anger, but White power, whether in the shape of the Independent Police Complaints Commission (IPCC), or the coroner, or the media (McCurbin had a criminal record, so presumably he deserved to die), they all had no problem ignoring our pleas for justice because in the final analysis, Black bodies and people who inhabit those bodies simply do not matter.

When I asked my white colleagues to support me in mounting a campaign to mark the callous killing of Clinton McCurbin way back in 1987, I was met with complete indifference. McCurbin's death did not resonate with them because the death of another anonymous Black man was no big deal. Every Black person knows that, in and of itself, George Floyd's death is not remarkable. Systemic racism didn't start with George Floyd's death, nor will it end with White people wringing their hands in liberal guilt, telling us how sorry they are for the racism that blights our lives and not theirs, while continuing to support the policies of a prime minister who can make racist remarks and has never apologized. A prime minister who defends the continued public display of statues erected in honour of White people who despised Black people and considered us lesser beings. The bitter truth is that Black lives have not mattered for a very long time and the church has long been complicit in this.

In 2017 the independent Angiolini report into police custody deaths found that 'a disproportionate number of people from BAME communities (and those with mental health concerns) have died following the use of force'.[48]

The report found that between 1990 and 2008 16 per cent of those in police custody who died from the use of force were Black, twice the proportion arrested. It summarized: 'Deaths of people from BAME communities, in particular young Black men, resonate with the Black community's experience of systemic racism.'[49]

Although Cone, as a contextual, African American, Black liberation theologian, writes for his context and immediate reality, his powerful words and brilliantly incisive theological ideas, nevertheless continue to speak to Black people all over the world.

Conclusion

The power of Cone's work has been to link the pointless ways in which Black people still die at the hands of White supremacist power, with the divine sacrifice of Jesus at the hands of colonial, ontologically White Roman imperial power. The latter provides the Christological framework for the former. Our lives matter because long before we were defined as chattel slaves, as heathens and natives, as brutes and savages, as rapists and work-shy welfare queens and illegal immigrants, Jesus Christ died like one of us. He died a miserable and vicious death that was humiliating and absolutely avoidable. Jesus' encounter with Pontius Pilate indicates the kind of death he died. Pilate knew he was innocent and that Jesus should have been released (and he had the power to do so) but the power of the mob and political expediency condemned him to death.

Cone's Christology does not doubt the metaphysical power of God to effect a miracle in releasing Jesus from the bonds of death and to new life, in terms of his bodily resurrection. Cone holds to this as an act of faith, as do many liberationists – as I stated in the previous chapter, Cone (like myself and many others) is a liberationist and not a theological liberal. We believe in the literal, bodily resurrection of Jesus because this speaks to the God who has the power to resist White supremacy and its blasphemous claims to be the final arbiter of life and death.

And yet Cone does not fall into the theological determinism that asserts Jesus *had to die* because God willed it. Rather, Jesus dies because it was inevitable given his stance against the corruptions of the human spirit willed by the Roman occupation and the greed and collusion of Jesus' countrymen, imbued with a spirit of internalized colonization that would rather surrender one of their own for the sake of self-preservation and preferment.

Rather, the nature of Jesus' struggle in confronting the cross is expressed in very eloquent terms by the Church of England priest and Black theologian, David Isiorho, who has stated that 'Jesus died *because* of our sins and not *for* them.'[50] In invoking this statement, Isiorho is agreeing with Cone in suggesting that Jesus died in solidarity with and as one of the oppressed peoples of his day. In doing so, Jesus is alongside all Black people who have died and continue to be crucified in our contemporary epoch. Jesus dies in solidarity with all colonized and marginalized and oppressed peoples for whom the cross of abusive power, often in the shape of systemic racism, remains a daily reality.[51]

The realities of the cross are light years removed from the sanctified and supine way in which many White Christians espouse racists' views on the one hand and adorn their necks with lifeless, abstract crosses that affirm their sense of entitlement and complacency on the other. For them, the cross has been brutally removed from the realities of colonized suffering, so much so that White supremacist groups like the Ku Klux Klan and Britain First can seek to claim the cross as their own, never seeing the irony that the person to whom the cross speaks was the very kind of person they are determined to hate, given that he was not a White Aryan man.[52]

Jesus dies like many Black people, forced into an existential encounter with White power which he will not survive, any more than did Trayvon Martin, Breonna Taylor, Eric Garner, Mark Duggan, and countless other Black people. Their deaths did not need to happen, but they happened, nonetheless, and political expediency, much like Pontius Pilate, explained it away as necessary to keep the wider mood of populism and White nationalism happy and contented. Jesus dies like a Black person caught between power and complicity. His death echoes those of so many in history who sought to be themselves and to resist the blandishments of White power and the sense of entitlement that wanted them to believe that their lives did not matter. Womanist theologian Jacquelyn Grant argues that Jesus is a co-sufferer with ordinary poor Black people, as they seek to confront unjust systems and powers in their efforts to fight for their freedom.[53]

This chapter has sought to provide a brief overview of the central claims of James Cone's understanding of Jesus within the corpus of his Black theology work across 50 years as a public intellectual. In the following chapter we shall look at the role of the church in Black theology, juxtaposing the best of its identity, in subversive creation of it through the lens of Black experience, and the worst, when it was and remains allied to White supremacy, entitlement and privilege.

Notes

1 James H. Cone, *Black Theology and Black Power* (Maryknoll, NY: Orbis Books, 1989/2009), p. 34.

2 For more details on this African American Black church tradition, see Ann H. Pinn and Anthony B. Pinn, *Fortress Introduction to Black Church History* (Minneapolis, MN: Fortress Press, 2001). See also Alton B. Pollard and Carol B. Duncan (eds), *Black Church Studies Reader* (New York: Palgrave Macmillan, 2016).

3 See Linda E. Thomas (ed.), *Living Stones in the Household of God: The Legacy and Future of Black Theology* (Minneapolis, MN: Fortress Press, 2003).

4 See James H. Cone, *For My People: Black Theology and the Black Church* (Maryknoll, NY: Orbis Books, 1984), pp. 99–121.

5 James H. Cone, *Said I Wasn't Gonna Tell Nobody* (Maryknoll, NY: Orbis Books, 2018), pp. 1–30.

6 See Howard Thurman, *Jesus and the Disinherited* (Boston, MA: Beacon Press, 1996 [first published 1949]).
7 Thurman, *Jesus and the Disinherited*, pp. 11–35.
8 Thurman, *Jesus and the Disinherited*, p. 15.
9 Thurman, *Jesus and the Disinherited*, p. 34.
10 See Jacquelyn Grant, *White Women's Christ and Black Women's Jesus: Feminist Christology and Womanist Response* (Atlanta, GA: Scholar's Press, 1989).
11 Cone, *Black Theology and Black Power*, p. 35.
12 Cone, *Black Theology and Black Power*, pp. 43–7.
13 See Noel L. Erskine, *Decolonising Theology: A Caribbean Perspective* (Maryknoll, NY: Orbis Books, 1998). See also Michelle A. Gonzalez, *Afro-Cuban Theology: Religion, Race, Culture, and Identity* (Gainesville, FL: University of Florida Press, 2009), and also Mokgethi Motlhabi, *African Theology / Black Theology in South Africa: Looking Back, Moving On* (Pretoria: UNISA Press, 2009).
14 James H. Cone, *God of the Oppressed* (San Francisco: Harper and Row, 1975), p. 119.
15 Cone, *God of the Oppressed*, p. 114.
16 Cone, *A Black Theology of Liberation*, p. 113.
17 The picture 'The Healer' was drawn by Harold Copping in 1915, commissioned by the then London Missionary Society, a forerunner of the Council for World Mission (CWM). For further details on this see Peter Cruchley, '"Savage healers", Rhetorics of Whiteness in the Council for World Mission/London Missionary Society Mission Archive' (Amsterdam: World Council of Churches, forthcoming).
18 Cone, *God of the Oppressed*, p. 122.
19 Cone, *God of the Oppressed*, p. 120.
20 See for example, Angus Cochrane, 'Tory MPs refuse to "pander to woke agenda" as they reject anti-racism training', *The National*, 22 September 2020, www.thenational.scot/news/18738661.tory-mps-refuse-pander-woke-agenda-reject-anti-racism-training/ (accessed 5.10.2021).
21 For a critical response to the government report, see Ceren Sagir, 'U.K. Conservative Party government report: "Institutional racism" doesn't exist', *People's World*, 21 April 2021 (accessed 510.2021).
22 Cone, *A Black Theology of Liberation*, p. 121.
23 See Reddie, *Working Against the Grain: Reimagining Black Theology in the 21st Century* (London: Equinox, 2008), pp. 81–90.
24 This was the case when this piece was published on 5 October 2021. For further statistics on Covid in Africa, see 'COVID-19 (WHO African Region)', *World Health Organisation* (accessed 5.10.2021).
25 Cone, *A Black Theology of Liberation*, p. 121.
26 Cone, *Black Theology and Black Power*, pp. 31–61.

27 Cone, *My Soul Looks Back*, p. 27.

28 The famed South African Black liberation theologian Allan Boesak makes connections between the Civil Rights movement, the Anti-Apartheid movement and Black Lives Matter in a recent book. See Allan Aubrey Boesak, *Pharaohs on Both Sides of the Blood-Red Waters: Prophetic Critique on Empire* (Eugene, OR: Cascade Books, 2017).

29 See Albert B. Cleage, *Black Messiah: On Black Consciousness And Black Power* (New York: Africa World Press, 2017 [first published in 1968]). See also his book, *Black Christian Nationalism: New directions for the Black church* (New York: William Murrow, 1972).

30 Cone, *A Black Theology of Liberation*, pp. 114 and 123.

31 Cone, *A Black Theology of Liberation*, p. 114.

32 Cone, *A Black Theology of Liberation*, p. 123.

33 See Kelly Brown Douglas, *Black Bodies and the Black Church: A Blues Slant* (New York: Palgrave Macmillan, 2012), pp. 93–105.

34 Cone, *A Black Theology of Liberation*, p. 123.

35 See Dele Ogun, *A Slave Ship Called Jesus* (London: Lawless Publications, 2021).

36 See Albert J. Raboteau, *Slave Religion: The 'Invisible Institution' in the Antebellum South* (New York: Oxford University Press, 2004).

37 Cone, *Black Theology and Black Power*, pp. 62–90.

38 Cone, *Black Theology and Black Power*, p. 73.

39 See the following for details of the nature of the racist abuse received by Revd Jarel Robinson-Brown: Harriet Sherman, 'C of E body criticises "social media lynching" of priest in Captain Tom row', *The Guardian*, 9 February 2021, www.theguardian.com/world/2021/feb/09/church-body-criticises-social-media-lynching-priest-robinson-brown-captain-tom-row (accessed 5.10.2021).

40 Cone, *The Cross and the Lynching Tree*, pp. 1–2.

41 Cone, *The Cross and the Lynching Tree*, pp. 1–29.

42 Anthony B. Pinn, *Terror and Triumph: The Nature of Black Religion* (Minneapolis, MN: Fortress Press, 2003), pp. 1–80.

43 See Anthony B. Pinn, *Why Lord? Suffering and Evil in Black Theology* (New York: Continuum, 1999).

44 See Anthony Pinn, *Why Lord?*, pp. 113–16.

45 Anthony Pinn, *Why Lord?*, p. 117.

46 Cone, *The Cross and the Lynching Tree*, pp. 30–64.

47 For further details on the life and death David Oluwale, see 'News', *Remember Oluwale for Social Justice*, https://rememberoluwale.org/index.html (accessed 8.10.2021).

48 For further details on the report see Home Office, 'Deaths and serious incidents in police custody', *Gov.uk*, 30 November 2017, www.

gov.uk/government/publications/deaths-and-serious-incidents-in-police-custody (accessed 8.10.2021).

49 Rt Hon. Dame Elish Angiolini DBE QC, 'Report of the Independent Review of Deaths and Serious Incidents in Police Custody', p. 86, available from www.gov.uk/government/publications/deaths-and-serious-incidents-in-police-custody.

50 Verbatim comment made by David Isiorho at the national Black Theology in Britain conference at the Queen's Foundation for Ecumenical Theological Education, July 2008. This comment was made in response to the paper he had presented, critiquing many of the traditional notions of Christ's sacrifice, particularly those that adhere to notions of 'penal substitution'. This paper was subsequently published in the international Black theology journal. See David Isiorho, 'Black Identities and Faith Adherence: Social Policy and Penal Substitution in the epoch of the SS Empire Windrush', in *Black Theology: An International Journal*, vol. 7, no. 3, 2009, pp. 282–99.

51 David Isiorho, 'Black Identities and Faith Adherence', pp. 284–92.

52 See Stephen Ray, 'Contending for the Cross: Black Theology and the Ghosts of Modernity', in *Black Theology: An International Journal*, vol. 8, no. 1, 2010, pp. 53–68. Ray demonstrates how White supremacy distorts the cross from being a symbol of God's solidarity with oppressed peoples on the margins to being a warped sign of White supremacy.

53 See Grant, *White Women's Christ and Black Women's Jesus*, pp. 212–18.

4

The Church in Black Theology

The church has always been an integral part of the story and the development of Christian theology. It is the church, coming into being at Pentecost, that provides the authority that confirms the composition of the Christian New Testament. It is the church that seeks to be the practical and collective expression and sign of God's Kingdom. The majority of Christian theologians will undertake their scholarly work in dialogue with the church, often as confessing believers in the very thing they are seeking to articulate as the truth. I am no exception and neither, of course, was James Cone. Christian theology exists to serve the church and the church in turn exists to serve Jesus Christ, in whose name she is consecrated and from whom she receives her identity and reason for existing.

In the early iteration of Black theology, Cone charts the developing understanding of the 'People of God', namely Israel, who throughout the Hebrew scriptures we see in a covenantal relationship with God.[1] God's relationship to an oppressed group of people whom God has elected provides the platform for 'God's revolutionary activity' to demonstrate God's righteousness to the world.[2] The fulfilment of this process of God acting in history culminates in the work and the person called 'Jesus of Nazareth'. With the coming of Jesus, the church comes into being to give practical expression to the teaching and the values shared by the activism, the message and the sacrificial death of the one in whom and from whom the church takes her identity and authority. Cone writes of the church: 'The Church, then, consists of people who have been seized by the Holy Spirit and who have determined to live as if all depends on God. It has no will of its own, only God's will; it has no duty of its own, only God's duty. Its existence is grounded in God.'[3]

In this regard, it is important to note that Cone has quite a 'high view' of the church. In making this remark, I do not mean to say that Cone sees the church in episcopal terms in the use of the term 'high', that might constitute a way of denoting a church with a pronounced sense of hierarchy that conforms to notions of apostolic succession. Rather, in using the term 'high' I mean Cone does not see the church in utilitarian terms as merely a human institution that seeks to do some good. For Cone, the church is understood as a gift of God, created in order to undertake the work of liberation to which God has given expression in the witness and supreme example of Jesus Christ. Because of the divine calling of the church, Cone expects much from it and is, therefore, scathing when it fails to live up to its high calling.

Of particular importance is how Cone differentiates between the 'White Church', that is, the church that emerges from the beliefs and social practices of people of White Euro-American heritage, and the 'Black Church'. The latter is the opposite of the former, the Black church grows out of the struggles of African Americans to give life to the liberationist impulse of God they witnessed in their lives in the power of the Holy Spirit, through their often limited engagement with the scriptures (many enslaved Africans were forbidden to read in general and not encouraged to read the Bible), and through their identification with Jesus as 'one of them'. The Black church, for Cone, although not beyond criticism as we shall see, nonetheless retains the identity of the 'true church' that seeks to be the authentic expression of Christian love, generosity and most crucially, aligned to Christ's liberating mission to bring freedom to those bound by systemic evil and social forms of injustice.[4]

The authenticity of the church is found not in its adherence to doctrines, dogma and creeds but rather through the extent to which it is willing to participate in the radical work of God revealed in Jesus Christ. To the extent that the church is willing to make a difference in the world and to contradict the false teachings of White supremacy and the jaundiced and biased operations of the status quo that upholds capitalistic greed and naked self-centredness, then she can be heralded as being what she was created to be. Yet, as Cone demonstrates throughout his work, the failure of the church and Christian theology to denounce White supremacy, White entitlement and privilege, is the damning indictment on the 'White church'.[5]

Central to the identity of the church is the clear sense that it is a countercultural agency that challenges and refutes any notion of injustice and the habitual selfishness of the world. Take for example this long quotation from *A Black Theology of Liberation*.

> The Christian church is that community of persons who 'got the hint', as they thus refuse to be content with human pain and suffering. To receive 'the power of God unto salvation' places persons in a state of Christian existence, making it impossible for them to sit still as their neighbors are herded off to the prison camps. The hint of the gospel moves them to say no to rulers of the world: 'If our brothers and sisters have to go, it will be over our dead bodies'. They are the ones who believe in the gospel of liberation, convinced that personal freedom is more important than 'law and order' ... Because the church is the community that participates in Jesus Christ's liberating work in history, it can never endorse 'law and order' that causes suffering.[6]

One can quickly deduce from this quotation that much of what happens on a Sunday in many parts of the world is not an authentic expression of the church according to the high expectations held of it by James Cone. For most churches, 'being church' entails the coming together to sing hymns, speak prayers, enact some form of liturgy (be it formalized and prescribed or implicit and improvised), listen to some form of address/sermon and then have coffee/tea and informal 'chitchat' afterwards. The aforementioned often takes place as a ghettoized experience separated from the wider world and the myriad problems and challenges that exist there. Of course, not every church is like this and there many notable exceptions, but in my very limited experience, the latter are the exceptions and not the rule.

Cone's words are anathema to the millions of White evangelicals in the US who voted twice for Donald Trump and his brand of populist White Christian nationalism. The noted African American Black theologian, Josiah Young, himself a former doctoral student of Cone's at Union Theological Seminary, has outlined the intellectual and faith gap between conservative White evangelicals who voted for Trump and the majority of Black Christians who opposed him through his presidency.[7] Charting the diametrically differing ways in which both groups saw and interpreted their Christian faith in the public square, Young writes, 'Many White conservative evangelicals are the progeny of racist privilege while many Black evangelicals are the progeny of enslaved African Americans.'[8]

The crucial difference between the foundational moments of 'White Christianity' and 'Black Christianity' provide the basic template and backdrop against which Cone makes his assessment on the authentic nature of the church.

Given the propensity of White Christians in the US to stand back and support the lynching of African Americans, one can see the extent to which White Christianity in America might be seen as anything but Christian. Cone reflects on the fundamental difference between these two modes of the faith when seen through the lens of the church. He writes:

> The cross has been transformed into a harmless, non-offensive ornament that Christians wear around their necks. Rather than reminding us of the 'cost of discipleship', it has become a form of 'cheap grace', an easy way to salvation that doesn't force us to confront the power of Christ's message and mission. Until we can see the cross and the lynching tree together, until we can identify Christ with a 'recrucified' black body

hanging from a lynching tree, there can be no genuine understanding of Christian identity in America, and no deliverance from the brutal legacy of slavery and white supremacy.[9]

Failure to be the church

In his 50-plus year career as a public intellectual, James Cone was concerned, constantly, with the need for the church to live out her mandate to be a lived and practised experiment in the liberationist expression of the gospel of Jesus Christ. Perhaps the most consistent and sustained critique of the failure to be the church can be found in a chapter in *Speaking The Truth* (1986).[10] In chapter 4, entitled 'A Theological Challenge to the American Catholic Church', Cone offers a coherent critique of American Catholicism that acts as a case study for a wider assessment of White American Christianity.[11] Cone makes it clear that he could write a similar critique of White American Protestantism.[12] Writing in 1986, Cone says 'The Catholic hierarchy in the United States is exclusively controlled by whites. Many black Catholics, therefore, find it difficult to challenge structures of authority in the church without enormous limitations being placed on their ministry.'[13]

This chapter offers an important precis of his landmark article in *Black Theology: An International Journal* 16 years later,[14] where Cone outlines the nature of White institutional myopia in witnessing to the nature of White supremacy. In this earlier book chapter Cone states:

> The evaluation of what purports to be real in the light of human experience is important in theology, because it is *people* who do theology and *not* God. As long as theology is made by human beings, it will be influenced by their history, culture, and interests. This may sound like an elementary point, but when blacks read the textbooks on Catholic theology, we find they are written as if the white experience is universal.[15]

Once again, the above point could have been written yesterday about much of the life of White majority, White-run, Euro-American churches across the so-called global North. I remember the moment I walked out of my final Connexional (National) Theological gathering in the Methodist Church (of Great Britain). It was the summer of 2006 and a gathering of Methodist theologians had come together to discuss the forthcoming 2007 Oxford Institute for Methodist Theological Studies gathering.[16] During the gathering, the participants were asked to name the important historical landmarks which the Institute should mark and respond to the following year. In a lengthy conversation, at which I was the only Black person present, my White Methodist colleagues managed to name every obscure and more obvious anniversary, except for the dominant one on which my Black mind and body was focused; namely, the bicentenary of the Abolition of the Slave Trade in Britain and her dominions. Not one White person mentioned the forthcoming commemoration and its huge significance for Methodists, given that our founder John Wesley's last major statement prior to his death in 1791 was a pronouncement on the evils of slavery.[17]

The failure of the meeting to note not only their Whiteness, but how the experience of being White was so normative that it had completely shaped their consciousness, was so palpable and nauseating, that I decided there and then that I would never frequent another Methodist theological gathering of that sort. At the time of writing, I have remained resolute in that decision.

Cone's critique of White Christianity is enshrined in the failures of White churches to be attentive to the concerns that were uppermost in Jesus' own ministry. Care for the poor, the marginalized and neglected *should* see all churches adopting a liberationist stance in terms of their relationship to power and vested self-interests. Most crucially, it should entail a severe critique of and action to denounce White supremacy, as the latter is a clear denial of the gospel. And yet, the absence of critique at best and downright collusion with the active and more veiled workings of Whiteness at worst, have continued to besmirch the legitimacy of the church in the global North.

The importance of the Black church

The core of James Cone's writing on the place of the church in Black theology is focused on the existence and the continued role of the Black church as an incubator of the radical, liberationist, revolutionary spirit of God, to which the Black experience seeks to testify.

In *My Soul Looks Back*,[18] Cone talks of his Christian formation in Macedonia AME church in Bearden, Arkansas. The Black church in the US speaks to the wider tradition of ecclesial bodies that emerge from the African American experience, with its roots in chattel slavery and the corruption of the Christian faith at the hands of White supremacy. Gayraud Wilmore (with whom James Cone formed a formidable partnership in co-editing two highly influential Black theology anthologies[19]) charts the historical development of the independent Black church tradition in the US, in his brilliant *Black Religion and Black Radicalism*.[20] The importance of this church tradition lies in its separation from the machinations of White power. It is in these Black independent churches, which emerged following the war of independence, that witnessed

> the desire of the slaves to have a place of their own in which to worship God. But it was, in fact, a form of rebellion against the most accessible and vulnerable expression of white oppression and institutional racism in the nation: the American churches.[21]

Historically, Black churches occupied the role of providing both 'safe space' for Black people to be fully human beyond the restrictions of institutional racism, and where the thrust for Black freedom could be rehearsed and organized. So, it is through the Black church that the 'Black Power' statement is issued by the 'National Committee of Negro Churchmen' on 31 July 1966, which is published in the *New York Times*.[22] The noted Black theologian and former doctoral student of Cone, Dwight Hopkins, highlights this statement as the birth of Black theology in America.[23]

The church that emerges from the Black experience has been the incubator for Black theology. The initial focus of Cone's work as it pertained to the church in Black theology focused on the United States. While commending the Black church for its radical roots, as outlined by Gayraud Wilmore, Cone also chastises it for failing to live up to that exalted history. Cone has been at pains to critique the Black church for its anti-intellectualism, the extent to which it has become a haven for neo-conservatism and often a retreat from the very kinds of political engagement that brought it into existence in the first instance.[24] Cone writes 'Unfortunately, black churches have allowed the historical and theological identity of black faith to be forgotten partly because of their promotion of the art of preaching to the exclusion of doing theology.'[25] Because Cone loves Black people (the subject of the following chapter) and therefore loves the genius within them, that is the 'spirit of liberation for us'[26] that helped to create the Black church, he is not sparing in his criticism of it. In many respects, some of Cone's more trenchant critiques of the Black church have been realized with the emergence and resurgence of the Black Lives Matter movement. Writing in the early 1980s, Cone was at pains to point out that the majority of Black churches did not participate in the Civil Rights Movement.[27] In my work I have spoken of Black Christianity being infected by bourgeois middle-class respectability politics that has seen Black Christians and the churches to whom they belong often disengage from any forms of praxis they deem as too 'political' or 'extreme'.[28] The noted womanist theologian (and another of Cone's brilliant doctoral students) Kelly Brown Douglas outlines the neo-conservative classism of Black churches that often sees them siding with the forces of respectability and non-radicalism.[29] Cone states:

During the 1960s and afterwards, it seemed to me that the AME church and many other black denominations did not regard the liberation of the poor as the central theme of the gospel. Most black denominations preached a 'spiritual' gospel that ignored the political plight of the black poor. By failing to connect the gospel with the bodily liberation of the poor, black churches forgot about their unique historical and theological identity and began to preach a gospel no different from that of white churches.[30]

The situation has grown considerably more acute with the rise of 'prosperity gospel'-informed models of Black church that emerge out of neo-Pentecostalism, in which the radical instincts of Black Christianity have become submerged even further beneath a stultifying weight of conservatism and respectability politics. It is in this context that one has witnessed the rise of Black Lives Matter and the growing gap between it and many traditional Black churches in the US. Reflecting on the heterogeneous, non-doctrinal iconoclasm of the Black Lives Matter movement, in comparison to the Civil Rights movement, one notices that the latter was led by Black church men and the former largely by Black lay women. The latter are not indebted to the church and many no longer see it as an incubator of Black liberation struggles in the US or across the world.

The later development in Cone's thinking, however, was to move discussions about the church beyond the shores of the United States, taking on the global dimensions of the fight for liberation and justice among the poor in the global South. In his essay entitled 'Black Theology and the Black Church' Cone writes:

> Black theologians and church people must now move beyond a mere reaction to white racism in America and begin to extend our vision of a new socially constructed humanity for the whole inhabited world. We must be concerned with the quality of human life not only in the ghettos of American cities but also in Africa, Asia, and Latin America. Since

humanity is one, and cannot be isolated into racial and national groups, there will be no freedom for anyone until there is freedom for all.[31]

Cone's final words are apposite given the lack of sharing of the vaccines for Covid by the White majority countries of the global North in relationship to the majority world, often located in the global South. We have seen little evidence of any commitment to freedom for all. Cone's committed internationalism saw him become a key member of the Ecumenical Association of Third World Theologians (EATWOT) in the 1970s, in dialogue with Latin American, liberation theologians and post-colonial scholars and activists from the African continent and also colleagues from South East Asia.[32] The international dimensions of Cone's reflections on the church have seen him wrestle with the significance of Marxism as a tool of social analysis for understanding global capitalism and the ubiquity of poverty across the world as it impacts on Black people and other peoples of colour. In *Speaking The Truth*, Cone writes:

> To liberate the poor requires social analysis that explains the origins and the nature of human poverty. Why are people poor, and who benefits from their poverty? This question places the church in the context of society and forces it to be self-critical as it seeks to realize its mission of bearing witness to God's kingdom that is coming in and through the human struggles to liberate the poor.[33]

Cone saw the church as called to be the catalyst through whom the liberating work of God in history would be enacted. The growing reach of his international fame and influence reached the UK on his visit in 1996 to the Queen's Foundation. Robert Beckford, tutor in Black Theology, had invited Cone to come and speak. What was clear from his speeches was the immediate relevance of his words and ideas to the nature and existence of colonial, Mission Christianity in Britain.

Cone's influence on the church in the UK

As Cone makes clear in *Speaking The Truth*, White Christians have been more concerned with unity around doctrinal and confessional issues than with socio-political ones such as race and poverty.[34] While the Body of Christ has been fractured by arguments over doctrine, denomination, issues of class, gender and sexuality, perhaps the most ongoing challenge and indeed the most persistent scourge has been that of racism. Black Christianity in Britain has constantly sought to challenge oppressive realities within the Body of Christ. In using the term 'Black Christianity in Britain', I am speaking of the broad phenomenon of Black people of African and Caribbean descent who are domiciled in Britain and within this context can be said to believe in the God revealed in Jesus Christ and seek to give expression to the central tenets of the Christian faith in myriad forms of social-cultural practices.

Black Christianity in Britain has challenged the scourge of racism as it has sought to effect unity within the Body of Christ. At its heart, has been the challenge to White Christianity to live out the gospel imperative to love one another as humanity has been loved by Christ. The challenges of John 13.31–35 are not new. I remember sitting in the Methodist Conference in 1998 when the church sought to recognize the 50th anniversary of the post-war Caribbean migrants who, on 22 June 1948, landed at Tilbury docks on the *Empire Windrush*. While we celebrated the rise of a more conspicuous, multicultural and plural Britain that had emerged through this epoch of African Caribbean and later South Asian migration (approximately 1948–1972), the church also had to reckon with the stories of lament of Black people sharing their pain of being rejected by the 'Mother churches'. The continued struggles of Black people within historic, White majority dominated churches, is a reminder of the continued necessity of James Cone's radical understanding of the nature and the liberationist identity of the church. A church committed to liberation and the full inclusion of those who are on the margins will not treat its

Black members and adherents so appallingly. The fact that in 2021 the Church of England needed to have a Commission on Racial Justice is surely an indictment of the failure to be church for all people, over the past 70 or so years, let alone the collusion with slavery and empire in the centuries preceding the Windrush.

Black people have displayed immense amounts of love for and dedication to their respective 'Mother churches', a love and dedication that is not deserved by these ecclesial bodies. White missionary Christianity sought to convert the 'natives' and the 'heathens', but even our conversion did not make the White institutional church love us as we deserved to be loved. Even when Black people became Christians there was little evidence of this love ethic displayed in the actions of many White Christians.[35] When many Black people travelled to the UK in the post-World War Two migration of the 1950s and 1960s, where was the outpouring of love for one another upon their arrival? It is no wonder, then, that many Black Christians have questioned the alleged nature of so-called White, British Christianity.[36] Looking from the outside in, some older Black Christians of the Windrush Generation have wondered whether many 'good White English Christians' have ever read and understood the New Testament at all.[37]

White English Christianity must be committed to a ruthless and fiercely argued critique of its Whiteness, in a manner that accords with the existential struggling for truth that Black people have been obliged and sometimes forced to undertake since the creation of modernity.[38] In critiquing Whiteness, I am talking about a thorough deconstruction of the toxic relationship between Christianity, empire and notions of White-British superiority.[39]

The recent research of Black British Pentecostal womanist scholar Selina Stone highlights the failure of progressive Black Caribbean Pentecostal churches in Britain to develop a form of theological praxis that engages holistically with those who are marginalized and disaffected within the body politic of post-colonial Britain.[40] Like Cone's critique of Black churches in the US, the logic of his work also resonances for Black majority churches in White historic denominations and Black Pentecostal ones like those identified by Selina Stone in her recent doctoral studies.

Speaking with my friend Revd Jarel Robinson-Brown, who was on the receiving end of the rejectionist homophobic attitudes of a Black-majority Methodist congregation, is a reminder of Cone's radical work, challenging the church to *be* the church. To read Jarel's book *Black, Gay, British, Christian, Queer*[41] is to read of the ways in which his Black queer body has been rejected by other Black people, who have bought into and internalized the tropes and ethics of a neo-colonial form of Whiteness, in which the strictures around the respectability of heteronormativity were constructed by White Victorian imperialists and not Black people themselves. To witness the rejection of Jarel's ministry, due to one facet of his life, as if all his eminent gifts and graces were rendered null and void by this specific and particular facet, is to see the painful internalization of Whiteness within the corporate edifice of Black Christianity writ large, to a sad and disappointing degree in twenty-first-century Britain.[42]

As I have read Jarel's brave but never bitter words of regret, as he has reanimated his story of his calling and passion to be one of 'Mr Wesley's Preachers', I have witnessed the ways in which internalized racism and the tropes of Whiteness, built on coloniality and notions of acceptability for some and rejection for others, still remains a toxic residue of empire within the body politic of our nation. As mentioned earlier, this was witnessed, quite viscerally, in his electronic lynching on social media for an innocuous tweet,[43] as well as within British Methodism. In my previous book, *Theologising Brexit*, I spoke of Black gay people being identified as 'enemies within'.[44]

As Cone reminds us, the quest for equity, liberation and justice is one that requires the committed determined action of all peoples, irrespective of faith commitment. But it also requires truth telling and a retreat from all forms of obfuscation that blind us to the structural and systematic forms of racism that continue to oppress Black and other minority ethnic people in Britain. Whether we wish to acknowledge it or not, privilege and notions of who is important have a colour. Similarly, systemic power and notions of belonging and what is deemed acceptable also has a colour. The failure to name and unmask these forms of unearned privilege has been, for me, the most telling indictment of White Christianity in Britain. The days of Black people having to struggle with the pernicious patterns of socio-cultural and religious 'double jeopardy' (we have to solve our own problems and those of White people also, who for the most part, have failed to address their own Whiteness) should be at an end.

The task of unmasking the privileged construct of Whiteness is not a task for Black theologians alone. Conversely, the task of effecting the systemic and structural changes that better reflect the Kingdom of God within the urban context is a task for us all. The power and importance of James Cone's understanding of the church in Black theology cannot be overstated!

Notes

1 James H. Cone, *Black Theology and Black Power* (Maryknoll, NY: Orbis Books, 1989/2009), pp. 63–4.

2 Cone, *Black Theology and Black Power*, p. 64.

3 Cone, *Black Theology and Black Power*, p. 65.

4 James H. Cone, *God of the Oppressed* (San Francisco: Harper and Row, 1975), pp. 138–62.

5 James H. Cone, 'Theology's Great Sin, Silence in the Face of White Supremacy', in *Black Theology*, vol. 2, no. 2, 2004, pp. 139–52.

6 James H. Cone, *A Black Theology of Liberation* (Maryknoll, NY: Orbis Books, 1970/1990), pp. 129–30.

7 See Josiah Ulysses Young III, 'Making America Great Again? An Essay on "The Weightier Matters of The Law: Justice and Mercy and Faith"', in *Black Theology: An International Journal*, vol. 16, no. 1, 2018, pp. 53–60.

8 Young, 'Making America Great Again?', p. 54.

9 James H. Cone, *The Cross and the Lynching Tree* (Maryknoll, NY: Orbis Books, 2011), pp. xiv–xv.

10 See James H. Cone, *Speaking The Truth: Ecumenism, Liberation and Black Theology* (Maryknoll, NY: Orbis Books, 1986).

11 Cone, *Speaking The Truth*, pp. 50–60.

12 Cone, *Speaking The Truth*, p. 55.

13 Cone, *Speaking The Truth*, p. 55.

14 Cone, 'Theology's Great Sin', pp. 139–52.

15 Cone, *Speaking The Truth*, p. 58.

16 This is a 5-yearly gathering of Methodist and Wesleyan scholars from across the world, meeting at Oxford University. For more details see 'Our Mission: Scholarship in Service', *The Oxford Institute of Methodist Theological Studies*, https://oxford-institute.org/ (accessed 13.12.2021).

17 For a critical reflection on John Wesley's views on slavery, see Michael N. Jagessar, 'Review Article: Critical Reflections on John Wesley', in *Black Theology: An International Journal*, vol. 5, no. 2, 2007, pp. 250–5.

18 James H. Cone, *My Soul Looks Back* (Maryknoll, NY: Orbis Books, 1999), pp. 64–92.

19 See James H. Cone and Gayraud S. Wilmore (eds), *Black Theology A Documentary History Volume One: 1966–1979* (Maryknoll, NY: Orbis Books, 1993) and James H. Cone and Gayraud S. Wilmore (eds), *Black Theology A Documentary History Volume Two: 1980–1992* (Maryknoll, NY: Orbis Books, 1993).

20 See Gayraud S. Wilmore, *Black Religion and Black Radicalism: An Interpretation of The Religious History of Afro-American People*, third edition (Maryknoll, NY: Orbis Books, 1986), pp. 74–98.

21 Wilmore, *Black Religion and Black Radicalism*, p. 78.

22 See '"Black Power" statement is issued by the "National Committee of Negro Churchmen" on the July 31, 1966', Cone and Wilmore (eds), *Black Theology A Documentary History Volume One*, pp. 19–26.

23 See Dwight Hopkins' interview with Ruth Wilde for Inclusive Church. See the following link for the recorded interview: 'Black Theology Series: No. 2 – Dwight Hopkins', *YouTube*, 24 July 2020, www.youtube.com/watch?v=1FNRTQqyQgY (accessed 20.01.2022).

24 Cone, *My Soul Looks Back*, pp. 64–92.

25 Cone, *My Soul Looks Back*, p. 69.

26 See Dwight N. Hopkins, *Head and Heart: Black Theology, Past, Present and Future* (New York: Palgrave Macmillan, 2002), pp. 77–90.

27 Cone, *My Soul Looks Back*, pp. 67–70.

28 See Anthony G. Reddie, *Theologising Brexit: A Liberationist and Postcolonial Critique* (Abingdon: Routledge, 2019), pp. 48–51.

29 Kelly Brown Douglas, *Black Bodies and the Black Church: A Blues Slant* (London: Palgrave Macmillan, 2012), pp. 93–105.

30 Cone, *My Soul Looks Back*, pp. 66–7.
31 'Black Theology and the Black Church', Cone and Wilmore (eds), *Black Theology A Documentary History Volume One*, p. 271.
32 Cone, *My Soul Looks Back*, pp. 93–113.
33 Cone, *Speaking The Truth*, p. 123.
34 Cone, *Speaking The Truth*, pp. 122–3.
35 It is important that I make the point that not all White Christians are guilty of this behaviour. Examples of alternative practices can be found in Kenneth Leech, *Through Our Long Exile* (London: Darton, Longman and Todd, 2001); Kenneth Leech, *Doing Theology in Altab Park* (London: Darton, Longman and Todd, 2005); Kenneth Leech, *Race: Changing Society and the Churches* (London: SPCK, 2005); Kenneth Leech, *Struggle in Babylon: Racism in the Cities and Churches of Britain* (London: Sheldon Press, 1988). See also David Haslam, *Race for the Millennium: The Challenge to Church and Society* (London: Churches Commission for Racial Justice, 1996); John L. Wilkinson, *Church in Black and White* (Edinburgh: Saint Andrew Press, 1990) and Timothy J. Gorringe, *Furthering Humanity: A Theology of Culture* (Farnham: Ashgate, 2004).
36 See Michael N. Jagessar, 'A Brief Con-version: A Caribbean and Black-British Postcolonial Scrutiny of Christian Conversion', in *Black Theology: An International Journal*, vol. 7, no. 3, 2009, pp. 300–24.
37 Anthony G. Reddie, *Faith, Stories and the Experience of Black Elders* (London: Jessica Kingsley, 2001), pp. 11–26.
38 Perhaps the best work that addresses issues of Whiteness and privilege in Christian theological terms is Alison Webster, *You Are Mine: Reflections on Who We Are* (London: SPCK, 2009).
39 I have addressed this issue in my republished book, *Is God Colour Blind?: Insights from Black Theology for Christian Faith and Ministry* (second edition, London: SPCK, 2020), pp. 37–52.
40 See Selina Rachel Stone, '"Holy Spirit, Holy Bodies"?: Pentecostal Spirituality, Pneumatology and the Politics of Embodiment', unpublished PhD thesis, University of Birmingham, 2021.
41 See Jarel Robinson-Brown, *Black, Gay, British, Christian, Queer: The Church and the Famine of Grace* (London: SCM Press, 2021).
42 Aspects of this form of rejection can be found in the work of Omari Hutchinson. See Omari G. Hutchinson, 'Into exile: theological perspectives on hearing the voices of Black queer Pentecostal men seeking asylum in the UK', in *Practical Theology*, vol. 11, no. 5, 2018, pp. 426–36.
43 For precis of the incident on twitter concerning Jarel Robinson-Brown see 'Racist attacks on Jarel Robinson-Brown "appalling", says Bishop of London', *Church Times*, 8 February 2021, www.churchtimes.

co.uk/articles/2021/12-february/news/uk/racist-attacks-on-jarel-robin son-brown-appalling-says-bishop-of-london (accessed 3.07.2021).
 44 See Reddie, *Theologising Brexit*, pp. 110–32.

5

Black Theology, Black People and Black Power

In the final chapter of Part 1, I want to reflect on the importance of Black people, primarily African Americans in the first instance, in the Black theology schema of James Cone. In some respects, the location of this chapter can be seen as odd, in that any brief excursion into James Cone's work and life will demonstrate the centrality of Black people and his love of and identification as one of them.

The answer to this lies in the early chapters of James Cone's final memoir *Said I Wasn't Gonna Tell Nobody*, in which we see how Cone fought to create a model of Black theology that would have theological credibility within the academy. Some of Cone's early detractors were quick to declare that Black theology was something of a misnomer as its connection to Black experience made it something more akin to sociology and anthropology than 'proper' theology. Cone refuted such notions and, in establishing the discipline largely as a form of systematic or constructive theology,[1] sought to ensure that Black theology was firmly embedded within the theological academy.

Hence, in this book I have begun by looking at Cone himself as a man and a theologian, and then moved on to his understanding of God and then Jesus, because it is through the lens of his commitment to his vocation to be a theological scholar and teacher, and his faith in God, that one understands his commitment to Black people and Black power. For Cone, the human nature of theology, that is, its identity as a human meaning-making process that is about God, but not done *by* God, means that the theologian needs to be clear as to their basic intent when undertaking *their theology*. What is it they are seeking to accomplish?

Reading and rereading Cone's work it is clear that his central intent is the dignity and self-determination of Black people, as agents of change, created in the image and likeness of God. For Cone, Black people are a sacred people because they are sacred to God. This is not to suggest that all people are not sacred and are special to God. But Cone's point of departure in asserting this for Black people is precisely because it has for too long been a contested claim. The history of racial terror unleashed on Black people across several centuries by White supremacy speaks to the salient fact that we have not been seen or treated as a gift of God to the world by the majority of White people. The travails of Black people have led to a continuing struggle to live with the implications of our Blackness. I would like to remind us of the searing contradiction to diasporan Black life, caught up in the brief description of the Black condition written by Fats Waller entitled 'Black and Blue' – the words are as follows:

> Cold empty bed, springs hard as lead
> Feel like Old Ned, wish I was dead
> All my life through, I've been so black and blue
>
> Even the mouse ran from my house
> They laugh at you, and scorn you too
> What did I do to be so black and blue?
>
> I'm white – inside – but that don't help my case
> Cause I can't hide what is in my face
>
> How would it end? Ain't got a friend
> My only sin is in my skin
> What did I do to be so black and blue?[2]

BLACK THEOLOGY, BLACK PEOPLE AND BLACK POWER

Slavery is long gone but anti-Black racism has long outlived the institution that helped to breath it into life. In our contemporary era, the underlying framework of Blackness, which still symbolically is seen as representing the problematic other, finds expression in a White police officer placing his knee on the neck of a Black man and despite the plaintive pleas of 'I can't breathe', the officer remains unmoved and maintains his violent posture until this Black man dies.[3] One cannot understand the futility of this death unless you understand that this is no new phenomenon. White power has viewed Black flesh as disposable for the past 500 years. The reason why Black theology came into being was simply to assert that our lives mattered in an era when we were viewed purely as chattel and objects to be placed on a financial ledger.

Long before the advent of Black Lives Matter James Cone was fashioning a theological movement whose sole intent was to assert that our lives mattered when White supremacy behaved as if that were not the case.

Across his 50 years as a public intellectual and the architect of Black theology, a constant refrain was the connection between Black theology and Black power. Not only was this the title of his very first book, but it was also the title of numerous book chapters and papers. In an early section of *Black Theology and Black Power*, Cone offers a basic definition of Black power. He says, 'Black Power, then, is a humanizing force because it is the black man's attempt to affirm his being, his attempt to be recognized as "Thou", in spite of the "other", the white power which dehumanizes him.'[4]

Much like the recent controversy around Black Lives Matter and All Lives Matter (the latter being a spoiler organized by predominantly White people to nullify the significance of the former), when Cone unleashed his theological model of Black theology, he had to counter a deluge of insincerity around the dangerous notion of Black power. Cone's invocation of the term was met with a withering torrent of accusations of hate-fuelled anger, often by White people who had remained steadfastly silent at the far more dangerous existence of White power. Black power did not create ghettos or invent a complex machinery that imprisoned and sanctioned the deaths of millions of people. Black power did not create segregation or Jim Crow. Black power did not assassinate advocates for justice such as Malcolm X or Martin Luther King.

Black power was the expression of the agency and self-determination of Black people in 1960s America. In some respects, it was an alternative reframing of a long-held desire of Black people to attain some semblance of mastery over their existence, given that the lives of the descendants of enslaved Africans remained circumscribed by systemic racism and White supremacy. Whether in the foundation of independent Black churches or in the Black nationalism of Marcus Garvey's movement in the years immediately following World War One, Black people had sought, through religion, to create social movements committed to self-determination and freedom.

Central to the edicts of Black power was the sense in which Black people would determine for themselves the agenda by which they might live their lives. Cone writes:

> When Black Power advocates refuse to listen to their would-be liberators, they are charged with creating hatred among black people, thus making significant personal relationships between blacks and whites impossible. It should be obvious that the hate which black people feel toward whites is not due to the creation of the term 'Black Power'. Rather, it is the result of the deliberate and systematic ordering of society on the basis of racism, making black alienation not only possible but inevitable.[5]

The thrust for self-determination and agency, namely the power to decide for oneself the direction of travel for a people and for that not to be influenced by those who have constrained and oppressed you, was made in clear terms. For too long, White liberals had tried to determine the pace of change for Black people. In *The Cross and the Lynching Tree*, James Cone compares the theological vision of Dietrich Bonhoeffer and

Reinhold Niebuhr. Cone demonstrates how Bonhoeffer spent time living in a Black community in Harlem despite only being in America for a year, which had an enduring impact on his consciousness for the remainder of his life. Reggie L. Williams argues that 'Bonhoeffer's experience of learning in Harlem was unique, as it required the modification of filters formed in Germany through which he was accustomed to seeing the world and understanding himself in it.'[6] In contrast, Niebuhr apparently engaged very little with Black experience, ignoring the voices of Black suffering and relativizing the atrocities that were going on at the time.[7]

The power of White liberals to determine the nature of the public conversation around social and political changes as they related to Black people was one that called for a dramatic change in the ways in which such discourse was conducted. Given the propensity for a White-run media to listen to the voices of conservative and 'moderate' Black people has not changed in over 50 years, we can see how White supremacy has always favoured the more moderate voices of those willing to collude with them than those seeking to challenge and overturn their hegemony. In our more contemporary era, one only has to witness the Conservative government's decision to put Dr Tony Sewell, a noted Black conservative, in charge of a report on systemic racism in Britain, to see the cynical ways in which White power seeks to control the narrative of systemic racism in White majority societies.[8]

Given the clear disparities in power between Black people and White people, it should not come as any surprise, then, that a central tenet of Black power has always been self-determination. Way back in 1996, when Cone first spoke at the Queen's Foundation, I recall him saying that partnership and notions of reconciliation as conceived by White people did not equate to equality. In a memorable phrase he stated, 'Being in partnership doesn't make you equal. The horse and the rider are in partnership, but they are not equals.' Since first hearing those words, I have added to the imagery by stating that the rider controls the horse with a bit in its mouth and beats it with a stick. The only agency the horse has is to throw the rider, at which point, it is *always* the horse's fault and not the rider's.

Given these dynamics, and led by the brilliant thoughts and writings of Malcolm X, Martin Luther King and James Baldwin, Cone fashioned a Black theology that puts Black activism and agency centre stage, as the primary interpreters for the meaning of God's righteousness in the world. Blackness becomes the hermeneutical lens through which God's revelation in Christ is made known.

Although not a narrative theologian like myself, in terms of using stories and personal experience as a means of generating theological reflection,[9] Cone, nonetheless, does provide the raw materials of how life experiences inform the Black theology work he was to pioneer. Two examples, from differing sides of his scholarly life, will suffice at this juncture as a means of making this point. In his very first book *Black Theology and Black Power*, James Cone outlines the ways in which his lived experience as a Black man in America informs the development of Black theology.[10] Central to the articulation of Black theology is the essential importance of Blackness and the recasting of that experience in positive terms that are understood as analogous to God's very self, revealed in Jesus Christ. For Cone, even as early as 1969, was clear that at the heart of Christianity is the claim to God's reconciling work in Jesus Christ, reconciliation in terms of God to human beings and within the scope of human relations as well. In terms of the latter, as it pertains to so-called 'race relations' Cone writes 'When we analyze the black–white relationship in the twentieth century in light of God's reconciling work in Jesus Christ, the message is clear. For black people it means that God has reconciled us to an acceptance of our blackness. If the death-resurrection of Christ means anything, it means that the blackness of black people is a creation of God himself.'[11]

It is for this reason that Black theology has always rejected the notion of 'colour-blind' approaches to overcoming 'race' and notions of intercultural and racialized forms of reconciliation. A Black theology that emerges from the realities of Black experience is one that seeks to rehabilitate and rethink how we conceive of Blackness and not attempt to circumnavigate it or to imagine it into non-existence, all the time enabling Whiteness to remain supreme by stealth and non-examination.

The promotion of Blackness *forces Whiteness to be visible and to own its existence*. Colour-blind approaches to Christian reconciliation still assume that it is our Blackness that is problematic, when the truth is that it is White supremacy that is the problem, not us. White people are not problematic per se, rather it is their propensity to assume a sense of entitlement, superiority and power that is the problem. Anti-racist White people who fight to reject the privileges of Whiteness or at least to confront them, are the kind of radical Christian disciples Black theology applauds.

At the other end of the scholarly continuum that marked James Cone's life work as a Black liberation theologian, we see in the first chapter of *Said I Wasn't Gonna Tell Nobody* a more explicit rendering of the significance of Black experience to the interpretation of the gospel of Jesus Christ.[12] For Cone, the love of Blackness and the rehabilitation of the experience of Blackness, into a divine love of self was non-negotiable. In speaking of the experiences and events that have given rise to the writing of *Black Theology and Black Power*, Cone narrates the socio-political and cultural climate of late 1960s America and the growth of the Black Power movement and its clear differentiation from the more moderate Civil Rights movement that had preceded it. Talking of this period, including learning from Revd Albert Cleage, Cone writes:

> I immersed myself in talk about black love, black unity, and black pride, black liberation, and the black revolution. The meaning of black power was clear; the self-determination of black people in every area of their lives by any means necessary. No one outside of the black struggle for justice could tell us what we could and couldn't say or do to gain our freedom. Not even Negroes![13]

Black culture and experience

For Cone, the sacredness of lived Black experience was such that it becomes an indispensable source for the construction of Black liberation theology. In *A Black Theology of Liberation* Cone says:

> Being Black is a beautiful experience. It is the sane way of living in an insane environment ... The Black experience is a source of black theology because this theology seeks to relate biblical revelation to the situation of blacks in America. This means that black theology cannot speak of God and God's involvement in contemporary America without identifying God's presence with the events of liberation in the black community.[14]

For Cone, the Black experience becomes the lens through which the enduring truth of biblical revelation is made. It is this ongoing struggle, between the text of scripture and the context of Black experience, that provides the ongoing platform on which Black theology and its hermeneutics of liberation are played out. An essential ingredient in the Black experience is that of Black culture. Culture is the creative means by which human beings make sense of the world through the materials, practices, expressions, traditions, and rituals that help them to constructing meaning. Cone, speaking of Black culture, states that it 'consists of the creative forms of expression as one reflects on history, endures pain, and experiences joy'.[15]

Black cultural expression is an important means by which and through which the divine communicates their creative engagement with Black people. The clearest expression of this aspect of James Cone's Black theology is found in his 1972 book *The Spirituals and the Blues*.[16] In this text, Cone, responding to the critique that the intellectual underpinning of his Black theology work was more dependent on Western intellectual sources such as Karl Barth and Paul Tillich than on anything that might be considered 'authentically' Black, argues for the significance of the historical legacy of the spirituals and the blues as ways of framing Black religiosity. The spirituals and the blues are two key cultural sources through which Black people navigate the journey in a world of often unremitting pain and suffering. The blues are Saturday night, and the spirituals are Sunday morning. Both speak to an ongoing struggle to make sense of Black existence that is often characterized by a sense of absurdity and 'non-sense'.

The importance of *The Spirituals and the Blues* lies in the ways in which it foregrounds later work that explores the historical development of African American cultures and artistic sensibilities that give rise to varied forms of religious expression. One can see this in the work of such scholars as Albert Raboteau[17] and Robert Hood.[18] Their work is characterized in particular by a pervasive sense of the work of the spirit(s) within Black life. The spirit of Black folk offers alternative ways of knowing,[19] and provides a different way of seeing and being in the world that seeks to make sense of Black existence.[20] Cone's work in *The Spirituals and the Blues* seeks to extend and amplify the foundational work of his first two books, in that it provides a more practical, expressive means of Black theology that is less dependent on systematic theological frameworks, but leans more on historic Black cultural practices. When Cone surveys the theological meaning of the spirituals and the blues, he is offering a narrative for how the basic building blocks for a liberative and radical expression of Black religiosity has always been in evidence, long before academic theologians like him began to chart these developments and write them down.[21]

Although Cone's attempt to mine the cultural resources of Black people as a means of constructing a platform for Black theology that rests on the centrality of Black experience is focused on the United States, there can be no doubting its significance for the UK. Within the UK context, as a member of the African diaspora, the religious and theological developments within the life experiences of the disenfranchised Black working class – who I have described as the voiceless[22] – have been accomplished by various cultural forms of production not that dissimilar to those highlighted by Cone. Whether in the music of Bob Marley as explored by Robert Beckford,[23] or in Anansi, as outlined by Michael Jagessar,[24] we see ways in which, for example, Caribbean arts and culture are used as ways of undertaking Black liberative God-talk.

What Cone demonstrates is that the means by which Black people have sought to challenge their ongoing dehumanization is through a dialectical spirituality, in which seemingly oppositional concepts and modes of thinking are juxtaposed and held in tension; much as the way in which jazz musicians use improvisation to hold together disparate and competing musical phrases and sources.

Cone's use of Black material cultures demonstrates how the practised and folk-orientated form of Black theology (interesting to note that Cone never wrote another book like this again), as opposed to the more formal systematic form of theologizing that was his forte, taps into the everyday lives of ordinary Black people. When it has been argued that Black theology is a purely academic, scholarly enterprise that has no links to ordinary Black people, this facet of Cone's work demonstrates otherwise. By demonstrating how the spirituals and blues can be interpreted theologically, Cone illustrates how Black theology derives its core identity, not solely from the Bible and the Judeo-Christian tradition, but also from the creative resources of Black peoples themselves. When using the term 'dialectical spirituality' I am speaking of the means by which Black people have sought to hold in tension differing ways of seeing the world, in which the hopes of self-actualization and their accompanying sense of belonging and value are juxtaposed with the realities of being considered 'less than' and even 'non-beings'. The vibrant spirit within Black people, the spirit that helps to create Black music and art and which is a bedrock of the Black experience, becomes the means by which Black people engage with formal religious phenomena like the Bible or church, for example.

Black experience and the Bible

One of the important aspects of Black theology is the sense that it has provided an element of freedom and creativity for Black people in how we engage with formal religious ideas and rituals. In the context of how Black people have engaged with the fluid creativity between text and context, I have described this as a form of 'dialectical spirituality'. When speaking of a dialectical spirituality I am referring to the ways in which the liberationist impulse of Black people has enabled us to critique existing orthodoxies and to assess them for their truth as it pertains to us, rather than for its applicability to those who are advantaged and powerful. This aspect of Cone's method is for me key, because it challenges the more dominant expressions of Black Pentecostalism and other forms of conservative Black Christianity that have been offered as a counterweight to Black theology.[25] Although the Bible, for example, remains an essential part of Cone's theological method in the construction of his version of Black theology, its significance, nevertheless, lies in dialectical tension with the realities of Black experience. James Cone illustrates how, through their engagement with the Bible, Black peoples' experiences sit in dialectical tension with the truths emanating from the Bible, where Black experience serves as the hermeneutical key to unlocking the continued revelation of God in the world, a world dominated by White supremacy. Cone outlines what I am calling a dialectical spirituality that has been used to subvert White hegemony.[26]

In this mode of theologizing, Black theology uses the resources of the Bible and Christian tradition but rereads them through the lens of Black experience, so that what emerges are creative ways of seeing the activity of God as a liberationist mode that challenges existing, White dominated norms. In speaking of a dialectical spirituality that underpins Black theology, I am interested in how Black people have sought to improvise on and manoeuvre through life in order to create space for them to find resources and strategies for resisting White hegemony.

I want to argue that repeated attention to the dialectical

and improvised qualities of diasporan African life can reopen the seemingly rigid and non-flexible approaches to our Black Christian engagement with the Bible, which seem to be an increasingly common phenomenon across the world in the last 20 years or so.[27]

In my own work as a theological educator over the past 25 years, it is fair to say that my greatest critics have not been White people, but more frequently, conservative Black Christians, often African Pentecostals. Their criticisms of my James Cone-inspired approach to Black theology has often centred on my perceived lack of fidelity to the Bible. But Cone himself is clear that the biblical tradition provides a guide to Christian ethics and is not a rule book. Speaking of how we see Jesus he says:

> We cannot use Jesus' behavior in the first century as a *literal* guide for our actions in the twentieth century. To do so is to fall into the same trap that fundamentalists fall into. It destroys Christian freedom, the freedom to make decisions patterned on, but not dictated by, the example of Jesus. Scripture, then, does not make decisions for us.[28]

The logic of Cone's hermeneutics through the prism of Black experience is a loosening of the rigid bonds of fundamentalism that is a manifestation of much of Black Pentecostalism and neo-Pentecostalism in the US, the UK and around the world. A Black theology inspired model of hermeneutics is one that looks at the Bible through the eyes of the poor and the marginalized, in a manner that takes seriously the realities of the concept of 'race' and the realities of systemic racism. Cone's Black theology methodology has given rise to radically new insights about what it means to be church and to be the people of God, instituted by the spirit, in order to bear witness to the gospel of Jesus Christ. Black theology has proposed a radical rereading of biblical texts, so that Paul's injunction in Galatians 3.28 is no longer seen as a proof text to justify a homogenized notion of sameness – in effect a colour-blind theology that has captured many Black evangelicals; but rather, it becomes a radical ideal in which distinctions between 'in groups' and 'out groups' are obliterated. A new reading moves us into a model that affirms difference, but outlaws preferential treatment based on ideas of election and preordained acceptance for some and the exclusion of others, on grounds of 'race', gender or sexuality.[29] By juxtaposing Black experience in dialogue with the Bible, where the former provides insights and perspectives for rereading the latter, Black theology offers a creative model of improvisation for Black people that makes the ultimate goal one of liberative praxis (faithful living out of the faith) and not adherence to an often oppressive status quo.

The sense of Black people improvising on the Christian faith in order to create new meaning and understanding for the continued fight for dignity and self-determination is central to the basic intent of Black theology. Cone's focus on Black experience, initially through the prism of the Black Power movement, was an exploration of the means by which the gospel of Jesus Christ might be decoupled from the weight of the imperialistic, top-down power to which it has been anchored since the epoch of Emperor Constantine and the capitulation of the faith to empire and later slavery and colonialism.

The continued existence of racism in Britain today, and in many parts of the so-called developed West, is testament to the continuance of an underlying Eurocentric Judeo-Christian framework that has invariably caricatured Africans as 'less than' and 'the other', and often placed White Euro-Americans as the apex of human civilization. The notion that human beings can be categorized into a fixed set of identities, which characterize human potential and capability, often effected in notions of morality and ethics, can be traced back to the first four centuries of the Common Era (CE). It was during this epoch that negative connotations pertaining to Black people as the 'other' began to surface in Christian thinking.[30]

The scourge of racism in Britain is nothing new for Black people. As Robert Beckford has demonstrated, one can chart a genealogy of racism in European intellectual thought that has exerted a disproportionately negative hold on the life experiences of Black people.[31] Scholars such as Emmanuel Eze have shown the extent to which the allegedly enlightened thinking of such 'luminaries' as David Hume and Immanuel Kant was infected with the stain of White supremacist thought.[32] The construction of the binary of Blackness (as bestial and less than) and Whiteness (as the personification of goodness and the basis of superiority) is a product of modernity.[33]

The chief legacy of transatlantic slavery was the unleashing of the rampageous and ravenous animal that is racism. The construction of racialized notions of fixed identity and restricted perspectives on Black human selfhood were the dangerous offspring of the chattel slavery of the 'Black Atlantic'.[34] The outworking of an immutable hierarchical manipulation of humanity did not disappear when the Act to abolish the British slave trade was passed in 1807. The Act brought the legal making of slaves to an end but racism, the notion of White supremacist norms, most certainly did not end.[35]

The backdrop against which diasporan African Christianity is rooted is one that has had to wrestle with the privations of slavery and colonialism. Diasporan Africans have lived for hundreds of years with the continued effects and ongoing trauma of the epoch of slavery. The Maafa (Swahili term relating to the African holocaust) remains a site for deep-seated trauma within diasporan Africans, to which Black pastoral theology and pastoral care has needed to respond.[36] This pastoral response, what Cedric Johnson calls 'Soul Care', which has its equivalents in other pastoral theology texts written by Black people of African descent,[37] seeks to attend to the deep-seated psychological malaise arising from the epoch of slavery. Delroy Hall, Britain's leading Black pastoral theologian, has undertaken work exploring the pastoral needs of African Caribbean people as they seek to make sense of their liminal experience living in post-colonial Britain.[38]

Black pastoral and practical theologians have sought to offer some form of amelioration for the suffering experienced by Black and working-class poor across the US and in other parts of the African diaspora, helping Christian communities to deal with the most deleterious of experiences related to the toxic machinations of neoliberal, global capitalism. These respective theological approaches of Black practical and pastoral theologians provide an important, prophetic diagnosis of the wider environmental milieu in which the church is immersed. As the old adage states, it is not sufficient to be in the noble cause of rescuing people from drowning in a river if one is not concerned with those who are deliberately throwing them into the water further upstream.

The impact of neoliberal economics and capitalism under the aegis of the 'global economy' have continued the long travails facing Black peoples across the world.[39] In using the 'global economy', I am concerned with the interconnected means by which countries undertake their economic activity. This can be seen in terms of how multi and transnational companies operate. Quite often the activities of multinational corporations take advantage of being located within large global markets, where they seek to maximize their profits, using the framework of technological capitalism.[40]

The idea of the global economy emerged in the nineteenth century, but perhaps came into its own in the last century. In the twenty-first century it is now commonplace. In fact, it is so much a part of the economic landscape that it is hard for us to remember a time when people did not trade across national boundaries, or that companies did not belong to or have their primary allegiance, to any one country. The national boundaries of so-called sovereign nations have been ignored and are now often overrun by multinational companies whose primary commitment is making profit for their shareholders.[41]

The current Covid-19 pandemic has led to an apocalypse-like existence as much of the world has ground to a halt and 'normal life' has ceased to exist for approximately 18 months. As the usual neoliberal financial activity was postponed and social distancing and lockdowns saw the near collapse of our usual embodied and embedded social, cultural and economic routines, we are increasingly seeing a marked tension between those who want us to return to our existing normal as soon as possible and those who are more hesitant. While some want us to return to our existing normal in order to preserve the 'old world order', often at variance with any scientific evidence to justify such a return, others are cautioning against the politics of return, feeling that a 'pause for thought' is necessary at this troubled time.

At the outbreak of the pandemic, it was often asserted that the deaths of people from across strata of society represented the virus as 'a great leveller'. However, the disproportionate deaths of Black people and those at the bottom of the socio-economic ladder has shown us that the pandemic is a 'great revealer' more than a leveller. Covid-19 is a revealer in that the disproportionate deaths of poor Black people, has shown us the iniquitous nature of global, neoliberal capitalism that has rendered the primary victims of this pandemic as disposable, collateral against a system that has been rendered as normal. The legacy of James Cone is one that argues that alongside the scourge of the Covid-19 pandemic there has been an older, perhaps more insidious pandemic, namely, that of White supremacy and systemic racism.

The significance of being Black cannot be lost on us when disproportionate numbers of Black people have died in the world and the first recourse of the experts was to speculate on whether Black people were predisposed to the virus because of our (faulty or inferior) genes. Given that at the time of writing, the continent on which most Black people live presently has less than 1 per cent coverage of the vaccine and that the richest, White majority countries have bought up most of the stocks of the Covid-19 vaccine, is testament to a world in which Blackness remains the despised and marginalized other. The depth of inequality of our present world order has been laid bare by the Covid-19 pandemic. The disproportionate deaths of poor Black people have shown the brokenness of the existing world order. We cannot and should not go back to the existing normal.

James Cone's focus on the realities of Black existential suffering is a reminder that colour-blind approaches to theological reflection remain flawed and faulty so long as the world is run by and for the benefit of White supremacy, under the guise of so-called 'fairness'. Black theology as conceived by Cone is a theology of Blackness. It seeks to speak into the threat of non-being and rejoices in the belief that it is in and through our Blackness that God speaks truth and justice to the world, a world painfully shaped by White supremacy.

A theology whose point of departure is Black experience is one that seeks to give Black people a sense of agency and self-determination that no other theological model or perspective can manage. Theological traditions and models such as 'World Christianity' are dominated by White people. It is still not uncommon to find posts dedicated to 'African Christianity' held by White people and not Black people. It is interesting to note that the adopted nomenclature of 'Public Theology' within one of the more recent theological texts emerging from South Africa refuses to name the specific racial-ethnic identities of those who are deemed the workers and the endemic poor within the country.[42] These generic categories mask the overwhelmingly Black African complexion of poverty in post-Apartheid South Africa. The movement towards adopting alternative nomenclatures for undertaking critical and constructive theological reflection in South Africa is, I believe, a problematic one. I am not entirely clear on how a departure from the iconic use of the term 'Black' can aid the continued need for a radical liberation struggle in South Africa. It seems to me that the continued importance of the nomenclature of 'Black' is precisely because it continues to unsettle and remains a difficult naming strategy with which to identify oneself.

At a time when the language of and the realities pertaining to Blackness continue to be disparaged, to advocate the uncritical use of the nomenclature of African (into which oppressive structures and persons can also claim an identity) is to cede elements of the radical and iconoclastic agenda for the more mainstream position into which all elements can coalesce, even those whose commitment to systemic, transformative change has to be questioned. This brings me to my other concern, namely, how does the movement from Black theology to African theology not become a subtle movement towards a 'business as usual' policy where patriarchy and male privilege are re-inscribed under a rubric of 'tradition' and 'historical precedent'? These are substantive questions for Black Theologians in South Africa and are not ones that I can answer, but they need to be asked![43]

In short, only Black theology has the unabashed commitment to Black self-determination. Global movements like Pentecostalism, for example, are often still led by White scholars, as is the case in the UK. Black theology is a theology of Blackness that is predicated on the experience of Black people who know their suffering and struggles first hand. This was the genius of James Cone. To realize that a theology which sought to free Black people could only be done by Black people, committed to the efficacy of affirming Blackness, as the unapologetic gift of God. Anything less simply will not do!

Notes

1 I have sought to broaden the methodological approaches to undertaking Black theology by using the methods more commonly found in practical theology as a way of undertaking constructive theological conversation. I have termed this 'participative Black theology', as I seek to combine the interdisciplinary approaches of practical theology with the constructive and systematic theological content of more traditional approaches to Black theology. For examples of this work, see Anthony G. Reddie, *Dramatizing Theologies: A Participative Approach to Black God Talk* (London: Routledge, 2006) and Anthony G. Reddie, *Working Against the Grain: Reimaging Black Theology for the 21st Century* (London: Routledge, 2008).

2 For more details, see '(What Did I Do To Be So) Black and Blue', *Wikipedia*, https://en.wikipedia.org/wiki/Black_and_Blue_(Fats_Waller_song) (accessed 19.01.2021).

3 On 25 May 2020, George Floyd, an African American, was murdered by a White police officer who placed his knee on Floyd's neck for 8 minutes and 46 seconds. For further details, see 'Murder

of George Floyd', *Wikipedia*, https://en.wikipedia.org/wiki/Killing_of_ George_Floyd (accessed 3.03.2021).

4 James H. Cone, *Black Theology and Black Power* (Maryknoll, NY: Orbis Books, 1989/2009), p. 7.

5 Cone, *Black Theology and Black Power*, p. 13.

6 Reggie L. Williams, *Bonhoeffer's Black Jesus: Harlem Renaissance Theology and an Ethic of Resistance* (Waco, TX: Baylor University Press, 2014), p. 79.

7 James H. Cone, *The Cross and the Lynching Tree* (Maryknoll, NY: Orbis Books, 2011), p. 47.

8 For the Conservative government's investigation into systemic racism in Britain, see Commission on Race and Ethnic Disparities, 'Commission on Race and Ethnic Disparities: The Report' (March 2021), available from https://assets.publishing.service.gov.uk/government/uploads/system/uploads/attachment_data/file/974507/20210331_-_CRED_Report_-_FINAL_-_Web_Accessible.pdf (accessed 14.10.2021).

9 I have done this in all books, but the most notable examples might be Anthony G. Reddie, *Working Against the Grain* and *Is God Colour Blind? Insights from Black Theology For Christian Ministry* (London: SPCK, 2010).

10 Cone, *Black Theology and Black Power*, pp. 8–18.

11 Cone, *Black Theology and Black Power*, p. 149.

12 Cone, *Said I Wasn't Gonna Tell Nobody* (Maryknoll, NY: Orbis Books, 2018), pp. 1–30.

13 Cone, *Said I Wasn't Gonna Tell Nobody*, p. 14.

14 James H. Cone, *A Black Theology of Liberation* (Maryknoll, NY: Orbis Books, 1970/1990), p. 25.

15 Cone, *A Black Theology of Liberation*, p. 27.

16 James H. Cone, *The Spirituals and the Blues* (Maryknoll, NY: Orbis Books, 1972).

17 See Albert J. Raboteau, *Slave Religion* (New York: Oxford University Press, 1978).

18 See Robert E. Hood, *Must God Remain Greek: Afro-cultures and God-Talk* (Minneapolis, MN: Fortress Press, 1990).

19 Cheryl Bridges Johns, *Pentecostal Formation: A Pedagogy among the Oppressed* (Sheffield: Sheffield Academic Press, 1998), pp. 62–137.

20 Robert Beckford, *Dread and Pentecostal* (London: SPCK, 2000), pp. 168–82.

21 Cone, *The Spirituals and the Blues*, pp. 53–127.

22 This term is used to invoke the sense of powerlessness and invisibility that affects Black British people in the UK. 'We' are invisible to the wider society, particularly in terms of religious or cultural significance. The all-embracing hegemony of Whiteness, on which Englishness

is predicated (see Paul Gilroy's *There Ain't No Black in The Union Jack*, London: Hutchinson, 1988) excludes the important contributions Black people have and continue to make to the body politic of the nation. This invisibility is secured on the basis of Black people being 'other' and thereby lacking any authentic sense of belonging to Britain. This sense of being 'other' and not belonging is exacerbated when one considers the tendency to pathologize the Black self, linking Black presence to structural and societal ills like crime, illness, unemployment and educational failure. In order to find a working heuristic for this ongoing phenomenon, I have constructed a notion of Blacks in Britain being 'voiceless'. This methodological and thematic construction is explored in more detail in my book *Dramatizing Theologies*.

23 See Robert Beckford, *Jesus is Dread: Black Theology and Black Culture in Britain* (London: Darton, Longman and Todd, 1998), pp. 115–52.

24 See Michael N. Jagessar, 'A Brief Con-version: A Caribbean and Black-British Postcolonial Scrutiny of Christian Conversion', in *Black Theology: An International Journal*, vol. 7, no. 3, 2009, pp. 300–24.

25 I explore aspects of this tension in a previous piece of work. See Anthony G. Reddie, *SCM Core Text: Black Theology* (London: SCM Press, 2012), pp. 162–71.

26 Cone, *The Spirituals and the Blues*, pp. 53–127.

27 Robert Beckford, *Jesus Dub: Theology, Music and Social Change* (London: Routledge, 2006), pp. 130–44.

28 Cone, *A Black Theology of Liberation*, p. 32.

29 See Demetrius K. Williams, *An End to This Strife: The Politics of Gender in African American Churches* (Minneapolis, MN: Fortress Press, 2004).

30 See Robert E. Hood, *Begrimed and Black: Christian Traditions on Blacks and Blackness* (Minneapolis, MN: Fortress Press, 1994), pp. 23–43.

31 Robert Beckford, *Dread and Pentecostal* (London: SPCK, 2000), pp. 95–130.

32 See Emmanuel C. Eze, *'Race' and the Enlightenment* (Oxford: Blackwell, 1997).

33 See James W. Perkinson, *White Theology* (New York: Palgrave, 2004), pp. 154–84.

34 Dwight N. Hopkins, *Being Human: 'Race' Culture and Religion* (Minneapolis, MN: Fortress Press, 2005), pp. 144–60.

35 One of the best texts in this regard from a Christian theological purview is by Richard S. Reddie, *Abolition!: The Struggle to Abolish Slavery in the British Colonies* (Oxford: Lion, 2007).

36 Cedric C. Johnson, *Race, Religion, and Resilience in the Neo-Liberal Age* (New York: Palgrave Macmillan, 2016), pp. 101–26.

37 See Lee H. Butler, *Liberating Our Dignity, Saving Our Souls: A New Theory of African American Identity Formation* (Des Peres, MO: Chalice Press, 2006). See also Homer U. Ashby Jr, *Our Home Is Over Jordan: A Black Pastoral Theology* (Des Peres, MO: Chalice Press, 2003).

38 See Delroy Hall, *A Redemption Song: Illuminations on Black British Pastoral Theology* (London: SCM Press, 2021).

39 See Keri Day, 'Global Economics and U.S. Public Policy: Human Liberation for the Global Poor', in *Black Theology: An International Journal*, vol. 9, no. 1, 2011, pp. 9–33.

40 Perhaps the best explanation for this phenomenon in terms of Black and womanist theologies can be found in Keri Day's recent work. See Keri Day, 'Global Economics and U.S. Public Policy: Human Liberation for the Global Poor'.

41 This issue is addressed with great alacrity by the renowned Sri Lankan liberation theologian Tissa Balasuriya. See Tissa Balasuriya, 'Liberation of the Affluent', in *Black Theology: An International Journal*, issue 1, no. 1, 2001, pp. 83–113.

42 Steve De Gruchy, Nico Koopman and Sytse Strijbos (eds), *From Our Side: Emerging perspectives on development and ethics* (Pretoria: UNISA Press, 2008).

43 More contemporary developments in Black theology in South Africa including wrestling with the impact of neoliberalism and globalization and the quest for Africanization and decolonizing the curriculum. For further details, see Allan Aubrey Boesak, *Kairos Crisis, and Global Apartheid: The Challenge of Prophetic Resistance* (New York: Palgrave Macmillan, 2015), Allan Aubrey Boesak, *Pharaohs on Both Sides of the Blood-Red Waters: Prophetic Critique on Empire* (Eugene, OR: Cascade Books, 2017) and Allan Aubrey Boesak, *Children of the Waters of Meribah: Black Liberation Theology, the Miriamic Tradition and the Challenges of 21st Century Empire* (Eugene, OR: Cascade Books, 2019). See also Rothney S. Tshaka, 'The Advocacy for Africanity as Justice Against Epistemicide', in *Black Theology: An International Journal*, vol. 17, no. 2, 2019, pp. 132–49. See also Jakub Urbaniak, 'Decolonisation as Unlearning Christianity: Fallism and African Religiosity as Case Studies', in *Black Theology: An International Journal*, vol. 17, no. 3, 2019, pp. 223–40. I have resisted addressing these issues out of deference to my colleagues living and working in South Africa, for whom these are a part of their lived reality.

PART 2

Perspectives on Key Texts

6

Black Theology and Black Power and *A Black Theology of Liberation*

In this second half of the book, I want to offer a brief overview of the key texts in James Cone's canon of work, *from my perspective*. I have emphasized these words because it is just that, namely, my perspective. Others would have chosen other books and for alternative reasons to the ones on which I have decided to focus. The following chapters outline the six books I think are the key to understanding the genius that is James H. Cone. I have not ranked them. That would be an even more invidious task than simply trying to choose one's favourite or best books, period.

In the second half of this introductory text, I have chosen to identify the key books in chronological order. With this in mind, therefore, we begin with Cone's first two books, published in 1969 and 1970 respectively. In the first instance, I was going to start with *A Black Theology of Liberation* and omit *Black Theology and Black Power*. However, after further thought I decided that this would be a mistake. It would be an error for two reasons. First, *Black Theology and Black Power* will forever be identified and decreed by many as the first authentic scholarly Black theology text. Notwithstanding the claims made for Albert Cleage, which I have addressed at the outset of this work, to my mind, *Black Theology and Black Power* is the first authentic Black theology text that outlines the theological basis for a theology of Black experience based on God's identification with Black suffering and struggle through the hermeneutical lens of Blackness. As such, to assess Cone's theological scholarship without accounting for this text would be a historical error. Second, and perhaps of greater importance, is the fact that this book provides the scaffolding that enables the appearance of *A Black Theology of Liberation* in the following year. While I am clear that *A Black Theology of Liberation* is the superior book of the two, there is no doubt in my mind, that without its predecessor, this later, early Cone classic would not have appeared.

In this chapter, therefore, I am juxtaposing the two books as one entity – a part 1 and part 2, if you will. Both texts outline a seismic shift in how we conceive the nature of academic theology and the nature of the Christian faith as it pertains to lived experience and God's activity and place in human affairs and history. Both texts create the foundation from which Cone's later key works, such *God of the Oppressed* and *Malcolm & Martin & America* can emerge.

Black Theology and Black Power

At the time of writing, I am looking at the 1989 20th anniversary edition of *Black Theology and Black Power*. Rather than provide a review of this text, I will, instead, offer an overarching assessment as to why it is an important text in the James Cone canon. What does it have to tell us about the modern world in which we live?

In the context during which *Introducing James Cone* was being written, we witnessed the resurgence of the Black Lives Matter movement. The radicalism of this heterodox movement, on which I have written previously, is one that has evoked a great deal of negative comment by many conservative and middle-of-the-road White people. The term 'woke' has been used as a pejorative with which to tarnish and traduce the credibility of the movement. Accusations of anti-Semitism, anti-police, violent anti-social tendencies and skewed and dangerous manifestoes have been levelled at the movement. Upon rereading Cone's first book, one is reminded of the skewed and partisan ways in which we have been fooled into seeing our current social, cultural and political norms as acceptable and having anything to do with God, justice or equity. That is the power of Whiteness – persuading us that racist norms are more acceptable than anti-hegemonic and anti-racist movements like Black Lives Matter.

The first and foremost task Cone sets for himself in *Black Theology and Black Power* is that of juxtaposing the false equivalence of 'White power' and 'Black power'. The critics of the latter were quick to demonize it as unchristian and extreme, often with little compunction and moral aptitude to criticize the former, when it has been the harbinger of death and suffering for countless millions of people. Even if Black power were extreme and unchristian it could hardly be any worse than that exhibited by White power. And yet, then as now, many White people will criticize 'woke' theologies and so-called 'Cancel Culture' without a word said against the status quo, because so long as that is construed in terms that favour White entitlement and the privileges that enable the flourishing of White supremacy then all is well and right with the world. An important intent of *Black Theology and Black Power* is the affirmation of Blackness and the belief that it is in and through our Blackness that God's redeeming work of transformative justice is to be found.

So, Black power, far from being a heretical and antithetical gospel phenomenon that is pitted against the gospel of Jesus Christ, is instead, consonant with it.[1] Black power is only a dangerous aberration when understood through the lens of White privilege. Reflecting on the first three chapters of *Black Theology and Black Power* one is reminded of the asymmetrical relationship between White power and Black power. The former provides the blueprint for Christianity as the unabashed religion of empire for over 1,000 years with little critique. This is an era of colonial expansion, and the mass incarceration and conscription of Black bodies, and yet Christian theology says nothing (to quote Cone – 'Theology's Great Sin: Silence in the Face of White Supremacy'). Yet when Black people push back with Black power, of which Black Lives Matter is a postmodern iteration, the same White power that was silent when unleashing epistemic violence and physical terror on Black people, now cries foul and accuses us of manipulating the gospel and distorting Christian theology. Talk about bitter ironies! How is it that even relatively benign and reasonable White Christians thought that stealing other people's lands was consonant with the gospel of Jesus Christ? Yes, missionaries built schools and colonial regimes brought medicine and Western forms of progress and development. But they also brought White supremacy and modes of Christian education that taught 'natives' and 'heathens' to abandon their ancient traditions and become third-class citizens in their own countries. It is interesting how the edicts of Whiteness see many 'reasonable' White people voting for Brexit in Britain and Trump in the US in order to take back control, because they believe they have lost elements of self-determination and agency. Yet when we then seek to bring these values and beliefs and apply them to the agency of Black people, especially those in the traditional 'mission fields', all of a sudden, Black people cannot be granted the same desire for self-determination as that assumed by White people.

In creating a theology of liberation predicated on the affirmation of Blackness, Cone writes, 'Black Power, in short, is an *attitude*, an inward affirmation of the essential worth of blackness.'[2] When speaking of the basic intent of the book Cone states that, 'This work, then, is written with a definite attitude, the attitude of an angry black man, disgusted with the oppression of black people in America and the scholarly demand to be "objective about it".'[3]

As I was getting ready to write this chapter I was reminded yet again of the mealy-mouthed 'reasonableness' of the political right in the UK that will happily attack Black Lives Matter and anti-racist activism as dangerous, all the while casting a White, entitled, status quo perspective as benign, normative and largely a reflection of God's righteousness.[4] As I stated previously, it is an astonishing piece of theological escapology that can construe the political machinations of Whiteness and empire that owe more to Pontius Pilate, a powerful apparatchik of empire, than to a colonized and oppressed Galilean Jew, and yet still clothe itself in the trappings of God's righteousness, telling others what is and what is not of God.

In his first book, Cone irrevocably casts a critical light on the dangerous hypocrisy of White power, juxtaposing it with the radical, revolutionary entity that is Black power. The latter, unlike White power, is not predicated on the false doctrine of White superiority. Rather, taking its cue from the gospel of Jesus Christ, whose point of departure was as a colonized and oppressed Galilean Jew, Black power, as the underpinning of Black theology, seeks to liberate Black people and White, but for radically different reasons. Cone writes: 'If the work of Christ is that of liberating men from their alien loyalties, and if racism is, as George Kelsey says, an alien faith, then there must be some correlation between Black power and Christianity.'[5]

As I have stated previously, this assessment of *Black Theology and Black Power* is written against the backdrop of the resurgence of the Black Lives Matter movement, following the murder of George Floyd. Cone's pursuit of the prophetic work as a Black liberation theologian was very much inspired by the radicalism of Jesus, whose resistance to Roman occupation, in support of poor, ordinary people on the margins, was seeking to speak truth to the power of the political establishment of his day. We can see this in Jesus' encounter with the money changers in the temple (Matt. 21.12), when his 'righteous anger' sees him railing against what was effectively the central treasury of his day, the equivalent of the economic heart of an occupied and colonized community. Jesus' opposition to the vested interests of the Jewish religious authority in Jerusalem and their collusion with Roman imperialism can be seen in his teachings to his followers. He counsels his followers not to lord it over others, but to make love their central ethic and not the seeming inflexibility of the Jewish law or the violence and the love of power exerted by the Romans (Matt. 20.25).

As a Black liberation theologian, I see Jesus' execution by the Romans as not simply a spiritual necessity to secure salvation, as is often asserted by traditional Christian teaching, but rather as the inevitable consequence of speaking Black truth to White power. The grisly nature of crucifixion, often a slow and painful suffocation as one's lungs collapse over three days or so, was a form of state-sponsored execution reserved for those deemed enemies of the state, those whose presence was upsetting to the status quo. The inspiration for Cone's writing of this first book was one of seeking to speak Black truth to White power, taking as his point of departure the inspiration of Jesus' own actions in confronting the powerful and cruel machinations of Roman imperialism and colonialism.[6]

Black Theology and Black Power forms the underpinning for the development of Black theology as it calls into question the ensnarement of the gospel by the egregious nature of White power, in which the oppression of Black bodies and the flourishing of White supremacy has gone unabated for centuries.

When approaching this iconic book in the pantheon of Black theology-inspired scholarship, the reader is brought face-to-face with a clear reminder that when we open the scriptures, we need to view the texts through the lens of colonial and oppressive power. We need to acknowledge that America and Britain, for example, have been possessors of lands and empires and control of peoples, that have rendered them not the allies of Jesus Christ, but his enemy. That a nation, such as the UK, once the possessor of the largest empire the world has ever seen, cannot easily pretend to be on the side of those who represent the powerless and the oppressed. Rather, we need to be careful that we clear off the dust of empire from our interpretive lenses when we open the Bible and proclaim the words, 'This is the word of the Lord ... Thanks be to God.'

What I find most poignant, as I reread Cone's opening salvo in the fight for a liberative theology that emerges from within the prism of lived experience and the affirmation of Blackness, is the Preface to the 1989 edition. In this preface, Cone, like the great scholar he is, freely acknowledges the blind spots and oversight in the initial work 20 years previously. One of the oversights is the American-centric nature of the work and its focus on the plight of African Americans. A telling comment of Cone is stated below:

> Another weakness of *Black Theology and Black Power* was my failure to link the African-American struggle for liberation in the United States with similar struggles in the Third World. If I had listened more carefully to Malcolm X and Martin King, I might have avoided that error. Both made it unquestionably clear, especially in their speeches against the U.S. government's involvement in the Congo and Vietnam, that there can be no freedom for African-Americans from racism in this country unless it is tied to the liberation of Third World nations from U.S. imperialism.[7]

While it would be a stretch to suggest that Cone's writing in this book sows the seeds for the later developments in post-colonial hermeneutics and theology, I would argue that the central affirmation of Blackness, in the guise of Black power, provides an important platform for the later decolonial theologies of the Caribbean, Africa and South-East and South Asia. Cone's first book represents a seismic break in how theologians engaged with issues of context, in terms of how one engages with the historical materiality of the time and space in which the Christian faith is being understood and interpreted and to what end. Primarily, in identifying God with Blackness and the lived realities of Black suffering, Cone is providing the logical outworking of faith of the Black prophetic tradition of which he is a part.

To be clear, Black people had been doing theology long before James Cone came onto the scene in the late 1960s. From the moment Absalom Jones and Richard Allen walked out of St George's church in Philadelphia in 1786, the independent Black church tradition is birthed. Along the way, we see such luminaries as Henry McNeal Turner speaking out against racism at the end of the nineteenth century and in the twentieth, figures such as Benjamin E. Mays and Howard Thurman and perhaps the greatest public theologian of them all, Martin Luther King Jr. All of the aforementioned and many others play key roles in articulating and arguing for a non-racist Christian theology in which Black people are seen as equal partners in the gospel of Jesus Christ. Cone's genius is to absorb their experiences, writings and activism, to synthesize them, but also and most crucially, to radically restate them in terms of what we are now describing as *Black liberation theology*. While the roots of this radical scholarly movement called Black theology can be traced in the lives of these earlier figures, Cone revolutionizes this existing tradition in order to create a radical, no-holds-barred, Black theology whose point of departure is the Black experience of suffering and struggle from within the prism of White supremacist forms of systemic racism. There would be no Black theology were it not for *Black Theology and Black Power* published in 1969!

A Black Theology of Liberation

Following the metaphoric seismic eruption that emerged with the publication of his first book, Cone came out with *A Black Theology of Liberation* that continued where the previous book had left off. In this follow-up 1970 text, Cone builds on the scaffolding provided in his previous work, to now deliver fully a conceptualized and complete building in which the fabric and substance has been added to an overarching structure. Now, we have not simply the contextual background to the necessity of Black theology, but here, in the first ever book to carry the nomenclature of 'Liberation' (before Gustavo Gutiérrez's *A Theology of Liberation*), Cone furnishes us with the content of this theological movement in greater detail.

Whereas the bulk of the previous text was an apologetic for the rationale of Black power and its relationship to Black theology, in his second book, a companion piece to the first, we have the worked through implications for the systemic theological development of Black liberation theology. While I still believe that the following book (and the subject of the next chapter) *God of the Oppressed* is Cone's single greatest scholarly achievement (and the single greatest Black theology book of them all in my opinion), if one were to read only one Black theology text as 'an introduction' to the subject, then I would always suggest *A Black Theology of Liberation*.

At the heart of *A Black Theology of Liberation* is the radical claim Cone makes for the God of the Judeo-Christian tradition, the God of the Bible, revealed in Jesus. Cone states:

It seems clear that the overwhelming weight of biblical teaching, especially the prophetic tradition in which Jesus stood unambiguously, is upon God's unqualified identification with the poor precisely because they are poor. The kingdom of God is for the helpless, because they have no security in this world. We see this emphasis in the repeated condemnation of the rich, notably, in the Sermon on the Mount and in Jesus' exclusive identification of his ministry with sinners.[8]

The single most important aspect of *A Black Theology of Liberation* lies in its articulation of the centrality of 'liberation' as the operative norm that runs through our understanding of Christianity and the message of God to the world, via the scriptures and the life of Jesus. Liberation from all that oppresses is consonant with the very nature of God's being. Time and again through the book Cone explicates the necessity of Christians being in solidarity with the liberating message of God in Christ as an expression of authentic discipleship.

I do not have the necessary facility with words to do justice to the significance of this book to my own conceptualization of Christianity the first time I read it back in 1992. When I first opened the pages to my 1986 edition of this book, I was confronted with these words:

Christian theology is a theology of liberation. It is *a rational study of the being of God in the world in light of the existential situation of an oppressed community, relating the forces of liberation to the essence of the gospel, which is Jesus Christ*. This means that its sole reason for existence is to put into ordered speech the meaning of God's activity in the world, so that the community of the oppressed will recognize that its inner thrust for liberation is not only *consistent with* the gospel but *is* the gospel of Jesus Christ.[9]

Having been raised within a relatively conservative church (theologically and politically in some respects), where there existed a chasm between theological reflection and the social context in which the mission of the church was expressed, these words came as a bombshell to me. By the early 1990s, I was no longer an evangelical in the way I had been nurtured within the faith in the church into which I was spiritually formed. Exposure to the radicalism of the Student Christian Movement, a very active Birmingham University Methodist Society, and many hours spent in the university chaplaincy centre at St Francis Hall had a major impression on me. I was a more socially conscious Christian committed to social justice, but still wedded to a Eurocentric conception of the faith. Five years after my graduation in 1992, I had an opportunity to read this first self-declared, systematic Black theology text. The rest, as they say, is history.

One of the important aspects of *A Black Theology of Liberation* is the way in which Cone shows the theological underpinning of Black theology as a legitimate form of academic, scholarly undertaking. Although some later scholars have been less than impressed with the ways in which Cone seeks to legitimize Black theology as an authentic theological enterprise,[10] Cone is clear that the work he is pioneering is a genuine form of scholarly work that is Christian theology. In chapter 2, when outlining the sources and norms of Black theology, using his training as a systematic theologian to the full, Cone details the ways in which this new scholarly movement adheres to and departs from the substantive set of ideas of the giants of modern twentieth-century theology, such as Barth, Tillich and Pannenberg.[11]

Given that not everyone will come to Black theology with a knowledge of the wider field of systematic theology and the ways in which, particularly, academic theology has been shaped by its wider tradition, *A Black Theology of Liberation* also provides a helpful framework for understanding the ways in which Cone's articulation of the discipline is both radical and relatively orthodox. Cone acknowledges his debt to his training in systematic theology for the character of his Black theology, in which 'revelation', particularly as it relates to Jesus Christ, is a central approach in his method for undertaking theological reflection.[12] While he admits in the preface to the 1986 updated edition that if he were writing the book again he would do so differently, I would still maintain that adopting the approach as he does – the form of neo-orthodoxy built on the work of Karl Barth – Cone provides a helpful structure to people whose formative studies are not in theology (my undergraduate degree was in history).

The orthodox character of Black theology outlined by Cone is very much on show in *A Black Theology of Liberation*. In the initial seven chapters of the book, Cone explores traditional theological categories through the lens of Black theology.

For those seeking to explore how Black theology sits alongside more 'classical' or 'traditional' forms of Christian theology, this book is hugely important. At this early juncture in his writing career, Cone was at pains to show how Black theology was not some strange aberration on the intellectual, scholarly scene, but was actually *the authentic* expression of Christianity. As I have demonstrated in the early chapters on Cone's doctrine of God and most crucially, the person and work of Jesus, the model of Black theology that emerges is a curious and interesting hybrid. The social and political concerns of Black theology are radical and yet the theological construction of the work is relatively orthodox and traditional.

If anyone were in any doubt from the first book, in this, his second text, we see clearly that Cone's Black theology is resolutely a Christian theology. The God who is the architect and the guarantor of liberation is the Judeo-Christian God of the Bible, with Jesus Christ at its heart. Cone is a Christian and the Black theology he crafts is reflective of his ancestry and the cultural milieu in which he was brought up. None of this is new, as I have demonstrated in previous chapters. But it is worth restating that Cone's Black theology is one that is anchored within the traditional mooring of Christianity as the seemingly self-evident religious identity of Black people across the African diaspora.

Anthony Pinn's work offered a radical challenge to the regulatory assumptions on what constituted diasporan African religious sensibilities. Those who have read his significant *Varieties of African American Religious Experience*[13] have undoubtedly been forced to reconsider the Judeo-Christian supremacist leanings, realizing that devotion to Jesus and adhering to seemingly normative Christian doctrines did not subsume the totality of 'authentic' Black religious experience, as dictated by James Cone. His later book *Terror and Triumph*[14] expands the religious and theological optics even further, as Pinn charts a non-essentialist, materialist perspective on Black religiosity that did not privilege the Black church, God, Jesus, the Holy Spirit, indeed, not even the axiomatic recourse to metaphysics. Drawing on the towering scholarship of Charles Long, to whom this work owes more than a little debt (while remaining a deeply original piece of work), I remember the extent to which Pinn was able to stretch the semantic meaning of Black religion, to become one that was not focused solely on experiential musings on church practice. All of this is a significant challenge to the Christian hegemonic framing of Cone's work, especially that which is found in *A Black Theology of Liberation*. The work of Anthony Pinn offers an important antidote to the doctrinal certainties of *A Black Theology of Liberation*. His work has opened the gates to a more materialistic, non-metaphysical, non-theistic conception of Black theology that moves beyond the parameters set by James Cone.

It is important that we acknowledge the alternate perspectives on Black theology that differ and depart from the frameworks provided by Cone's second book because of the long shadow cast by *A Black Theology of Liberation* on the early and subsequent development of Black theology. As my friend and colleague in the Black Theology in Britain movement, Michael N. Jagessar has shown, the dogmatic, Christian theological framework provided by James Cone has led to a particular circumscribed way in which the development of the movement has operated in the UK.[15] Jagessar responds to the question, 'Is Jesus the only way?' by effusively arguing 'no' and seeks to demonstrate the extent to which liberative God-talk can be effected through the prism of other religious traditions.

Perhaps the greatest achievement of *A Black Theology of Liberation* is to rearticulate the radical and revolutionary potential of Christian theology. In the UK, given the proximity of Christian theology and the church to the establishment (especially the Church of England) and the vested interests of the status quo, Black activists have long shunned Christianity, the church and Christian theology. Two of the early progenitors of Black theology in Britain, David Moore and Gus John, both of whom had trained as Anglican priests, abandoned the Church of England in favour of careers in education. In the British Methodist Church, an early 1990s programme at the Queen's Foundation[16] to provide access opportunities for predominantly Black British-born young people of Caribbean descent yielded only one person to continue into ordained ministry. The majority of people who moved into ministry were largely Black people who were born overseas in the Commonwealth, as opposed to those born in the UK.

One of the factors that has mitigated against Black British born or educated people is the 'colour-blind', 'context-less' stationing (deployment) of ministers and deacons in the British Methodist Church. This is predicated on the fallacy that 'all bodies are perceived as equally acceptable in all spaces',[17] so we match people to contexts, and contexts to people with seemingly little regard for the socio-political and cultural norms at play in how various bodies and people are perceived in differing settings.

So, in short, this form of activity operates on the basis that 'everyone can go anywhere'. In theory that is true, but for many Black and minority ethnic people, we know from bitter experience, there are particular places and spaces where we feel safe and others where we do not. The notions that 'people can go anywhere' is one that is reserved for educated, White heterosexual men. It is a product of an unreflective form of Whiteness that pervades how we conceive the nature of our church. The truth is White people can go anywhere and make themselves at home – the British empire and colonialism proves that.

It is no surprise, then, that the norm for many Methodists remains the iconic figure of John Wesley who was an Oxbridge White man. And let us not forget that across 270 years or so of having people involved in representative ministry, until the last 30–40 years, most of our ministers would have fitted this category precisely – educated, White, heterosexual men. Is it any wonder, then, that those who do not fit this particular norm are the ones who often experience difficulties in stationing and in the exercising of their ministry across this colour-blind Connexion?[18]

I was one of those who had felt a call to ministry in my teenage years but knew instinctively that I would never permit myself to offer for ordained ministry and put my fate in the hands of White officialdom and a White, Eurocentric institution. And yet for me, the route into a scholarly form of ministry came through the inspiration of James Cone's *A Black Theology of Liberation*. His radical reworking of the traditional understanding of Christianity and the committed, social and political outworking of Christian theology inspired me to believe that there was an alternative means of interpreting the central intent of the Christian faith and the church. While much of what I had imbibed in my Christian education and formation seem to cast the church as perennially on the side of the forces of the conservative and the preservation of the status quo, Cone's Black theology clearly located God on the side of the marginalized and the oppressed. James Cone's Black theology is a revolutionary interpretation of the Christian faith that is committed to Black self-determination, agency, dignity and self-respect.

Cone's *A Black Theology of Liberation* establishes Black theology as a theology of liberation that is the specific self-named enterprise of reinterpreting the meaning of God as revealed in Jesus Christ, in light of the ongoing struggles of Black people in America and across the world. This approach is one that engages with the Christian tradition, seeking to rethink and recontextualize it for the purposes of lived experience of liberation within history. In this regard, it is not unlike other forms of liberation theology found in Latin America and later in areas such as South-East Asia. Cone shows that his point of departure is the lived experience of Black struggle in a world of White supremacy and hegemony. This lived experience is placed in dialogue with Holy Scripture, namely, the Bible and development of church and Christianity across 2,000 years.[19]

Cone's Black theology which emerges from *A Black Theology of Liberation* is one that sees the necessity of seeing faith-inspired, radical, social and political action as the norm rather than having to adhere to the often abstract limitations of Christian orthodoxy. For Cone, this work is committed to challenging the ways in which traditional Christianity is often disengaged from the realities of Black suffering such as slavery and colonialism. In this book, Cone is concerned with showing that in God and through the supreme example of Jesus Christ, the ultimate purpose of Christianity is to provide a means by which ordinary people can be inspired to engage in the radical praxis of acting and resisting in their lived struggles to overcome systemic racism and whatever confronts them in the world. This work, like his first book, has been an immense inspiration to the development of Black theology and the challenges that continue to face Black people across the world, including in my context, in post-colonial Britain.[20] *A Black Theology of Liberation* challenges Black people to seek in God a means of making sense of situations that often seem inherently senseless.

The iconic nature of this work includes his admission that the original work had sexism and patriarchal elements in it. Cone's sexism was a direct contributory factor to the development of early womanist theology and the scholarly work of

Delores Williams[21] and Jacquelyn Grant.[22] James Cone's *A Black Theology of Liberation* offers a radical form of thinking and contextual praxis that simultaneously seeks to empower marginalized and disenfranchised Black people alongside the need to challenge and inspire White power to act differently. This book is the herald of the mature development of Black theology.

It can be argued that the Christian moorings of the work have limited the broader utility of Black theology across the world, especially in those places where Christianity is a minority religious tradition. Conversely, Cone's Black theology which emerges from this book is one that resists any form of colour-blind approach to disembodied forms of spirituality which convince many that our means of resisting racism is to pretend that not seeing Blackness is the way forward. Cone's affirmation of Blackness reminds us that one cannot rehabilitate the demonization of our Black skin by pretending that it doesn't exist – as if such a thing were possible. James Cone's Black, contextual rereading of the Christian faith, gives rise to a model of Black theology that provides a systemic, liberationist interpretation of the gospel of Jesus Christ. *A Black Theology of Liberation* creates the template for the radical development of a movement that seeks to directly challenge White hypocrisy juxtaposed with the affirmation of Blackness. I will restate my earlier bold assertion – if you were to only read one Black theology book, then *A Black Theology of Liberation* should be that book!

Notes

1 James H. Cone, *Black Theology and Black Power* (Maryknoll, NY: Orbis Books, 1989/2009), pp. 31–61.

2 Cone, *Black Theology and Black Power*, p. 8.

3 Cone, *Black Theology and Black Power*, p. 2.

4 A classic example of this is the right-of-centre magazine *The Critic* that offers a seemingly benign religio-cultural view of the world

that is nothing less than a White-dominated, reactionary push back against all and any forces that are seeking to bring about equity and justice for the global majority. For further examples of their reporting, see Michael Collins, 'The Church of Woke', *The Critic*, 29 June 2020 (accessed 1.11.2021).

  5 Cone, *Black Theology and Black Power*, p. 39.
  6 Cone, *Black Theology and Black Power*, pp. 31–61.
  7 Cone, *Black Theology and Black Power*, pp. xii–xiii.
  8 Cone, *A Black Theology of Liberation*, p. 117.
  9 Cone, *A Black Theology of Liberation*, p. 1.
  10 See Elonda Clay, 'A Black Theology of Liberation or Legitimation? A Postcolonial Response to Cone's Black Theology and Black Power at Forty', in *Black Theology: An International Journal*, vol. 8, no. 3, 2010, pp. 307–26.
  11 Cone, *A Black Theology of Liberation*, pp. 21–38.
  12 Cone, *A Black Theology of Liberation*, pp. xiii–xix.
  13 See Anthony B. Pinn, *Varieties of African American Religious Experience* (Minneapolis, MN: Augsburg Fortress Press, 1998).
  14 See Anthony B. Pinn, *Terror and Triumph: The Nature of Black Religion* (Minneapolis, MN: Fortress Press, 2003).
  15 Michael N. Jagessar, 'Is Jesus the Only Way? Doing Black Christian God-Talk in a Multi-Religious City (Birmingham, UK)', *Black Theology: An International Journal*, vol. 7, no. 2, 2009, pp. 200–25.
  16 Brief details of this programme can be found in Robert Beckford, *Duppy Conqueror* (London: Darton, Longman and Todd, 2021), pp. 20–1.
  17 Important theological work has been undertaken by womanist theologians exploring the significance of Black bodies and the ways in which they have been viewed deleteriously by Whiteness. See M. Shawn Copeland, *Enfleshing Freedom: Body, Race, and Being* (Minneapolis, MN: Fortress Press, 2009) and Eboni Marshall Turman, *Toward a Womanist Ethic of Incarnation: Black Bodies, the Black Church, and the Council of Chalcedon* (New York: Palgrave Macmillan, 2013).
  18 Clearly, it is the case that I am guilty of making broad generalizations, as not every Black or person of colour has faced difficulties in candidating, training and stationing in terms of expressing their ministry as Methodist presbyters and deacons. Similarly, the Methodist ministry is demonstrably more diverse than was once the case. But as Jennings and my own work has shown, increased diversity does not mean that the underlying template for what constitutes our conceptual norms has changed. See Anthony G. Reddie, *Nobodies to Somebodies: A Practical Theology for Education and Liberation* (London: Epworth Press, 2003), pp. 132–40. See also Anthony G. Reddie, *Is God Colour*

Blind: Insights from Black Theology for Christian Faith and Ministry (London: SPCK, 2020), pp. 3–22.

19 See Michael N. Jagessar and Anthony G. Reddie (eds), *Black Theology in Britain: A Reader* (London: Equinox, 2007), p. 1.

20 In using this term, I am referring to the historic and continued frameworks of British life that have been shaped by and continue to respond to the theories and practices that arise from the phenomenon that was and is colonialism and neo-colonialism. For an explication of this in light of British life, see R. S. Sugirtharajah, *Postcolonial Reconfigurations: An Alternative Way of Reading the Bible and Doing Theology* (London: SCM Press, 2003) and R. S. Sugirtharajah, *The Bible and Empire* (Cambridge: Cambridge University Press, 2005), pp. 60–97.

21 See Delores Williams, *Sisters in the Wilderness: The Challenge of Womanist God-Talk* (Maryknoll, NY: Orbis Books, 1993).

22 See Jacquelyn Grant, *White Women's Christ and Black Women's Jesus* (Atlanta, GA: Scholars' Press, 1989).

7

God of the Oppressed

James Cone's next great book was the fourth in his literary canon and was entitled *God of the Oppressed*. It was published in 1975, three years after his third text, *The Spirituals and the Blues*. I believe *God of the Oppressed* to be Cone's greatest book. I am not sure if it is my favourite Cone book, but it is right up there in my top one or two.

If you were to read only one Black theology book, then *A Black Theology of Liberation* is that book. But, for me, *God of the Oppressed* is the most complete Black theology book. Cone's towering genius and mastery of his subject is on complete display here. The central argument is the confirmation that the God of the Judeo-Christian tradition is one who sides unequivocally with those who are oppressed. If liberation is the central norm that guides the overarching framework of the Christian faith, then underpinning it is a God of the oppressed. Not a disinterested God or one who is neutral and identifies with oppressed and oppressor equally.

The Spirituals and the Blues was a methodological departure from his first two books, as he responded to the criticism that his initial work was too indebted to White intellectual sources. So, Cone sought to show the Black religious and cultural foundations of Black liberation theology from within musical and linguistic traditions of African Americans, namely, the spirituals and the blues.

In many respects, *God of the Oppressed* represents a kind of 'return to the main theme' as the book, in style and method, owes more to *A Black Theology of Liberation* than it does to the book that most immediately preceded it. In not including

The Spirituals and the Blues I know I am making a bold statement in terms of my own preference for what constitutes the most vital aspects of Cone's canon and legacy. *The Spirituals and the Blues* is an amazing text, but it is interesting to note that, until his final book, *Said I Wasn't Gonna Tell Nobody*, one does not witness Cone returning to more cultural and artistic modes of engagement as to primarily historical, constructive doctrinal and systematic forms of theological inquiry.

The summation of what has been

What makes *God of the Oppressed* so important to my mind is the expansive range of the theological topics with which he engages his critical skills as the premier Black theologian. The book was, with the exception of *Martin & Malcolm & America*, the largest text James Cone wrote and remains among the most, if not *the* most comprehensive Black theology text as it relates to the exposition of the discipline as a systematic theological subject. If *A Black Theology of Liberation* is the thematic sequel to *Black Theology and Black Power*, then *God of the Oppressed* is the summation of the previous two and the completion of the trilogy of ground-breaking formative texts that help to define the nature and identity of Black theology as an academic discipline.

This text begins with Cone restating the nature of Black theology and its relationship to the lived experience, culture, traditions and history of African Americans.[1] Cone reminds us that revelation is always an embodied and a contextually specific phenomenon. Just as God discloses God's self, among a marginalized and oppressed community within the Hebrew Bible, then God continues to be revealed from within the historic experiences of suffering Black people. Therefore, the sacred songs of lament, the preaching, the hymnody and testimonies of continued struggle represent the expressive data that constitute God's revelation within human history in more contemporary times.[2]

In charting the social context in which Black Christianity in the US developed, from which emerges Black theology, Cone shows the crucial difference between the often arcane and abstract theologizing of White Christians and that of their Black counterparts. Speaking on this subject Cone says:

> White theologians built logical systems; black folks told tales. Whites debated the validity of infant baptism or the issue of predestination and free will; blacks recited biblical stories about God leading the Israelites from Egyptian bondage, Joshua and the battle of Jericho and the Hebrew children in the fiery furnace ... Blacks did not ask whether God existed or whether divine existence can be rationally demonstrated. Divine existence was taken for granted, because God was the point of departure of their faith. The divine question which they addressed was whether or not God was with them in their struggle for liberation.[3]

The existential and experiential nature of Black theology is what aligns it with other 'Theologies of Liberation'. This title refers to a group of socio-political theologies that seek to reinterpret the central meaning of the God event within history, particularly, in terms of the life, death and resurrection of Jesus Christ. They provide a politicized, radical and socially transformative understanding of the Christian faith in light of the lived realities and experiences of the poor, the marginalized and the oppressed.[4] Building on the work of his first two books, in particular, *God of the Oppressed* outlines the wider scope of God's activities within the Bible and in contemporary history, in which the God revealed in Jesus is in *actual* solidarity with ordinary Black people, the majority of whom have suffered directly under the impact of White supremacy.

One of the key elements of this book is the way in which Cone carefully marshals his argument for a strident and ideological construction of God as being on the side of the oppressed. In using the word 'ideological' I am speaking of the pointed and 'biased' way in which Cone is seeing the God of the Judeo-Christian tradition in terms that are very different to how many of us have been taught in churches. As I have stated previously, Cone dispenses with any sense that God is neutral and refuses to take sides. God is not solely concerned with spiritual matters and saving people for heaven, based on faith in God's son Jesus Christ, with no sense of how social and political matters are effected between human beings in the world, prior to any one being saved. In using the term 'ideological' I am not suggesting, as many critics have charged, that Cone is creating a distorted conceptual approach to Christianity that is more humanistic than theological. Ironically, that is what White colonial Christianity has done! Rather, in using the term 'ideological', much as I did in my previous book for SCM Press where I spoke about Black theology as a form of 'subversive ideology',[5] I am speaking to the way in which Cone is identifying God with a particular cause in history – the liberation of oppressed peoples – in which God is taking sides and is asking those who say they follow God's son, Jesus Christ, to do so as well.

This radical challenge of 'taking sides' and not effecting a false truth of being 'neutral' (for that is also to side with the status quo, the powerful and those who are the oppressors) is what makes *God of the Oppressed* such an arresting and challenging text. Cone juxtaposes the alternative perspectives of 'freedom' and 'oppression'. Much like Paulo Freire[6] before him (my PhD in 2000 pitted James Cone and Paulo Freire together as joint perspectives for creating a practical, educational model of Black theology), Cone asserts that only those who have been oppressed can then be truly and fully free.[7] Cone notes, as Freire in *Pedagogy of the Oppressed*, that those who identify with the oppressors, whether overtly or covertly, can never be free unless they are freed by the humanity of the oppressed. By this, Cone means that it is only in surrendering the false claims to superiority found in White supremacy and being in solidarity with Blackness and the struggle for equity and justice propagated by Black people, can White people be set free.[8] Cone's assertions in *God of the Oppressed* are ideological because they force White people to choose. Either they are on the side of righteousness as their faith suggests, which means siding with Blackness and rejecting White supremacy or siding with the latter, and then rejecting the pretence that they are on the side of God or should have the nerve to call themselves Christians. Cone writes:

> While pretending to be concerned about the universal character of the human condition, oppressors are in fact concerned to justify their own particular status in society. They want to be oppressors and Christians at the same time. Since the oppressed are the only true Christians, oppressors claim to be victims, not for the purpose of being liberated but for their own social interests retaining a 'Christian' identity while being against Jesus Christ. This is what Dietrich Bonhoeffer in another context called 'cheap grace'. I call it hypocrisy and blasphemy.[9]

One can be in no doubt as to the prophetic radicalism of this quotation. It should be self-evident that one cannot be a racist and a Christian. The way of salvation for oppressors is to refuse racism, White supremacy and notions of White entitlement, and to enter into the struggle for the liberation of the oppressed, which given the interconnected ways in which humanity is linked, is in fact, to fight also for one's own redemption and liberation.

At the time of writing this book, I, along with many others, have heard the racist counterclaims of the 'Cancel Culture' brigade asserting that the tyrannies of 'wokeness' are distorting and polluting our discourse, not once acknowledging how racism and White supremacy have been doing that long before the so-called exponents of 'woke' got to work. The theological basis of Cone's work rests not on critical theory, but on the gospel of Jesus Christ. The notion that White oppressors should enter into solidarity with oppressed Black people finds its echoes in Jesus' assertion that to be counted as one of his followers, one has to 'deny self and carry the cross' (Matt.

16.24 and Luke 9.23). Of course, countless years of Christianity's enslavement to empire and White supremacy has seen the potency of these words spiritualized, so that the charges of 'carry the cross' often mean nothing more than buying one less fancy consumable and being nice to the poor through charity.

Cone is clear that liberation remains the defining character of the gospel of Jesus Christ. But this liberation is not the spiritualized version often asserted by missionaries, where the freedom that comes from being liberated, was one that rejected the 'wages of sin' but had no currency when one sought to cash it out in terms of material sovereignty from slavery and colonialism. All of a sudden, such protestations for liberation are circumscribed by the pernicious, false doctrines of White supremacy. So, even the teachings of 'freedom in Christ' are limited to the spiritual realm in order that White hegemony, in the form of empire and top-down forms of authority and power, can continue to flourish unencumbered by the radical teachings of Jesus Christ.

In the current age when the counter assertions of the 'Alt-Right' and social conservatives are seeking to relativize their opposition to anti-racism as being a reasonable counter discourse of opinions and theory (as if racism is a contestable argument rather than a dangerous phenomenon that kills people), Cone's work in *God of the Oppressed* remains a necessary and important champion against the forces of White microaggression.

When Black and Asian government ministers such as Kemi Badenoch and Priti Patel are prepared to mount the cultural barricades and defend the status quo against supposed 'wokeness' one has to see this for what it is, the co-option of neo-colonialist tropes of White supremacy now being marshalled through Black and Brown bodies. Cone's work makes the ideological nature of the gospel clear in that it confronts the naked, vested interests of empire and forces us to choose sides. Are we on the side of the oppressed or the oppressors? Modern and postmodern scholars will have us believe that the contemporary complications of human intersectionality are such that one can no longer speak so clearly of 'oppressed' and 'oppressors'. Well, tell that to the Black Caribbean people of the Windrush Generation still languishing in exile having been deported erroneously by a White racist government and then having Black and Brown ministers serving a government seeking to 'explain away' why this wasn't state sanctioned, systemic racism? There are still oppressed and oppressors in this world and we can spot them if we have eyes to see!

Naming the elephant in the room

In the years before I became an academic, I worked briefly as a racial equality advisor for a local authority. One of the exercises we used to develop was that of exploring 'What was the elephant in the room?' What was the foremost issue about which no one wanted to talk or give utterance? Invariably, it was the question of 'race'. It would take too long to explain the exercise here, but suffice it to say, one of the ways in which it operated was on the basis of displaying the lengths to which many White people would go in order to preserve their sense of normality by not having to talk about issues pertaining to 'race' and racism. The former, although a fictional construct with no basis in empirical fact, nevertheless, gives rise to the latter.

One of the enduing truths of *God of the Oppressed* is that Cone, writing in the mid-1970s, is sure about the nature of White obfuscation that wants to rest easy in the assumed superiority that comes with White privilege. This happens while refusing any of the necessary challenges of giving up power and repenting, in order to be aligned with God's righteousness, as that same God is in solidarity with the very people White supremacy wishes to dismiss. Much of the quiet status quo of Whiteness is content to hold a major oxymoron in place, namely, that Christianity and White entitlement and power belong together. So, until the murder of George Floyd in May 2020, the majority of White-run institutions in the UK were happy not to talk about 'race' or racism, or the absence of non-White people in their midst. The pretence that there is not an elephant in the room has been a feature of British ecclesial life for decades.

Cone's constant mining of the biblical context and the social context of Christian theology – a basic reminder that (quite ridiculous that people even needed reminding, of course) *all theology is contextual* and is shaped by the time and space in which it was developed – was to illustrate that Christian theology *should be concerned with liberation of the oppressed*. The fact that students training for ministry in many of our theological colleges could, until recently, undertake those studies without any recourse to Black theology is a telling indictment in itself. If, as Cone so eloquently shows, the biblical tradition contains a plethora of texts that pertain to God's liberating activities and given the 1,500 years of imperial power that has become enshrined with Christianity, the past 500 or so coinciding with European expansion, slavery and colonialism, how could theological education not see this?

I remember teaching a class on James Cone at a not-to-be-named theological college back in 2008. The charge made to me then was that, with the recent election of Barack Obama that year, the continuing need for Black theology had become superfluous. I argued that the election of one Black man, no matter how powerful, was not going to change the world if many White people remain committed to the status quo in which the sense of entitlement and privilege that surrounds Whiteness continued. At the time of writing, not even I with my pronounced sense of cynicism and 'keeping it real' could have accounted for the four years of horror that would be unleashed on us by Donald Trump.

God of the Oppressed demonstrates the necessity of choosing sides and acknowledging that the God who is on the side of the oppressed has chosen sides and demands that we do the same.

The historic naivety surrounding the election of Barack Obama back in 2008 should not surprise us. Many White people could vote for a Black president so long as he was not going to change anything systemically, requiring White privilege to have to account for its undeserved pre-eminence. The controversy surrounding Obama's collusion with Black theology via the prophetic ministry of Jeremiah Wright Jr is an example of the White media wanting a sanitized and neutered version of Blackness in the White House. Obama was attacked for attending a predominantly Black, radical megachurch in Chicago, Trinity United Church of Christ (the senior pastor was Revd Dr Jeremiah Wright Jr). The efficacy of Obama attending this pro-Black church (and therefore, presumed to be anti-White) was questioned at length in the media. Nowhere did anyone remark that every White candidate and president before him had attended all-White (and therefore, anti-Black?) churches!

While no one was uttering the 'r' word, we all know it was lurking in the background. The elephant is still in the room, smiling nonchalantly at the scene of self-conscious indifference going on around her.

Cone's incendiary theological work in *God of the Oppressed* is to challenge the complacency of mainstream White Euro-American Christianity. Ten years on from the question of Obama's election, I was asked by the URC magazine *Reform* to write a brief piece on whether 'Christianity had made the world a better place.'[10] For the three other White writers, all of whom addressed the question from differing perspectives, the phenomenon of Whiteness did not figure in their appreciation of the question. The short piece I wrote drew primarily on James Cone and his writings in *God of the Oppressed*.

The question of whether Christianity has made the world better depends on which 'Christianity' we are speaking about. In this, his most complete theological work to my mind, Cone's immense genius is his unflinching critique of White Euro-American Christianity, denouncing it as an aberrant form of faith that owed more to the anti-Christ and manifest evil than the effusive, life-giving force of the Jesus of the gospels who sided with the downtrodden and the marginalized. The theology developed by Cone in this book is the complete antithesis of that which endorsed slavery and the vicious oppression of Black bodies, alongside the colonization of other peoples' lands and the brutal suppression of indigenous cultures.

God of the Oppressed outlines a model of faith that shows up the mendacity of White Christianity and the collusive deals it has made with White supremacy and capitalism. Cone's writings lay the groundwork for James Perkinson's provocative ideas in his book *Shamanism, Racism, and Hip Hop Culture: Essays on White Supremacy and Black Subversion*, which argues that White Mission Christianity was effectively a form of witchcraft in its relationship to White and Black people, empowering and justifying the empires of the former and the suppression and marginalization of the latter.[11]

In an age when 80 per cent of White evangelicals in the US voted for Donald Trump in the 2016 presidential election and a great deal of European Christianity has closed its hearts and borders to refugees from the South, one can argue that White Christian faith continues to scar the world for the worst.

Black development and transformation

As someone whose earliest paid work, post undergraduate study, was that of a youth worker, perhaps the greatest aspect of *God of the Oppressed* that has remained with me since first reading it was the impact it had on my Black psyche. This book, perhaps, more so than any other, gave me the grounds for wanting to become a Black theology-inspired youth worker and activist. As a cradle Methodist, Cone's work introduced me to a rich Black church tradition, in which Methodism had played a significant part. So, while my own church so often seeks partnership with the White-majority 'United Methodist Church', there are other forms of Methodism from the US in which the impulse for pro-Black Christian-inspired mission and ministry has flourished for around 200 years. There are three de facto Black Methodist Churches: the African Methodist Episcopal Church (AME), the Christian Methodist Episcopal (CME) and the African Methodist Episcopal Zion (AMEZ).

The latter Black-majority churches share similar doctrines and polity to their White-majority counterparts UMC, but they are separated by the historical fissure of 'race' that runs through the body politic of the US.

Reading *God of the Oppressed* exposed me to the many ways in which Black Christians have sought to create an alternative template by which we might understand the liberating work of God in the world. The God who is revealed in the lives of those who are oppressed and marginalized is one who has a profound love for Blackness and Black people. This God, revealed in Jesus, is one who seeks to empower Black people to continue to resist the noxious presence of imperialism. In the first two decades of the twenty-first century, Black people are still trying to come to terms with and exist within a context that both validates and legitimizes the institutional and casual incidences of racism against people of colour.[12]

It is within this climate that Black people are struggling with forms of microaggression, such as the attempts to relativize racism, to the point where anti-racists are being dubbed 'racists' and not the White people upholding White privilege and exceptionalism. The persistent presence of microaggression is what often leads to forms of 'low-level rage'. Beckford defines the latter as 'related to internalised rage in that it is experienced in mind and body. It is manifested in anger, depression and anxiety.'[13] The high incidence of mental ill health (particularly schizophrenia) among African Caribbean communities in Britain adds substance to Beckford's contentions.

Beckford's notion of 'low-level rage' is one that continues to impact on Black people. I know of a number of Black people who, having witnessed the death of George Floyd, found themselves experiencing anxiety attacks and heart palpitations as the visceral nature of Black suffering and death confronted them once more. Black life in twenty-first-century Britain is being lived out under the shadow of a Conservative government that can issue a report refuting the visceral nature of systemic racism.

My continued reading of *God of the Oppressed* has challenged me to want to find ways of making a difference in the lives of ordinary Black people. Perhaps, the most significant importance of Cone's work was the inspiration it gave me to undertake my own doctoral studies in the mid-1990s. The process I underwent in attempting to develop an authentic, contextualized Christian education curriculum for Black young people and young people in general was an exciting experience and one that changed my life. Inspired by James Cone, especially *God of the Oppressed*, I began to think about how I might apply his ideas and locate the central teachings from the book into an African-centred educational theory.

My doctoral project was sponsored by the Methodist Church and remains one of my proudest achievements. The research project sought to provide a means of raising the social, political and cultural consciousness of young Black people as they were growing up in a White dominated and racist society. The project that ran from 1995 to 1999 was titled the 'Birmingham Initiative'. Right from the outset the project was inspired by James Cone and his book *God of the Oppressed*.

One of the significant points of learning when undertaking the work, something that I learned from Cone and his detailed articulation of a God who is in solidarity with oppressed peoples, was the significance of creating a structure of learning that was founded on the affective, or the ways in which our emotions and feelings about self, others and the world are shaped by the deepest impulses of love as we have experienced it or not, in our formation as human beings. Namely, one cannot construct any kind of theological or educational framework for liberation if it is not underpinned by love. In educational terms, James Michael Lee reminds us that all the best forms of pedagogy are underpinned by the necessity of engaging with the affective domains on what it means to be human, that is, the need for people to feel loved, affirmed and having a sense that they belong to others. The educational work I undertook with churches in Birmingham in the mid to late 1990s was focused on learning from James Michael Lee and the importance of recognizing how our emotions and sense of connectedness to others is not incidental to learning but is, rather, the core of it. Lee states, 'The path to humanity and to divinity lies not through power or politics or cognition, but through affect and value and love. Thus it behoves the religious educator to center a good deal of his attention on the affective content of religious instruction.'[14]

My doctoral studies were very much concerned with wanting to put Cone's radical theology into an educational curriculum framework in order that the insights of Black theology might assist churches in becoming centres for radical theological thinking and committed forms of praxis, or reflective, prayerful action.

In *God of the Oppressed*, like much of his earlier and later work, Cone displays a profound love for Black people, anchored within the necessity for creating safe space in which the rubrics of liberation and radical commitment to justice can be rehearsed and learned. As I have demonstrated previously, this means we must contend with the significance of Black churches as potential incubators for justice.[15]

The desire of Black people to form their own ecclesial spaces was the process of a long period of history, arising from the 'Great Awakening' in the middle of the eighteenth century. One cannot underestimate the importance of Black existential experience and context to the historical manifestation of Black churches. Black churches were born of the existential need to create safe spaces in which the Black self could rehearse the very rubrics of what it meant to be a human being.[16]

The birth of the independent Black church in the Caribbean can be traced to the arrival in Jamaica in 1783 of approximately 400 White families, who migrated from the United States, preferring to live under British rule than the newly independent Thirteen colonies. Among the White migrants were two enslaved Black people, George Liele and Moses Baker.[17]

The mass migratory movement of Black people from Africa and the Caribbean in the years following the end of World War Two has often been termed 'Windrush'.[18] The post World War Two presence of Black people within inner cities in Britain and the churches to be found there is a phenomenon that has been described by a great many sociologists and historians.[19] This influx is perceived as commencing with the arrival of 492 Caribbean people at Tilbury docks on the *Empire Windrush* on 22 June 1948.

A radical agenda for the Black church in the twenty-first century

The development of Black churches is an ideological and theological product of history. While scholars such as Aldred have argued for a non-contentious and missiological rationale for the development of Black churches in Britain,[20] I am arguing that this interpretation of that narrative is a conservative and a-historical reading of Black Christian tradition. Drawing on the inspiration of James Cone, I will continue to argue for the radical reappropriation of a prophetic tradition within Christianity as espoused by Black churches as a means of galvanizing them to challenge the absurdities of White supremacy while affirming and supporting Black people.

Black theology is distinguishable from other theological movements or trends by the fact that its formative developments did not come from the academy starting with professional scholars, but rather from the committed beliefs and actions of ordinary Black people in the Americas.[21] In *God of the Oppressed*, James Cone draws on the inspired radical actions of enslaved Africans to create the raw materials that would later lead to the academic development of Black theology, of which this book, is in my opinion, the apogee of the systematic treatment of this discipline. While some Black religious scholars have lamented the gap between academic Black theology and the often less strident and ideologically driven faith of ordinary Black Christians,[22] there is, nonetheless, an agreement among the majority of Black religious scholars that Black theology and the Black church should be working hand-in-hand in their attempts to work for equity, justice and peace for all people.

James Cone has established Black theology as the radical

reinterpretation of the revelation of God in Christ, in light of the struggles and suffering of Black existence in order that dehumanized and oppressed Black people might see in God the basis for their liberation. As we have seen previously, Cone's Black theology is resolutely Christian and unapologetically Christological. Cone writes, 'Christ's salvation is liberation; there is no liberation without Christ. Both meanings are inherent in the statement that Jesus Christ is the ground of human liberation.'[23]

In rereading this book, I remain convinced that the major themes of it have not dated. Rather, as we continue to move through the twenty-first century, witnessing the continued push-back of White supremacy and the rich countries of the global North hoarding vaccines for Covid and denying access to Black people in the poorer, global South, we need more than ever a radical restatement of the liberative potential of the Christian gospel. This movement has to work in partnership with Black churches (of all guises, denominations and traditions), inspired by Black theology, to counter the worst excesses and the continued existence of systemic racism.

Back in the late 1990s, inspired by the systematic brilliance of James Cone and reading *God of the Oppressed*, I embarked on an intellectual odyssey to attempt to create a Black theology-based approach to a Christian education curriculum that could offer an important corrective to the practice of teaching the Christian faith to Black young people. This work would also assist in developing greater levels of self-esteem, and connectedness for such individuals to the cultural heritage and antecedents that helped to shape their sense of identity. This model of transformative learning would, I hope, assist in changing the practice of Christian education and faith formation in inner city faith communities across the UK.

My work with Black young people was completed in November 1999. The attempts to create a new model for Christian youth work with Black young people gave rise to two significant developments. The first was a then wholly new attempt for the UK, an exercise in seeking to submerge the central ideas of Black theology within Christian education curricula. The developments of this form of Christian formation and learning in the UK based on Black theology, were later documented in my doctoral thesis.[24] The practical research that was conducted in Birmingham served to challenge the dominant theories of Christian youth work in this country at the time, which have sought to normalize the experiences of White people and, as a corollary, disparaged, marginalized and pathologized Black youth.

The practical expression of this work is contained in the two volumes of African-centred Christian education work I created, which emerged as the major catalyst in the quest to create new models and approaches to the theory and practice of Christian youth work with reference to Black young people in Britain. The two volumes were first published in June 1998.[25] Since they were first published, copies of the books have been sold in The Netherlands, Sweden, Jamaica, Barbados, St Vincent, Trinidad and Tobago, the United States of America, Canada, Australia and New Zealand.

None of the aforementioned would have been possible without the inspiration of James H. Cone and, most significantly, his magnum opus *God of the Oppressed*. I have highlighted this work, not to turn the spotlight away from Cone onto myself, but rather to show the enormous impact this book had upon my own developing consciousness as a then fledgling postgraduate researcher. Essentially, without James Cone, there would have been no doctoral studies for me and without, principally, *God of the Oppressed* there would have been no *Growing into Hope* and the later developments in my own scholarship since that time.

As I stated at the outset of this chapter, I believe that *God of the Oppressed* is the single greatest book in the canon of Black theology that has been written thus far and there is a very good chance that it may never be surpassed. I still believe it is the most complete Black theology text that has been written to date and remains a must read for anyone serious about understanding the nature and intent of the discipline.

Notes

1 James H. Cone, *God of the Oppressed* (San Francisco: Harper and Row, 1975), pp. 16–61.
2 Cone, *God of the Oppressed*, pp. 39–61.
3 Cone, *God of the Oppressed*, pp. 54 and 55.
4 For an important recent text that delineates the comparative developments in 'Theologies of Liberation' see Marcella Althaus-Reid, Ivan Patrella and Luis Carlos Susin (eds), *Another Possible World* (London: SCM Press, 2007).
5 See Anthony G. Reddie, *SCM Core Text: Black Theology* (London: SCM Press, 2012), pp. 1–26.
6 Paulo Freire juxtaposes freedom and oppression in his classic book *Pedagogy of the Oppressed* (London: Heineman, 1970).
7 Cone, *God of the Oppressed*, pp. 146–51.
8 Cone, *God of the Oppressed*, pp. 146–51.
9 Cone, *God of the Oppressed*, p. 148.
10 See the following link for details on this issue of *Reform* and the short piece I wrote: Anthony G. Reddie, 'A good question: Has Christianity made the world better?', *Reform*, September 2018 (accessed 9.11.2021).
11 See James W. Perkinson, *Shamanism, Racism, and Hip Hop Culture: Essays on White Supremacy and Black Subversion* (New York: Palgrave Macmillan, 2005).
12 Robert Beckford, *God of the Rahtid* (London: Darton, Longman and Todd, 2001), pp. 11–30.
13 Beckford, *God of the Rahtid*, p. 8.
14 James Michael Lee, *The Content of Religious Instruction* (Birmingham, AB: Religious Education Press, 1985), p. 257.
15 See chapter 6 in Anthony G. Reddie, *Working Against the Grain* (London: Equinox, 2008), pp. 111–36.
16 Henry H. Mitchell, *Black Church Beginnings; The Long-Hidden Realities of the First Years* (Grand Rapids, MI: Wm. B. Eerdmans, 2004), pp. 8–45.
17 Noel L. Erskine, *Decolonizing Theology: A Caribbean Perspective* (Maryknoll, NY: Orbis Books, 1983), pp. 41–5.
18 This term emanates from a pivotal event on 22 June 1948, when 492 Jamaicans arrived at Tilbury docks on SS *Empire Windrush*. These post-war pioneers ushered in a wave of Black migration to Britain from the Caribbean, which (for the most part) forms the basis for Black African and Caribbean communities in Britain. For further information see Mike Phillips and Trevor Phillips, *Windrush: the irresistible rise of multi-racial Britain* (London: Harper Collins, 1999).

19 Selective literature includes R. B. Davidson, *Black British* (Oxford: Oxford University Press, 1966); R. A. Easterlin, *Immigration* (Cambridge MA: Belknapp Press, 1982); Paul Hartman and Charles Hubbard Charles, *Immigration and the Mass Media* (London: Davis-Poynter, 1974); Edward Scobie, *Black Britannia: A history of Blacks in Britain* (Chicago, IL: Johnson Publishing Co., 1972); Ken Pryce, *Endless Pressure* (Bristol: Classical Press, 1979); Winston James and Clive Harris, *Migration, Racism and Identity* (London: Verso, 1993).

20 See J. D. Aldred, *Respect: Understanding Caribbean British Christianity* (Peterborough: Epworth Press, 2005).

21 Dwight N. Hopkins, *Introducing Black Theology of Liberation* (Maryknoll, NY: Orbis Books, 1999), pp. 7–13.

22 James H. Harris, *Pastoral Theology: A Black Church Perspective* (Minneapolis, MN: Augsburg Fortress, 1991). See also Dale P. Andrews, *Practical Theology For Black Churches: Bridging Black Theology and African American Folk Religion* (Louisville, KY: Westminster John Knox Press, 2002).

23 Cone, *God of the Oppressed*, p. 141.

24 See Anthony G. Reddie, *The Christian Education of Black Children in Birmingham: Creating a new paradigm through developing better praxis*, unpublished Ph.D. thesis, University of Birmingham, 2000.

25 See Anthony G. Reddie, *Growing into Hope* (Peterborough: Methodist Publishing House, 1998). This curriculum is published in two volumes. Volume one is subtitled *Believing and Expecting*. Volume two is entitled *Liberation and Change*.

8

Martin & Malcolm & America

Way back in 1996 when I first met James Cone, I remember vividly him speaking about the two great architects of his Black theology work. Cone said that the 'Black' in Black theology came from the great Malcolm X. Malcolm's brand of uncompromising Black nationalism, at least in the earlier part of his career as a public spokesperson, provides the compelling espoused Black focus that underpins the discipline. Malcolm X's radicalism and keen sense of Black agency and Black self-determination help to create the intellectual break with the seemingly self-evident belief that Christianity is the natural home and for some, the only home in which Black religiosity is housed. But this is balanced by the second half of this nomenclature. The 'theology' in Black theology comes from Dr Martin Luther King, or Martin King as Cone always preferred to name him. For Cone, King provides the resolutely Christian character of Black theology. As we have seen in previous chapters, Cone's Black theology is a Christian theology of liberation focused primarily on God's revelation in Jesus Christ.

Having heard Cone speak about these twin architects in 1996, it was not surprising, therefore, that upon further investigation into his canon of work, I came across *Martin & Malcolm & America: A Dream Or A Nightmare*, first published in 1992. This text is an interesting departure for Cone because, unlike much of his earlier work (*The Spirituals and the Blues* excepted), it is not a straightforward theological book. It is, to my mind, a Black theology-inspired commentary on the parallel lives of two of the most important Black world figures of the second half of the twentieth century. To be clear, these two great men were, first and foremost, African American. They were born into and shaped by the cultural milieu in which they were nurtured and socialized. Cone's meticulous research helps the reader to appreciate and understand the 'backstory', so to speak, of these two major figures in the twentieth-century Black liberation story.

In highlighting the lives of these two great Black men, James Cone is attempting to address two major existential questions that have long faced Black people, especially, diasporan Black people. The first is the nature of America as the 'Promised Land' of opportunity and dreams fulfilled. This has particular resonance for someone born of Caribbean parents, because the nature of endemic poverty in the region has always meant that their major export has not been material goods or services, but people. Caribbean migration was a constant feature of the region throughout the twentieth century. Members of my own family travelled to Panama to help build the Panama Canal at the dawn of the last century. Had it not been for the US passing the McCarran–Walter Act of 1952[1] that reimposed immigration quotas on unskilled labour coming into America, my own parents and their respective siblings would most likely have migrated to the comparatively closer shores of the US than the longer distance to the so-called 'Mother Land' of the UK.

For many Caribbean people, America has been a mecca in which travel to get work and the dubious promise of the 'American Dream' has loomed large. So, in narrating the Black African American experience in the 'Land of the Free and the Home of the Brave', Cone is using Malcolm X and Martin King as archetypes to explore the extent to which this experience is 'A Dream or a Nightmare'.[2] This theme is a key one, for there is a sense in which, for many Christian theologians, notions of 'Development' and 'Progressive' often have an American tinge to them. America is the richest and most powerful nation the world has ever seen. Her success is often linked to notions of manifest destiny and a sense of exceptionalism, often learned from the British who handed on this mantle as 'God's nation' through an Anglo-Saxon inheritance to the US.[3]

The second substantive area that Cone addresses through these two titans of the Black liberation struggle is the extent to which either 'integration' or 'separation' is the best means by which Black freedom will be achieved. In some respects, this is not only a macro question for Black people, but also a more micro one for the discipline of Black theology itself. To what extent is Black theology focused primarily on Black freedom 'by any means necessary', in which the Christian faith is a helpful, but not necessary, conduit for this movement to take place? Or, conversely, is Black theology primarily a discipline that is seeking to reform the warped and distorted identity of Christianity and the theology it espouses, the major beneficiary of which will be Black people, who will gain their freedom as a result of this wholesale reformation?

On the face of it, the clear answer would appear to lie in the first contention, because Cone says as much. As we have seen, Cone argues that the sole purpose of Black theology is that of freeing Black people. And yet, the lengths to which Cone seeks to anchor his work within the Judeo-Christian tradition, seeking to justify the authentic and legitimate identity of Black theology as a reputable Christian theology,[4] would seem to suggest that there is also a healthy dose of the latter in his modus operandi.

Martin (Luther) King

Although Cone cites Martin King and Malcolm X as the twin architects for Black theology, and equal treatment and time is given to both in the book, as Earle Fisher has shown in his recent article in *Black Theology*, Cone is not *really* even-handed in this engagement. Fisher argues that Cone is much less searching in his critique of King than he is of 'Brother Malcolm'.[5] The fact that Cone commences with King, about whom already a great deal more is known than Brother Malcolm, is instructive. Cone reflects on the formative influences that shaped King's early life, especially that of his father 'Daddy

King Sr'. Cone writes, 'Martin Luther King, Sr, the son of a sharecropper, was a classic example of a person who pulled himself up by his own bootstraps, thereby becoming a persuasive symbol of the merits of thrift, service, responsibility, and sacrifice.'[6]

Cone outlines the formative influences that gave rise to the towering social prophet that begins to emerge in the Montgomery Bus boycott of 1955. For King, education and the church – from Moorhouse, to Crozier seminary to Boston university and being ordained into the Baptist Church – these provide the developmental steps towards him becoming arguably the greatest public Christian theologian of the twentieth century.

Malcolm X

Cone's reflections on the social, cultural and political formation of Malcolm X are no less compelling. Cone shows how in stark contrast to King's comfortable, middle-class upbringing, as one of the elites of his community in the American South, Malcolm Little grew up among the dispossessed masses, in Omaha, Nebraska. Cone addresses head on the legacy of misconception, White demonization and vitriol aimed at Malcolm X, all of which tells one more about White people and their warped and skewed version of the world than it did about this complex personality in his own right.[7] As Cone makes clear, what characterizes Malcolm X's religious and political formation is not so much his hatred for White people and the deeply ingrained nature of systemic racism they have created, but rather, the embracing of Islam and his unwavering love for Black people.[8]

The story Cone paints of Malcolm X's formative years, prior to him being paroled from prison in 1952 and his meeting with Elijah Mohammed and the Nation of Islam, is a vivid picture of the precarious nature of Black life for many in the US, prior to the Civil Rights movement. The paralleling of their formative lives offers an intriguing picture of the often marked and differing ways in which Black liberation activism is born, either through a form of top-down, patrician privilege or the bottom-up, more grassroots form of activism. Both impulses remain in evidence within many Black communities across the world. Also, as Cone outlines, the formative development of their respective, religiously inspired philosophies begins to take shape in their respective early years. Once again, the compelling beauty of Cone's writing is that he shows us that, while ostensibly his book is about two huge personalities, it is also about something much more elemental and existential. How are Black people to live in a world of White hegemony? Are we to follow an integrationist or separatist logic? Is humanity more alike than unalike, or is nationalism the natural disposition that frames the ways in which human beings live? These remain marked questions for Black activists and those committed to the cause of Black liberation.

Two sides of the same coin

Throughout the book James Cone juxtaposes the alternate public activism of both men. We oscillate between Martin's dream and Malcolm's nightmare. The Christian-inspired hope of Martin and his belief in the redemptive power of the human spirit to change and Malcolm's more clear-eyed view of the tribal nature of humankind, especially when allied to notions of White superiority and White hegemony.

What emerges from this constant parallel reflection on the differing lives and approaches of Martin King and Malcolm X, is that they are not diametrically opposed as one might well imagine or has been reported in popular mythology. A few years ago, I attended a conference on MLK in Birmingham, organized by a friend and colleague working within the Baptist Union. The conference was to mark the 50th anniversary of the death of King. Of particular note for this conversation was the trenchant view of one of the speakers that MLK was a hero, and that Malcolm X's legacy was irrelevant to modern-day sensibilities and was certainly one that should be shunned by Black Christians. This was 2018! But as Cone makes clear, while their methods might have differed markedly, the overarching goal for which each fought remained remarkably similar. Cone puts it like this:

> The most important similarity between Martin and Malcolm was the *goal* for which they fought. From the beginning of their ministries, they both sought the unqualified liberation of African-Americans from the bonds of segregation and discrimination to self-determination as a people, from a feeling of inferiority and nobodyness to an affirmation of themselves as human beings. To be sure, Martin's and Malcolm's great differences in historical and social origins led them to choose different paths to the goal, yet the method of each complemented that of the other.[9]

The problem with individuals who want to assert the comprehensive difference between the two is that often the proponents of such sentiments want to position Martin within a paradigm of colour-blind evangelicalism. They often cite his famed comments of wanting his children to be judged by the content of their character and not the colour of their skin, which has invariably been taken out of context. As Cone shows in his exploration of Martin's non-violent, direct-action form of activism that was underpinned by love, this was not a colour-blind, let-us-all-transcend-race-at-all-costs form of struggle.[10] King's comments, indeed all his public pronouncements, were uttered within the wider context of the search for racial justice and other forms of equity for poor and marginalized peoples in the US and internationally. But at the heart of it all, Martin was a Black man, deeply connected to the plight of the people from whom he had been plucked to carry the burden of leading a Civil Rights movement.

The above is important because of the ways in which people of all ethnic and political perspectives have attempted to appropriate the life and legacy of Martin Luther King Jr.

As Richard Reddie shows in his excellent work on King, the legend of the man has now turned into myth and hagiography, to the point where both right and left on the political spectrum seek to claim him as their own.[11] The attempts of conservatives to deradicalize King are often based on a fossilizing of the moment of the March on Washington in August 1963, when he declaims his now iconic 'I Have a Dream' speech.[12] But as Cone and many others have shown, the seemingly utopian and pious rhetoric of this speech may have been the high watermark of his popularity in the public imagination of America, but it was not the end point. The King who was assassinated nearly five years later was someone calling for an end to militarism and espoused an economic outlook that very much resembled democratic socialism[13] – this was not the cuddly, benign, colour-blind dreamer!

Martin & Malcolm & America is notable for the ways in which Cone locates both men as representing different sides of the Black liberation coin. In their respective ministries they are not seeking to avoid 'race' or to transcend it, as if it does not exist, but rather, they are seeking to deconstruct and dismantle it. For both figures, the salient issue is one of Black freedom from the systemic scourge of racism and economic exploitation that has impacted all people. Long before the more recent talk of conceptualizing Whiteness that has become more de rigueur, particularly through the work of Willie James Jennings,[14] both Martin and Malcolm were challenging Whiteness to be deconstructed and reconstituted, shorn of its worst excesses of notions of exceptionalism and spurious superiority. This was especially true in terms of their critique of American Christianity, Martin from within the tradition and Malcolm from beyond it.[15]

For both figures, as has remained the case for the Black theology tradition of which Cone is the great exemplar, Black liberation will be accomplished when two parallel and yet differing moves are effected. First is that of Black empowerment, agency and self-determination. The second is the necessity for White people to change and to become anti-racist allies.[16]

Martin and Malcolm, even from their vantage point of undertaking public ministries that ended in the far-off decade of the 1960s, knew that White people being 'non-racist' was not sufficient for there to be equity and justice for all people in the US and across the world and for the realization of Black liberation to be effected.[17] Rather, White people needed to be *anti*-racist. This has become an even more pointed choice following the murder of George Floyd in May 2020. Are moderate and even progressive White people willing to move from non-racism to anti-racism?

Black theology in action

What is enormously enjoyable about *Martin & Malcolm & America* is the skilful way in which Cone weaves a narrative that frames the essential and substantive questions posed by Black theology into the socio-political and cultural background that is the America of Martin and Malcolm. In many respects, this is the book you buy a friend whom you want to engage with Black theology-based ideas, but who are either not much interested in theology or have no time for any reflections on formal religion. As I will demonstrate shortly, *Martin & Malcolm & America* is probably Cone's most popular book, one that a non-specialist reader can engage with, not knowing that they are surreptitiously imbibing the central tenets of Black theology from within what appears to be a straightforward biography of two great Black leaders.

As I demonstrated at the outset, one of the key aspects of Black theology is that its point of departure is the Black reality of suffering and not abstract theologizing in the first instance. Yes, Cone and many others (including myself, of course) have sought to reflect on the ways in which Black theology might be understood as a legitimate form of scholarly, theological enquiry (obviously opening it up to the charge that this has in fact dominated its identity), but this was always seen as a necessary second step. The first step was the activism of Black ministers and lay people, during the Civil Rights and Black Power movements.

On the many occasions I have taught Black theology, I have often used an experiential learning exercise first devised in one of my previous books, *Acting in Solidarity*.[18] In the exercise, a tall, powerful White man is in a fight to the death with a shorter, weaker Black woman. In this imaginary scenario (not as imaginary as one might imagine in all truth), God is suddenly seen walking on the other side of the road. Both the Black woman and the White man appeal to God to intervene on their side. In the exercise, I split the class into two, with one side adopting the identity of the woman and the other of the man. I ask each side, what do you want God to do? In summary, those thinking through the experience of the White man would preferably like God to endorse their actions and to sanctify their sense of superiority. But if needed, they are prepared for God to do nothing and to remain inactive, given that all things being equal, without some form of external intervention, they are going to win this fight. So, effectively, those representing the powerful White man are content with a non-interventionist or non-active God. Conversely, those representing the woman *want God to do something*. In other words, for them, an absent or distant God who will not intervene or take sides serves no purpose given their existential plight.

The responses from both sides provides a way into the relative points of departure between academic White theology and Black liberation theology. The latter has always presupposed that for God to be God and true to God's nature as seen in the scriptures and in history, then God is on the side of those struggling for justice. The exercise has always served as a way of helping predominantly White ministerial students to understand the passionate urgency of Black theology when it first came to life back in the mid to late 1960s. With Black people literally dying under the yoke of White supremacy, Black theology was never developed in order that a Black educated elite could show White people how clever they were. Rather, it burst into life due to the necessity of providing hope to a besieged and colonized set of people.

When I first developed this exercise, the reading that went with it was drawn from *Martin & Malcolm & America* because the latter describes vividly the socio-political and cultural backdrop to Black theology. Cone explores the nature of the systemic racism in 1960s America that resulted in poverty, social alienation, poor educational attainment and rampant substance abuse in the many Black ghettoes of America.[19] Malcolm X described these conditions as part of the 'American nightmare' for Black people, the often unmentioned reverse side of the illusory American Dream, so often invoked in American public consciousness.[20] The nightmare to which Malcolm X speaks is the searing reality to which Black theology seeks to respond, in the belief that God is in real solidarity with Black peoples across the world in this struggle.

In utilizing the lives of Martin and Malcolm, Cone hopes to create an opportunity that will enable readers who want to begin a journey into learning more about racial justice issues, to do so through the lens of these competing and yet complementary narratives. Cone's work counters some of the so-called common-sense type ideas of racism that are often put forward by many 'right wing' publications, such as some of our tabloid and broadsheet national newspapers. Martin and Malcolm provide differing ways of wrestling with systemic racism and the complacency and seeming blindness of White people to their unearned privilege around the nature of Whiteness.

Martin & Malcolm & America seeks to demonstrate the ways in which these two key figures sought to get White America to wrestle with the overarching difficulty of trying to get beyond the fragile and insecure subjectivity White people carry when dealing with issues of 'race'.

The tensions regarding issues of 'race' are all too evident in much of our contemporary discourse, whether inside of or external to the church. To quote Richard Reddie, 'The Church often avoids race-related discussions through fear, ignorance and a sense of seeming irrelevance.'[21]

The central defining metaphor of being the united body in Christ makes many Christians unable or unwilling to deal with issues of difference and the racism that arises from our refusal to engage with or even acknowledge that reality which separates and divides us. Writing with reference to the Eucharist, Tee Garlington reminds us of the ethnic tensions, and the inherent inclusivity that should embrace these differences, both of which reside within Jewish and Christian traditions.[22] Garlington continues, reminding us that the early church had to struggle with issues of ethnic or national intolerance, but that the praxis of those first Christians sought to move beyond the cultural superiority of facets of the existing faith.[23]

Martin King attempted to persuade White people, via the ethic of love, to live up to the unifying thread within Christian theology that the church has been propagating for centuries, but rarely practising when it comes to effecting racial justice for Black people.

These tensions had been endemic in Christianity and the church and wider American society for centuries and Martin King recognized the ways in which the ongoing phenomenon of racism is one that holds many of us hostage. Writing on the legacy of Martin King, Enoch Oglesby has employed the metaphor of the mountain in his attempt to make sense of and grapple with the often unnamed and unspoken sin that is racism.[24] Oglesby attempts to use Christian ethics to challenge the reality of racism in the US. He argues that the Black church in America has become absorbed into a White middle-class form of complacency that wants to ignore the reality of racism and identify it as someone else's problem – specifically, that of secular society. Oglesby writes:

> Thus, Black folk are faced, in this regard, with a double-barrelled moral dilemma: the sinful scandal of racism within the comfortable pews of the church, on the one hand; and on the other, the immorality of bourgeois power arising from the church's uncritical identification with the dominant class values of the status quo.[25]

Martin King reminds us that the challenge that has faced all Christians in America is one of attempting to live out the belief in the united and yet diverse body of Christ. The salient question remains one of how we find ways of being open about our differences (as well as that which unites us) and to name the sin that corrupts our sense of corporate unity. Martin King's life's project was the attempt to convince White people to be willing to get to a place where racism can be recognized and repelled in order to bring about justice for all people.

For Malcolm X, all the aforementioned was steeped in centuries of denial and White obfuscation and hypocrisy. His rejection of Christianity was born of a life lived in close proximity to White supremacy, in which the promises of democracy and equality, seemingly guaranteed through the twin foundations of the American constitution and the teachings of the church, had proved illusory. Unlike Martin, Malcolm saw human nature not through an appreciative, faith informed belief in the intrinsic goodness of humanity that is created in God's image and likeness. For Malcolm, the starkness of Black suffering arising from centuries of White supremacy, often aided and abetted by Christianity, was not an aberration of the faith, but was an indication of its true nature, a faith founded and built on White privilege as the White man's religion. The move to the Nation of Islam and later, more orthodox Islam, was inspired by the need to find an alternative, uniting principle and faith around which Black people could unite, in their constant fight for agency, self-determination and freedom. The universal humanism he found from his travels beyond America in 1964, the year before his death, allowed him to transcend the more strident anti-White doctrine he had espoused earlier in his ministry. And yet this more emollient formulation of his ministry and public activism did not see him embrace the religion of empire.

Cone, while attempting to be even-handed in his assessment of the respective ministries of Martin and Malcolm, quite naturally leans slightly towards King as he, like him, remains a Christian. For Cone and King, they had the problem of trying to contest and contextualize the shared faith of their oppressors. As I have shown earlier in this book, the God of the Judeo-Christian tradition cannot be on the side of both the oppressed and the oppressor. The inheritors of the profits of slavery and those whose bodies made those profits, both cannot be right when appealing to this same one God, in their plea to the truth.

Malcolm X had no such problems. Moving beyond Christianity allowed him to create an alternative philosophy of truth that did not have to contend with White people. Basically, the Nation of Islam simply bypassed White people and any claims they might make towards giving public utterance to, or living out the truth. This separatist perspective is one that has challenged and enticed Black theologians since the inception of Black theology.

Some, like Albert Cleage, who I mentioned in Part 1 sought to create a distinctly Afrocentric form of Christianity that effectively operated as an alternative form of Black hermeneutics that removes White people from the equation.[26] Chaz Howard's exploration of Black theology as a mass movement investigates the public ministry of Marcus Garvey and his form of Christian-inspired Black nationalism at the dawn of the twentieth century.[27] Jamaican-born, Black theologian Noel Erskine explores Rastafari as an alternative means of developing Black theology that once again bypasses the necessity of having to wrestle with developing forms of Black hermeneutics that disentangle truth from the corruptions of White supremacy.[28] Haitian scholars Celucien Joseph and Nixon Cleophat offer an approach to Black theology through the prism of Haitian Vodou.[29] Given the significance of vodou in providing the spiritual and philosophical underpinning for the Haitian revolution between 1791 and 1804 for Black enslaved Africans against the White 'Christian'-inspired French troops, one can see the immediate attraction of this religious tradition as a form of Black liberation theology.

In *Martin & Malcolm & America*, Cone offers us the compelling narrative of these twin identities of Black theology. Can

Black theology offer a compelling alternative form of Christian hermeneutics that wrestles truth and theological legitimacy from the realm of Whiteness? The extent to which this has been achieved or not is of continued significance if the church and Christianity is to harness the radicalism of Black youth, particularly that of the Black Lives Matter generation.[30]

Alternatively, does Black theology need to move beyond the parameters set by Christianity, because the move to create a parallel form of hermeneutics has ultimately failed and the Christian church remains within the iron grip of Whiteness, even when so-called 'World Christianity' has become increasingly in vogue in more recent times?[31] And yet, despite the compelling argument that Black self-determination cannot be effected from within the prism of Christianity and Christian theology, the bulk of Black theologians have remained within the Christian hermeneutical tradition.[32] Frederick Ware, in outlining the different methodologies to undertaking Black theology, shows how the Christian approach to the discipline, anchored in a reinterpretation of the Bible and its accompanying tradition focused through the church and its mission, has remained the normative methodological approach for most Black theologians.

Cone's book uses the towering ministries of Martin King and Malcolm X to address the wider development and character of Black theology as it is expressed in American life. Should Black liberation follow the identity of Martin King and his attempt to harness the power of the Christian narrative as a means of effecting Black liberation through the orienting power of Jesus Christ? Conversely, would the Black liberation project be better achieved through the prism of alternate, non-Western and more heterodox forms of religious expression that move beyond the parameters of the doctrinally framed theology of James Cone?[33]

James Cone's *Martin & Malcolm & America* is his most popular book. One does not need to be interested in academic theology or the intricacies of theological method to appreciate its significance. It taps into the broader questions of how we interpret the Black experience and the thrust for Black liberation. This book, Cone's least theological, remains the one that non-churchy people can read and find some sense of the wider socio-political contexts that gave rise to the development of Black theology.

Cone's searing truth telling is one that does not seek to mythologize or sanctify Martin King and Malcolm X. Just as he refused to be eulogized in his own life, Cone seeks to affirm the collective nature of Black liberation struggles that are best achieved through the mass participation of ordinary people who are inspired and convicted by the belief that the future can be better than the present, but that future needs to be fought for and wrestled with in order to free it from the iron grip of White supremacy. Cone of course can say this far better than me:

> People frequently ask: 'Who are the Martin King and Malcolm X of our time? The Reverend Jesse Jackson and Minister Louis Farrakhan?' In desperate situations, people look for messiahs to deliver them out of their misery ... Charismatic leaders, however, cannot liberate Black people from their misery. They may even hinder the process. Thus, it is important to emphasize that Martin and Malcolm, despite the excessive adoration their followers often bestow on them, they were not messiahs. Both were *ordinary* human beings who gave their lives for the freedom of their people. They show us what ordinary people can accomplish through intelligence and sincere commitment to the cause of justice and freedom. There is no need to look to messiahs to save the poor. Human beings can and must do it themselves.[34]

Cone sums up the continued challenges facing the wider Black liberation movement. The collegiality and non-mythologized, non-cult of personality style of leadership espoused by the Black Lives Matter movement is one that is very much in the mould of the cautionary words of James Cone. It is an attempt to broaden the leadership among a wider franchise of activists and is less dependent on charismatic, alpha-male leadership. And yet so much of modern Black Christianity, especially that which comes out of a neo-Pentecostal sensibility, is often focused on the very kind of charismatic, top-down, alpha-male leadership that Cone cautions us against.

Martin & Malcolm & America is a brilliant distillation of the Black liberation struggle in America, that spread across the world in anti-imperial movements, seeking to bring about Black self-determination and freedom, alongside the seeming necessity of service and sacrifice to the wider cause. Black theology remains committed to Black liberation and is indebted to Martin King and Malcolm X for providing the template for many to follow since their tragic deaths in the 1960s.

Notes

1 For brief details on this act, see 'The Immigration and Nationality Act of 1952 (The McCarran-Walter Act)', *Office of the Historian*, https://history.state.gov/milestones/1945-1952/immigration-act#:~:text=NOTE%20TO%20READERS-,The%20Immigration%20and%20Nationality%20Act%20of%201952%20(The%20McCarran%2DWalter,controversial%20system%20of%20immigrant%20selection (accessed 14.11.2021).

2 James H. Cone, *Martin & Malcolm & America: A Dream Or A Nightmare* (Maryknoll, NY: Orbis Books, 1992), pp. 1–17.

3 One of the best texts that explores this historical dynamic is Kelly Brown Douglas, *Stand Your Ground: Black Bodies and the Justice of God* (Maryknoll, NY: Orbis Books, 2015).

4 See the following article by Elonda Clay for an important critique of the tendency of James Cone's Black theology project to be more concerned with 'legitimation' than it was with 'liberation'. See Elonda Clay, 'A Black Theology of Liberation or Legitimation? A Postcolonial Response to Cone's *Black Theology and Black Power* at Forty', in *Black Theology: An International Journal*, vol. 8, no. 3, 2010, pp. 307–26.

5 See Earle J. Fisher, 'Brother Malcolm, Dr. King, and Black Power – A Close and Complementary Reading', *Black Theology: An International Journal*, vol. 18, no. 3, 2020, pp. 263–87.

6 Cone, *Martin & Malcolm & America*, p. 22.

7 Cone, *Martin & Malcolm & America*, pp. 38–57.

8 Cone, *Martin & Malcolm & America*, pp. 51–7.

9 Cone, *Martin & Malcolm & America*, p. 246.
10 Cone, *Martin & Malcolm & America*, pp. 120–50.
11 See Richard S. Reddie, *Martin Luther King, Jr* (Oxford: Lion, 2011).
12 Cone, *Martin & Malcolm & America*, pp. 83–8.
13 Cone, *Martin & Malcolm & America*, pp. 232–43.
14 See Willie James Jennings, *After Whiteness: An Education in Belonging* (Grand Rapids, MI: Wm. B. Eerdmans, 2020).
15 Cone, *Martin & Malcolm & America*, pp. 295–7.
16 I address aspects of the latter change in the following article. See Anthony G. Reddie, 'Reassessing the Inculcation of an Anti-Racist Ethic for Christian Ministry: From Racism Awareness to Deconstructing Whiteness', in *Religions*, vol. 11, no. 497, 2020.
17 Cone, *Martin & Malcolm & America*, pp. 288–314.
18 This exercise was first developed for a previous study. See the introduction to 'The Plain Old Honest Truth' in Anthony G. Reddie, *Acting in Solidarity* (London: Darton, Longman and Todd, 2005), pp. 144–5.
19 Cone, *Martin & Malcolm & America*, pp. 89–119.
20 Cone, *Martin & Malcolm & America*, pp. 89–119.
21 Richard Reddie, 'Book Review of "Making a Positive Difference" (Naboth Muchopa)', in *Black Theology: An International Journal*, vol. 1, no. 1, Nov. 2002, p. 120.
22 Tee Garlington, 'The Eucharist and Racism' in Susan E. Davies and Sister Paul Teresa Hennesee SA (eds), *Ending Racism In The Church* (Cleveland, OH: The Pilgrim Press, 1998), pp. 74–80.
23 Garlington, 'The Eucharist and Racism', pp. 75–8.
24 E. Hammond Oglesby, *O Lord, Move This Mountain: Racism and Christian Ethics* (St Louis, MO: Chalice Press, 1998).
25 Oglesby, *O Lord, Move This Mountain*, p. 8.
26 See Jawanza Eric Clark (ed.), *Albert Cleage Jr and the Black Madonna and Child* (New York: Palgrave Macmillan, 2016).
27 See C. L. Howard, *Black Theology as Mass Movement* (New York: Palgrave Macmillan, 2014).
28 See Noel Leo Erskine, *From Garvey to Marley: Rastafari Theology* (Gainesville, FL: University of Florida Press, 2007).
29 Celucien L. Joseph and Nixon S. Cleophat, *Vodou in the Haitian Experience: A Black Atlantic Perspective* (Lanham, MD: Lexington Press, 2016).
30 See Alease Brown, 'Re-imagining Sacred Texts: Recognizing the Ways in Which Protests, Tattoos, and Hashtags Constitute Vibrant Articulations of the Christian Faith', in *Black Theology: An International Journal*, vol. 18, no. 1, 2020, pp. 61–74.

31 See Adrian Hastings, *A World History of Christianity* (Grand Rapids, MI: Wm. B. Eerdmans, 2000). See also Lamin O. Sanneh, *Disciples of All Nations: Pillars of World Christianity* (Oxford and New York: Oxford University Press, 2008).

32 Frederick L. Ware, *Methodologies of Black Theology* (Eugene, OR: Wipf and Stock: 2008).

33 See Robert E. Hood, *Must God Remain Greek?: Afro Cultures and God-Talk* (Minneapolis, MN: Fortress Press, 1990).

34 Cone, *Martin & Malcolm & America*, p. 315.

9

The Cross and the Lynching Tree

The Cross and the Lynching Tree (2011) is James Cone's last great masterpiece, and was a book that was a long time in the making. I first heard Cone speak of the link between *The Cross and the Lynching Tree* at that memorable occasion at the Queen's Foundation in 1996.

The brilliance of the book is that it puts into plain view so many aspects of Christianity and the theology that emerges from it which has been hidden from so many, for so long. Cone outlines the symbolic power of the cross as a sign of transformation.

Cone's book highlights the broader Black theological work around the cross. Within the Black theology tradition, various writers have written about the cross and have located within the suffering of Jesus a sense of divine solidarity with their own historical and contemporary experiences of unjustified and unmerited suffering. Scholars such as Douglas[1] and Terrell,[2] and others, have all explored the theological significance for Black people of Jesus' suffering on the cross.

Writing with reference to this theme, Terrell states:

> Yet the tendency among Black people has been to identify wholly with the suffering of Jesus because the story made available to them – Jesus' story – tells of his profound affinity with their plight. Like the martyrs, they are committed to him because his story is their story. Jesus' death by crucifixion is a prototype of African Americans' death by *circumscription*.[3]

This radical identification with the undeserved suffering of an innocent individual has exerted a powerful hold on the imagination of many Black people and other marginalized and oppressed groups in the world.[4] Cone's work creates a visceral interaction with this tradition. James Baldwin, the third in the triumvirate of Black figures who are the architects of Black theology stated, 'White people in this hemisphere discovered Christ by way of the Bible. Black people discovered Christ by way of the cross.'[5] What Baldwin means here is that Black people discovered the God of the Bible 'the hard way', via unremitting suffering, especially that which emerged through the privations of slavery.

Cone taps into a resonance felt by many Black people to the visceral nature of Jesus' suffering that maps onto the historic nature of their own oppression. The identification with Jesus arises from the recognition that, just as Jesus challenged injustice and called for people to turn away from their old ways of living and behaving, which led to his unpopularity and death, then so also for Black people. Cone outlines the ways in which the cross speaks to the disruptive ways in which Black bodies have challenged the body politic of White majority-run nations in the global West and North. To put it bluntly, 'uppity negroes' were often the recipient of the grisly imposition of lynching.

For Cone, the cross is linked to the lynching tree and to every facet of Black suffering in the world, whether on the continent of Africa or beyond, by virtue of the fact that Jesus Christ participates in that suffering. Therefore, for Cone, notwithstanding the vociferous critique of the cross offered by Delores Williams,[6] Christ's participation in our suffering makes a qualitative change to the nature and purpose of that suffering. Cone is not justifying the cross as essential to human redemption, but he nevertheless does see redemptive qualities in it. The cross represents God's solidarity with all people wrestling under the yoke of underserved suffering and oppression. Cone's meditation on the cross in relationship to the lynching tree is linked to the wider struggle for Black liberation from the agonies of slavery through the more contemporary trials of colonialism, as outlined by a number of African biblical scholars.[7]

Central to Cone's exploration of the cross is the insistence that we move beyond a mere spiritualization of it, in order that we see it in both its historical context and the divine revelation through which God is speaking, as a means of understanding its resonance in the contemporary world. Cone writes, 'No theme was more important to King's thinking about the cross than the hope that emerges out of terrible circumstances.'[8] For Cone, the terrible circumstances of the cross and the resonance it has to the lived realities of suffering and oppression, especially of Black people, is what makes the cross of salvific value. Prior to reading this book, the significance of the cross had remained an intellectual and emotional site of tension for me. It's not that I doubted the historicity of the cross and Jesus' death on it, but I had witnessed too many White evangelicals eulogize about 'preaching Christ crucified' and there being 'Power in the blood', with little or no recourse to the social and political price expended by Christ on the cross and the contemporary crosses carried by many. I remember having a conversation with a group of relatively conservative White ministerial students in a theological college where I was then working, trying to help them see the natural connections between the cross and the socio-political and cultural contexts in which their ministerial formation was taking place. I asked them why it was that in a city built on the profits of the slave trade, with their training taking place in a large, ornate Georgian building, which was erected from the profits of slave owners, in one of the most fashionable parts of the city, in which most Black people are conspicuous by their absence, there wasn't one conversation about the social context of the city, not even one. In the year in which I worked in that city, I did not see one Black person walking the streets of the area in which this theological college was based. So I pressed the question, why was it that these students could proclaim the redeeming power of the cross but could not see the contemporary resonance of the cross in what continues to be a deeply racially divided city.

The people at the top of the hill are, invariably, White and affluent. The people living at the bottom and often across 'the way' separated by the end of a motorway, are invariably Black and minority ethnic peoples. There are two different worlds.

The fact that in the year in which I worked there not one mention was made of the slave trade or the fact that the beautiful building in which we worked had been owned by someone involved in the slave trade, made the point perfectly. The cross was so spiritualized that any resonance to contemporary experience was lost. The cross was the supreme expression of salvation but had little ethical charge on how human beings should relate to one another and to wider issues of justice and equity in the world.

The strength of this amazing late classic from Cone (written when he was in his early seventies) is the way in which he highlights the differing forms of obfuscation among White theologians and Christians of the social and political implications of the cross. One of the most resounding of ironies between the last two ex-presidents of the United States, is that while one was caught on a recording boasting about grabbing women's 'private parts' and being defended by White evangelicals in America and Britain as 'locker-room talk', his predecessor was quoting Reinhold Niebuhr. Niebuhr is often seen as America's pre-eminent Christian ethicist. His Christian realism had exerted a profound influence on generations of thinkers since his death in 1971. Obama's identification of Niebuhr's influence on his foreign policy is a reminder of the high bar Black people have to attain when compared to one's White peers.[9] While his successor had a penchant for mangling the English language, Obama was smart enough to be quoting leading intellectuals as the source for a seemingly (but not achieved) ethical foreign policy.

Cone's theological development was informed by Reinhold Niebuhr's Christian theological realism. But as Cone proceeds to demonstrate, even a clear-sighted and committed justice-oriented ethicist such as Niebuhr was blinded by his own Whiteness to the demonstrable and persistent nature of Black suffering in the US.[10] Cone writes of Niebuhr, 'Although Niebuhr is often called a "prophet" and claimed that "all theology really begins with Amos", he was no prophet on race.'[11]

Although Cone is resolutely a liberation theologian and not a post-colonial one, I nevertheless, see a number of interesting connections between the two categories. I have always seen liberation theologies and post-colonial theologies as different sides of the same coin. Although the latter is often more critical of the overarching Christian tradition than the former, invariably questioning the normativity and viability of Christianity as a site for the liberation of formerly colonized subjects, what links the two, however, is the constructive critique of Whiteness. For Cone, in juxtaposing the neo-orthodoxy of Karl Barth with the more critical liberalism of Reinhold Niebuhr, he is able to show that the myopia of Whiteness is alive and well in all forms of the phenomenon, irrespective of theological perspectives.

So, whether in the case of these relatively conservative White ministerial students in my former place of work, or in the following years when working for the Connexional team of the Methodist Church, one could see White people's aversion to wrestling with White privilege and the systemic racism evoked by the cross. In terms of the latter, I remember the occasion of the 50th anniversary of the historic Program to Combat Racism created by the World Council of Churches in 1969. This historic piece of prophetic, anti-racist Christian activism had its roots in a WCC consultation held at Notting Hill Methodist Church in May 1969. The 50th anniversary event was held on Sunday 19 May 2019 at which I was invited to be the guest preacher in the morning act of worship. In the afternoon, there was an unveiling of a blue plaque to mark the site at which the consultation had taken place 50 years earlier.[12]

In both the service itself in the morning and the unveiling of the plaque in the afternoon, not one person from the wider leadership of the Methodist Church was present: no President, Vice President, Secretary of Conference, Chairs of the London district nor any of the Directors of the Discipleship and Ministries Learning Network. I am sure people had busy diaries and a pressing number of events at which their attendance was necessary. But this was like the absence of any White Methodist church leaders at the Racial Justice fringe meeting at the 2016 annual Methodist conference in London that year. I remember at the time speaking passionately at the apparent lack of regard White leaders in the Methodist Church seemed to have for racial justice, given that none of them could be bothered to attend a meeting to be in solidarity with Black people.

In the later event in May 2019, the Methodists who did attend the event, beyond those in the hosting church, were radicals from a previous era. So, many of my formative Methodist heroes were present, such as Revds David Haslam and Donald Eadie, plus Lord Paul Boateng, the former Labour Party frontbench MP in Tony Blair's New Labour government of the late 1990s. There was no current leader in the Methodist Church present. Clearly, given the priorities facing the Methodist Church back in 2019, racial justice would appear to be an insignificant one at that juncture.

Sitting on the train heading back to Birmingham following the conclusion of the event, I had a profound sense that the Methodist Church in which my theological radicalism had been nurtured had sadly disappeared, and I was a man out of time, given that my fellow travellers were people some 25 or so years my senior. For present day or contemporary Methodists, racial justice did not appear as important as getting more people to join the church. All of this predates the murder of George Floyd and the present upsurge of performative responses to systemic racism.

The significance of *The Cross and the Lynching Tree* for the purposes of these reflections lies in the fact that, like the other examples I have cited, many White people seemed unable to connect the centrality of the cross with the existence of systemic racism and White entitlement and privilege in Britain and in many other parts of the world. Cone makes it clear that the lack of connection between these two realities represents a fundamental flaw in White Christianity.

Writing on the latter, Cone states:

> But we cannot find liberating joy in the cross by spiritualizing it, by taking away its message of justice in the midst of powerlessness, suffering and death. The cross, as a locus of divine revelation, is not good news for the powerful, for those who are comfortable with the way things are, or for anyone whose understanding of religion is aligned with power.[13]

Conversely, for those whose lived experience is marginalization and powerlessness, the cross and identification with it holds a powerful and seductive importance. It can be a means of convincing ordinary Black people to spiritualize their sufferings, holding onto the idea that suffering itself is redemptive, because Jesus himself suffered. Identification with Jesus' suffering on the cross can lead to theological passivity, as suffering is seen as the means by which one is made holy and closer to God. Cone does not endorse this view, but it can be argued that in focusing clearly on the cross, he runs the risk of sacralizing it, that is, making it appear as an essential spiritual value through which God's presence is made manifest in the lives of Christian believers.

For Cone, however, the focus on the cross and its links to suffering, exploitation and oppression are of such importance, that the dangers of it being made into a spiritual exemplar for justifying suffering, is worth risking. Cone is not arguing that suffering is necessary per se. In fact, Cone is clear that he is most definitely not saying that.[14] Rather, suffering is the natural consequence of standing up against oppressive forces and those who are seeking to impose their will and power on others. Cone's book provides theological impetus for looking beyond the spiritualized and the abstract in order to assess the ways in which the symbol of the cross that stands at the heart of Christianity has become debased and robbed of its power to challenge and affect people.

INTRODUCING JAMES H. CONE

Against theological pietism

The Cross and the Lynching Tree is perhaps, after *God of the Oppressed*, my favourite of all Cone books. One of the reasons I love it is because it offers a critical challenge to the pietism that has plagued predominantly White Christianity in the West for the past 1,000 years. For many ordinary Christians, Christianity is often caricatured as simply loving an invisible God who makes little or no demands on most believers. So long as one can say that they are saved and believe in the salvific work of Christ on the cross, then this same faith makes little or no demands on whom they vote for, how they treat their neighbours or to what social groups they choose to belong. Essentially, being a Christian is simply a lifestyle choice much like joining the Rotary club or gym. Yet, from my earliest days in the church, my central concerns were always ethical ones. As one of only two Black families in the Methodist Church in which I was raised and confirmed, and certainly one of the poorest families in it, the gap between the rhetoric of what we said we believed and how we acted was always a stark one.

When I became a student at the University of Birmingham, I was struck by the thought that what made life difficult as a Christian was not the metaphysical or supernatural elements of it at all; the reality of God, Jesus rising from the dead or the presence of the Holy Spirit in our lives. For me, all that was child's play. What was hard was the second of the great commandments of Jesus: loving your neighbour as yourself. Loving a God who is invisible and can be silent for very long periods can be quite easy. Loving your neighbour whom you can see and who may make serious demands upon you is a much harder proposition.

As a Black person who was born in this country and has lived here all my life, I have been aware of the continuing contradictions in the practice of Christianity in this country. I have seen people supposedly love God with all their heart, soul, mind and strength, and then in the next breath casually discriminate against their neighbour. I have witnessed good Christian people say one thing and most definitely and self-consciously do another, without even the merest hint of irony as they did so.

This can be seen in the church, having read the parable of the Good Samaritan (Luke 10.25–37), then conveniently making a rather pungent homeless person definitely unwelcome! Or the fellowship that closes its ranks to those who 'are not our sort of people'. In both contexts, the church stands accused of perverting the gospel of Christ. Cone's book has been a reminder that my commitment to Black theology has arisen from this experience of always being on the sharp end of such contradictions.

The Cross and the Lynching Tree speaks to the power of theological connections in that Cone is linking a powerful theological truth with the continued revelation of God in and through the oppressed and marginalized bodies of Black people. Cone recognizes that evangelical White Christians in North America will venerate the cross. They will see it as a holy symbol and blithely wear crucifixes around their necks as fashionable adornments. Their ability to remain indifferent to, at best, or to actively collude with Black oppression, at worst, results from the continued ability crucially to distinguish between that which is holy – an abstract cross – and that which is deemed to be of no significance, namely, Black bodies and Black suffering. Cone's genius is to make the two so synonymous that one cannot entertain the one without engaging with the other.

I would be so bold as to say that *The Cross and the Lynching Tree* is in many ways the great intellectual summation of Cone's scholarly career. Earlier in this book, I demonstrated how Cone's doctrine of God and Christology both argued persuasively that the God of the Judeo-Christian tradition was committed to the liberation of the oppressed. Cone agrees with Barth that God's self-revelation in Christ, through the scriptures, represents the authentic starting point for Christian theology. But unlike Barth, Cone makes that revelation contextual and specific. This means that it is through an oppressed, colonized, Galilean Jew that God is revealed. This revelation then speaks to God's continued revelation through the ongoing suffering and oppression of Black people.

Several centuries of White theological escapism have rendered the Christian gospel one that is friendly to White supremacy, colonialism and empire. While Cone's earlier books explore the wider Christian tradition, in order to explicate the necessity for liberation to be seen as a theological norm underpinning Christian theology, *The Cross and the Lynching Tree* creates a microcosm around the cross as its primary focus for rearticulating the central features of Black theology. Speaking of his intellectual journey from *Black Theology and Black Power* to *The Cross and the Lynching Tree* Cone writes:

> All of my work since that first book has involved an effort to relate the gospel and the black experience – the experience of oppression as well as the struggle to find liberation and meaning. Inevitably, it has led to these reflections on the cross and the lynching tree: the essential symbol of Christianity and the quintessential emblem of Black suffering.[15]

Cone continues to challenge White theological pietism by resolutely linking the spiritual and the theological to the socio-political and the ethical. Cone makes it clear that unless one is willing to face the grisly connotations of the cross, with its links to imperialism, greed and oppression and then juxtapose that with the suffering and exploitation of those on the obverse side of this, then one will never understand the true power and significance of the cross. In fact, the charge of 'cheap grace' that was thrown at comfortable White middle-class Christians from the epoch of Søren Kierkegaard and later Dietrich Bonhoeffer to the present day, rings true. Cone identifies Martin Luther King's commitment to racial justice as analogous to that of Bonhoeffer, both of whom paid the ultimate price for having the courage to live out their convictions to carry the cross of Christ in solidarity with others, having denied themselves the luxury of contentment by doing so.[16]

For Cone, authentic discipleship is nothing less than denying self and the carrying of the cross in solidarity with others (Matt. 16.24 and Luke 9.23). This challenge is aimed primarily at White people to see God's revelation not in abstract terms but rather in the lived experience of Black suffering, marginalization and oppression. It is to be committed to the denial of White privilege and to see in the cross a marker for the kind of solidarity that joins forces with God in Christ, in standing alongside all those who are crucified at the behest of untrammelled power and oppressive forces.

The challenge to neo-Pentecostalism

To my mind, the power of *The Cross and the Lynching Tree* lies in its critique of all aspects of religious pietism, whether that is of White origin, in terms of the inability to engage with Black suffering and oppression, or alternatively, a critique of Black neo-Pentecostalism and its propensity for 'prosperity-led' approaches to personal and social transformation.

In terms of the latter, Cone's work illustrates the costly nature of grace. For Cone, there is no short cut to any form of redemptive change. While Cone does not name newer forms of Pentecostalism as a fault line in contemporary Christianity, I am making that connection because I feel his theological analysis is useful in confronting another unhelpful form of religious pietism that has hindered Christian praxis in recent years. In this connection, I am reminded of a spirited conversation with a leading Black Pentecostal theologian in Britain who wanted to press me on whether 'prosperity gospel' teachings might be understood as a new, radical branch of Black theology. I was emphatic in my denunciation of this assertion. Nothing could be further from the truth. I would argue as to whether prosperity teaching can be understood as being *authentically Christian*, and perhaps is no more so than White supremacist notions of Christianity.

At the heart of Cone's theological project is the necessity of redemptive struggle as the only means of bringing about genuine transformation of predominantly poor Black communities. At the conclusion of the previous chapter, I detailed Cone's own critique of Black messiahs, predominantly Black alpha-males through whom God was going to rescue Black people, in order to show the dangers of looking to others to rescue us. If that is the case in terms of the forlorn and misguided hope of discovering the next Martin Luther King or Malcolm X, then it is equally the case for the new generation of megachurch leaders, be they TD Jakes or Matthew Ashimolowo, or anyone else.

The redemptive struggle at the heart of the cross arises from the necessity of seeking to confront evil and injustice. Black followers of Jesus, working in the prophetic, liberationist tradition, have long recognized that the only authentic way of bringing about social change from within the auspices of faith was to follow the example of Jesus. This meant confronting inhumane situations, with prayer and action, working collectively so that the 'least of these' would experience a sense of a measure of freedom, in the belief that full liberation would happen in the world to come, in heaven. Caribbean-American theologian, Delroy Reid-Salmon exemplifies this tradition in his theological exploration of the life and death of Sam Sharpe.[17] Sharpe was the embodiment of this tradition in that he gave his life for the fight against British-run slavery in Jamaica. Sharpe and many others in the long continuum were committed to fighting for justice through the collective, the sense of 'Ubuntu', in which Black communitarian action is the means by which transformation is achieved.

When I was growing up in inner-city Bradford, our way of dealing with urban, post-industrial poverty was through collective action such as the pardna.[18] We were poor and our relative poverty had nothing to do with the hard work or otherwise of my parents. We lived in one of the poorest parts of the city due to the structural inequalities and racism of British society. For those who peddle the prosperity gospel that the many poor Caribbean families simply did not pray hard enough or work sufficiently hard to earn God's favour: this is a damned insult. As a Black liberation theologian, therefore, I find it hard to engage with a form of Christian practice in which the poor can be blamed for their own socio-economic plight.

Prosperity teaching is often founded on a form of manipulation of people attending their meetings. These forms of Christianity prey on the vulnerability of the poor. The poor and oppressed, whose lot in life is so often one of abject poverty and absurd nothingness are quite naturally vulnerable to this kind of shameless exploitation.

Robert Beckford has written on this issue and states:

> Prosperity doctrines have nurtured an interest in finance and living debt free in many deprived communities in America and Britain. It is right to direct people to the fact that God will meet their needs, including their financial needs. The problem is that 'need' has exploded into legitimation of materialism in Black Churches, so that sacrifice, sharing and suffering have been banished from the meaning of the cross.[19]

Cone's broader work and this book in particular is one that critiques the shameless exploitation of the needs, cares and concerns of poor and marginalized people by slick, North American influenced capitalists who use the gospel for their own materialistic empire-driven ends. The likes of McConnell[20] challenge the basic flaws and distortions of capitalistic, money-driven approaches to Christianity that distort the message of Jesus and the necessity of engaging with the challenges of the cross. In attacking the prosperity-driven approaches to Christianity, it is not my intention to somehow glorify economic and material poverty as being intrinsically a good thing. Quite naturally, we all want to progress and develop, as individuals, communities, societies and nations. Alternative approaches to empowering and supporting the poor and excluded have been forwarded by activists such as Ron Nathan[21] and Paulette Haughton.[22]

Central to *The Cross and the Lynching Tree* is the clear

bias Cone has for the poor. God's solidarity with ordinary, poor, marginalized and oppressed Black people is such that the notion that God is going to work through rich, powerful and exploitative leaders is antithetical to the central intent of Black theology. Cone's book asks the critical question as to what the truth of the gospel is in our present age, regarding wealth, the accumulation of material goods and those who are denied even the basics.

Supporters of prosperity teaching or those more sympathetic to this phenomenon will argue that Cone's focus on the cross as a means of redemptive struggle is too narrow an understanding of this phenomenon and is an overly political reading of this central symbol in Christianity. Cone is an unabashed liberation theologian and so, of course, he is never going to be a fair or a balanced theologian. One only has to witness the personnel who populate the God Channel on satellite television or the work of well-known speakers such as Creflo Dollar[23] or Joyce Meyer[24] to see the truth of Cone's critique of 'cheap grace'.

While Cone's theological analysis might appear to be focused purely on the liberationist reading of the Christian faith, given the extreme nature of this form of ministry and the claims they make for themselves and for God, I think Cone's theological analysis in this book is spot on. Those who still feel I have been overly harsh on the proponents of this form of ministry would no doubt point to such proof texts as 'The blessing of the Lord, it maketh rich'[25] or will point to biblical figures such as Abraham (Gen. 13.2; 24.35); Solomon (1 Kings 10.23); Hezekiah (2 Kings 20.12–18); Job (Job 1.3) and Joseph of Arimathaea (Matt. 27.57). These individuals are all examples of wealthy believers blessed by God.

James Cone's uncompromising theological analysis of the cross, given its polemical nature, is one that has little rapprochement towards this form of Christianity. This form of globalization has become almost as much a homogeneous brand commodity sweeping through the poorer countries of the world as Coca Cola or McDonald's.[26] The challenges thrown up by prosperity teaching are real. The Black and Liberation theologians who have most shaped my own work, such as Cone,[27] Boesak[28] and Balasuriya,[29] continue to inspire me to hold out for a critical form of Christianity that does not exploit the poor or offer them false hopes for the eradication of their economic problems. The form of Christianity I am holding out for is a critical one that challenges believers and adherents to be in solidarity with others in order to be co-creators with God in transforming the world, rather than focusing on the narrow and limited gains for the individual.[30]

Conclusion

The Cross and the Lynching Tree was the final great original work by James Cone. He was in his seventies when the book came out and it had been a long time in its gestation process. Cone's work is an incendiary device at the heart of conventional Christianity. Cone demonstrates the continued radical and prophetic nature of his scholarly ministry. From 1969 to 2011, that 42-year time span sees Cone moving from an articulation of Black theology through the lens of the Black Power movement to a theo-cultural and political reading of the cross. This is a remarkable intellectual range and is one of the reasons why Cone will remain the pre-eminent Black theologian for many years to come, if not for all time. The book offers the ultimate theological challenge to all those who seek to uphold a form of Christianity that supports the socio-political status quo, often colluding with the machinations of White entitlement and privilege. By juxtaposing the cross and the lynching tree, Cone makes the central symbol of the Christian faith one that is no longer an abstract, ahistorical and spiritualized article of faith, but rather, a contextualized and radical emblem of Black liberation for African Americans and for all oppressed Black peoples across the world.

Notes

1 See Kelly Brown Douglas, *The Black Christ* (Maryknoll, NY: Orbis Books, 1993).
2 JoAnne Marie Terrell, *Power in the Blood?: The Cross in the African American Experience* (Maryknoll, NY: Orbis Books, 1998).
3 Terrell, *Power in the Blood?*, p. 34.
4 See Robert Beckford, *Jesus is Dread* (London: Darton, Longman and Todd, 1998) and Riggins R. Earl Jr, *Dark Salutations* (Harrisburg, PA: Trinity Press International, 2001), pp. 1–16.
5 See James Baldwin, *The Evidence of Things Not Seen* (New York: Holt, Rinehart and Winston, 1985).
6 See Delores Williams, *Sisters in the Wilderness: The Challenge of Womanist God-talk* (Maryknoll, NY: Orbis Books, 1993).
7 See Cain Hope Felder (ed.), *The Original African Heritage Bible Study Bible* (Nashville, TN: The James C. Winston Publishing Company, 1993), pp. 998–9.
8 James H. Cone, *The Cross and the Lynching Tree* (Maryknoll, NY: Orbis Books, 2011), p. 91.
9 For a brief article on President Barack Obama's connection to the thought of Reinhold Niebuhr, see John Blake, 'How Obama's favorite theologian shaped his first year in office', *CNN Politics*, 5 February 2010, http://edition.cnn.com/2010/POLITICS/02/05/Obama.theologian/index.html (accessed 22.11.2021).
10 Cone, *The Cross and the Lynching Tree*, pp. 30–64.
11 Cone, *The Cross and the Lynching Tree*, p. 61.
12 For details on the 50th anniversary event, see World Council of Churches, 'Marking the 50th anniversary of the Programme to Combat Racism', *World Council of Churches*, www.oikoumene.org/news/marking-the-50th-anniversary-of-the-programme-to-combat-racism (accessed 22.11.2021).
13 Cone, *The Cross and the Lynching Tree*, p. 156.
14 Cone, *The Cross and the Lynching Tree*, p. 150.
15 Cone, *The Cross and the Lynching Tree*, p. 154.
16 Cone, *The Cross and the Lynching Tree*, p. 70.
17 See Delroy A. Reid-Salmon, *Burning for Freedom: A Theology of the Black Atlantic Struggle for Liberation* (Jamaica: Ian Randle, 2012).
18 Jamaican Pardna is an informal saving scheme not unlike a voluntary credit union. For more details, see Sara Williams, 'How Pardners work – friends save & borrow in an informal club', *Debt Camel*, 15 June 2020 (accessed 22.11.2021).

19 Robert Beckford, 'Theology in the Age of Crack: Crack Age, Prosperity Doctrine and "Being There"', in *Black Theology in Britain: A Journal of Contextual Praxis*, vol. 4, no. 1, November 2001, p. 20.

20 See D. R. McConnell, *A Different Gospel: A Biblical Look at the Word and Faith Movement* (Peabody, MA: Hendrickson, 1988).

21 Ron A. Nathan, 'Prosperity through Empowerment: A Tribute to the late Revd Leon H. Sullivan (1922–2001)', in *Black Theology in Britain: A Journal of Contextual Praxis*, vol. 4, no. 1, November 2001, pp. 25–31.

22 Paulette Haughton, 'At the Coalface: Fighting Deprivation' in Michael Simmons (ed.), *Street Credo: Churches in the community* (London: Lemos and Crane, 2000), pp. 75–87.

23 For more information, see Creflo Dollar Ministries, www.creflodollarministries.org.

24 See Joyce Meyer Ministries, www.joycemeyer.org.

25 Proverbs 10.22.

26 See Simon Coleman, *The Globalisation of Charismatic Christianity: Spreading the Gospel of Prosperity* (Cambridge: Cambridge University Press, 2000).

27 Harry Singleton III, *Black Theology and Ideology: Deideological dimensions in the theology of James H. Cone* (Collegeville, MN: Liturgical Press, 2002).

28 See Allan Aubrey Boesak, *Children of the Waters of Meribah: Black Liberation Theology, the Miriamic Tradition, and the Challenges of 21st Century Empire* (Johannesburg: Afrika Sun Media, 2020).

29 Tissa Balasuriya, *The Eucharist and Human Liberation* (London: SCM Press, 1979).

30 Inderjit S. Bhogal, *A Table For All* (Sheffield: Penistone Publications, 2000), pp. 11–34.

10

Said I Wasn't Gonna Tell Nobody

James Cone's final book is his most personal, and I have included it purely because it is Cone speaking in more personal terms than was ever the case in his more formal academic books, perhaps with the exception of his two more autobiographical works, *For My People* and *My Soul Looks Back*. I am open to the charge that my choice of including this text as a key one in his canon speaks to the strong sense of nostalgia and the emotional impact it had on my own consciousness when I first read this book in the summer of 2018.

When I received the invitation from Orbis Books to write a brief endorsement for *Said I Wasn't Gonna Tell Nobody*, I became very emotional. This moment of affirmation was in stark contrast to the then wholesale rejections I was receiving from the many university theology and religious studies departments I was applying to for academic teaching and research posts. On receiving a hard copy of the final proofs I had the opportunity to read the manuscript before the general public and many of my academic colleagues. I remember reading the relatively short manuscript on a train journey to London and finding Cone's words bringing me to tears. Having had the privilege of meeting James Cone on many occasions and remembering the distinctive light, high-pitch lilt to his voice, I could hear the cadence of his words through the pages of the book. In *Said I Wasn't Gonna Tell Nobody*, Cone narrates the antecedents that helped him to invent the scholarly, systematic dimension of Black theology.

This book offers a more dialectical and conversational approach to engaging with James Cone's intellectual biography. It gives a sense of the inner character and expression of the man within the context in which he was formed, which also provided the intellectual background to his development as a scholar. The book gives us the distinctive voice of James Cone and his development as a Black theologian. As I have stated previously, my initial and subsequent meetings with Cone have shaped me directly as a person and a scholar. Cone was my primary academic inspiration from the moment I first met him in 1996. He is the reason why I wanted to become a theologian. Without James Cone, I may still have wanted to become a comedy scriptwriter.

Context is everything

In the midst of writing this book, I travelled to Cambridge to give the 2021 Michaelmas term university sermon at the university church of Great St Mary's. I had planned to stay the night in Cambridge, as I was also preaching at a Cambridge college Evensong later that day. While in Cambridge I had decided I would take the opportunity to catch up with an old friend from my undergraduate days at the University of Birmingham who is now a distinguished academic theologian working at Cambridge University. In the midst of a very convivial chat in the garden of his house we got talking about our respective interests in Karl Barth (for him) and James Cone (for me). We spoke about the things they had in common and what made them very different sorts of theologians. My friend stated that one significant difference was that Cone was very explicit about how context shaped his subsequent theological work, namely, that the impetus for a Black theology of liberation arose from the existential absurdity of Black suffering. For God to be God, in a world of White supremacy and unremitting structural and systemic racism, God could be nothing less than a God of the oppressed, whose inclination is to seek the liberation of all those who are cast as non-beings in history. The link between the aforementioned and the subsequent theological work that Cone produces is utterly transparent. We are in no doubt as to the role that context plays in the development of Black theology.

According to my friend, notwithstanding the brilliance of Barth's work and its continued importance to the development of modern theology, he is nowhere near as transparent about the contextual and subjective influences that shape his ground-breaking scholarship. What is at issue here isn't the importance of either person's work. I am not arguing that Cone is greater than Barth, although for a Black working-class boy growing up in an inner-city, racist environment, I know which of the two has been more relevant to my life. Rather, the issue is the transparency with which one writes and cites the factors that influence their respective approaches to contextual theology, in light of the fact that *all theology is contextual*, recognizing that one largely eschews the latter term, to be claimed as simply a 'theologian'. Barth is perceived neither as a contextual theologian nor as a White one, when he is clearly both of those things.

Perhaps Cone's greatest achievement, as the most influential Black theologian of them all, is his unflinching ability to root systematic theology within context and to show the significance of particularity to the development of what one might discern as universal truths. To my mind, there is no doubting the universality of Cone's writings. As he outlines the historical, religious, cultural and political contexts against and through which his theological vision arose, it is clear that the ideas he develops have universal application, as they relate to the very nature of Christian theology and why it matters. But Cone's way of arriving at this sense of universality is by means of his deep engagement with the contextual soil in which his Black liberation theology is earthed.

If Cone has made the Blackness of his context explicit (even while his theological method is deemed to be somewhat White and European), the same cannot be said for the myriad White academic theologians who preceded and succeeded him. Whiteness remains the elephant in the room. Cone not only created the academic conceptualization of Black theology, he also forced many White people to have to admit that they are, in fact, often doing 'White theology'. Although there is little in the way of contextual analysis, let alone subjective lived experience, in a great deal of academic, White systematic or practical theology (the latter guild to which I belong in the UK is really no better than any other discipline in the UK), often operating as if neither of these factors had any impact on the subsequent scholarly theological reflections as they arose, there is no doubt in my mind that a conceptual norm called 'Whiteness' pervades much of what we call 'mainstream' academic White theology. Karl Barth was as resolutely a White theologian as James Cone was a Black one. It is just that one of them was searingly honest about this point of departure.

From the moment one reads the opening pages of *Black Theology and Black Power*, there is no doubt that in James H. Cone we are not only reading the first great Black theologian, but that he will become one of the great exemplars for 'contextual' theologies. The juxtaposition of culture, context, history and lived experience alongside formal theological reflection, is intertwined in a fashion that meant one could not easily separate the former from the latter. It is why some of his critics doubted whether his brand of systematic theology was indeed theology at all.[1]

As stated previously, having queried the reasons why Cone was so resolutely focused within the discipline of systematic theology, especially given his early claim that Black theology was not an academic discipline but a form of practical theology in its orientation, this all became clearer to me upon reading his final book. Given the prejudice and clear intellectual blockages he faced in late 1969 and early 1970, when formulating Black theology as an academic, theological discipline, anything less than securing its moorings in systematic theology would have seen it let loose on the open waters, drifting aimlessly between the distant shores of anthropology, sociology or later, cultural studies. And while Black theology has important contributions to make to each of these respective disciplines, it is nonetheless, a resolutely theological discipline, largely Christian in character and outlook.

Cone, in writing this way, has nevertheless begun to force some White theologians to reckon with their Whiteness as an important contextual factor in the process of undertaking constructive and critical God-talk in this early part of the twenty-first century.[2]

James Cone's ground-breaking approach to Black theology has, in effect, outed Whiteness and lead to an increasingly more honest appraisal regarding the *actual existence* of White theology.

The ubiquity of Whiteness

In his latest text, *After Whiteness*, Jennings critiques the phenomenon of Whiteness, arguing how the conflation of European mastery, White, male, colonial power, and the internalization of notions of White superiority, become the means by which knowledge and truth is developed. Whiteness is not about the epidermis of those who are racialized as White.[3] Rather, it is the whole edifice of reality and how we even discern what is normality, how particular ideas and practices emerge and under whose gaze and imprint are notions of truth discerned and developed.

Whiteness has rarely been acknowledged in any intellectual discourse. It has always been the unspoken presence. Jennings illustrates how Whiteness became conjoined with patriarchy and colonialism to unleash an ethic of mastery, self-sufficiency and control, as the defining elements for what constitutes notions of development and progress.

Jennings' work, which is aimed primarily at theological education,[4] distils the means by which the production of knowledge and pedagogical insights on the craft of ministry have been informed by coloniality and Whiteness. Jennings is clear that this analysis is not about White people per se. Rather, it is the intellectual underpinning of a set of theo-cultural constructs, systems and practices that govern how theology and education operate, which inform our ways of being and its resultant praxis.[5]

In moving into an understanding of Whiteness as not simply about the epidermis of those 'racialized as White', Jennings is illustrating how this is better understood as the wider conceptual and practised template that defines truth, acceptability and belonging. The best way I would describe this rethinking is by use of a long-held analogy. Historically, liberation theologians saw White supremacy as analogous to ravenous sharks who patrolled the ocean seas preying on weaker, smaller fish.[6] The problem with this analogy was that most ordinary White people are not metaphorical sharks. Most do not burn effigies of crosses into lawns, or are violent towards non-White people, either physically or verbally. Yes, White supremacy does exist and has a long litany of actions that have manifested themselves in the body politic of many nations across the world, but this largely is not the province or the ethical stance of most ordinary White people.

Scholars like Jennings are now arguing that Whiteness is not the shark, but the very sea itself, arguing that the whole world in which we live has been shaped by Whiteness and the ethics of control and mastery that grow out of European expansion and colonialism.[7] As a Methodist, I know that the tradition into which I was born has been infected by Whiteness as much as any other denomination. The world in which John Wesley was formed and through which Methodism came into being was one that was shaped by the all-enveloping ethic of Whiteness. Wesley, to be sure, was a more enlightened exemplar of the nature of Whiteness in his eighteenth-century epoch than many of his contemporaries, but he, nonetheless, was immersed in a thought world that always assumed the superiority of Whiteness over other forms of epistemology, in which hierarchy and power often go hand in hand.[8] If most White people are not metaphorical sharks, they are, nonetheless, the beings that are most advantaged by an all-enveloping world of Whiteness. And while not all White people will experience a marked sense of immediate cultural, political or social benefit from being White, not one White person is systematically and procedurally disadvantaged as being designated as such. To cite a close Black friend, 'We wake up as Black people faced with innumerable challenges from being born in this skin. White people wake up also with innumerable challenges but being White isn't one of them.'

Cone's legacy has been to create the platform on which Jennings and other neo-traditional constructive theologians can critique Whiteness and how it has become embedded in our theological norms, in ways that would have been impossible without his pioneering work preceding them.

Telling our own story

The other important factor in Cone's final work is the significance it places not solely on context, but most crucially on personal experience and lived faith. While Cone was not a practical theologian like myself, his work, nevertheless, creates the foreground for how theology emerges not just from context but also from existential experience and the ways in which the former can become generative for how we conceive the task of undertaking theological reflection.

In *Said I Wasn't Gonna Tell Nobody*, Cone details the formative experiences that have shaped his intellectual and emotional outlook. For one destined for greatness, Cone's formative years are nothing exceptional. Born in the American South, Cone's intellectual brilliance is born of hard work and a self-determination ethic instilled in him by his father.[9] Prior to the publication of this book, I knew I identified with Cone's intellect and passion, but now with publication of his final memoir, he provides inspiration for all of us who might describe ourselves as being 'unpromising material'.

As I stated in the introduction, my ambition prior to meeting James Cone was to be a comedy writer, a playwright, or a TV scriptwriter. James Cone changed all that. Meeting him helped me to narrate a new story of my life. Cone speaks of how writing *Black Theology and Black Power* changed his life and enabled him to find his life's calling.[10] Reading Cone for the first time and then meeting him in 1996 inspired me to want to become a Black theologian. When I completed my first two books, popular Christian education material that arose during my doctoral studies looking at Christian formation and discipleship of Black young people by means of Black theology, I included a special commendation to James Cone.[11] After the long-held ambition to be a writer, the sight of my first two books was very much a dream come true, and the greatest inspiration for that work was James H. Cone, though the material was very different to anything that Cone would have written himself.

First and foremost, Cone's memoir is the narrative of the making of a Black hero. In writing *Growing into Hope*, the first piece of Black theological learning material I created was a short piece on Black heroes, identifying Moses as a prototypical leader of a liberation movement.[12]

Within the developing material, I identified other Black heroes and heroines from history, such as Nanny of the Maroons (eighteenth-century Jamaican national heroine) and Harriet Tubman (nineteenth-century African American heroine) as both were seen as Moses-like figures due to their leadership qualities.[13] The material asks young Black people to consider who are the Moses-like figures in the present age.[14] Cone's narrative is that of a seeming everyman who achieves greatness, and who in turn, inspires us to believe that we can be heroes also. What is ironic in seeing Cone as a hero is that he himself comes to represent the very kind of totemic figure he warns us against. The critical difference between Cone and the more modern Black religious and political leaders in Africa and across the African diaspora, is that his commitment to collectivist, liberationist inspired change, saw him work with countless Black men and women, training them to find their own voices to continue the work of Black theology and later womanist theology long after he had gone.

At the heart of Cone's transformation into one of the greatest of academic theologians is his focus on 'personal experience'. Black experience is key to the development of Black theology as Cone identifies God's revelation from within the prism of Black realities in the world. The power of personal experience is of course not invented by James Cone. Normative, classical Christianity claims that an individual can gain a personal experience of God in Christ by means of the Holy Spirit. In one of my earliest pieces of writing, I argue that many older Black people living in the UK have a very personalized and literal affirmation of Jesus in their lives.[15] God in general and Jesus in particular are not simply rationalized concepts but are experiential truths. Jesus becomes the best friend, the fellow struggler in solidarity, in the midst of myriad trials and tribulations.[16]

This facet of Christianity is both one of its enduring strengths as well as being a major weakness. In terms of the former, countless men and women have been inspired by the realness and nearness of God in order to create change in their individual lives and in the lives of others.[17] I remember Cone speaking powerfully in that same seminal address at the Queen's Foundation in 1996, stating that the most dangerous people in the world are those who claim to have an untrammelled line of communication to God and to know exactly what God wants and what can be construed as God's will. In effect, these are the scary people who later claim, 'God told me to do it' when they are arrested for some extreme atrocity. Personal experience can be a dangerous thing.

And yet Cone affirms the significance of personal experience because he realizes it is central to the intellectual force of Black theology. The legitimacy of personal experience lies in its connection with other sources, such as scripture and revelation, the latter seen as important correctives to the prism of human encounter with the divine. Black theology's method is one that holds in tension personal experience, alongside other sources, much like classical Christianity, the difference being that the relative power relations between these different elements is rethought. For Cone, the personal experience of disenfranchised and often silenced Black people is elevated and affirmed, but not to the point where Black people can claim that 'anything goes' when asserting that they have had an encounter with God.

The power of Cone's narrative and the significance of his theological method can be seen in how his work creates a wider form of enfranchisement, in which he offers ordinary Black people, like his parents, to be the bearers of a Black religious culture in which God's revelatory truths can be shared in the world. As I stated at the outset, James Cone did not invent the prophetic Black church tradition of which he was a noble and honourable part. Rather, Cone's work formalizes what ordinary Black people had long known to be true, namely, that a God who was on the side of the poor and marginalized did not speak only through the privileged lens of White entitlement and spurious superiority. Just as God spoke through Moses, a stuttering outcast, and also through David, a young man with a sling and some stones, and of course, through a colonized, Galilean Jew from a less than salubrious outpost called Nazareth, then God would, and did, speak through the experience of ordinary Black people. Cone's Black theology initiates the shift in how we see God's revelation from Whiteness into Black experience.

Cone's commitment to Black experience and the dignity of Black life is such that he has created an intellectual landscape that has seen the transformation of how many of us, people such as myself, see the world. People like myself can now dare to call ourselves Black theologians. When I was at university as an undergraduate, of all the people I knew who were studying theology, not one was Black like me. In three years of studying Church history, I did not read one book written by a Black person and in three years of my study, I was the only Black person on the course. How many of the scholars that populate most theology reading lists in universities are still White European males? How many are Black people of African origin? To what extent have specific African or more generally, non-European concepts influenced our theological thinking?[18]

INTRODUCING JAMES H. CONE

I remember in my first academic job at the Queen's Foundation, I was teaching a very experienced ministerial student who had already studied theology at bachelor, masters and doctorate levels; yet when I mentioned James Cone to him in an introductory lecture to Black theology, this student had never heard of him. He had never heard of Black theology and was somewhat surprised to hear that Black men and women had made scholarly contributions to academic theology.

Speaking personally, engaging with James Cone provided answers to a host of long-held existential questions that had long stalked me. I was always interested in and intrigued by theological questions in my formative years. I chose church history as opposed to theology to study at university because there was no tradition of religious studies at the large state school I attended. In the conservative church in which I was nurtured in the Christian faith, academic theology was viewed like a swear word, something never spoken about or acknowledged. So I opted for the safer ground of studying history, particularly that of the church, but certainly not studying God. If I had heard of James Cone in my teenage years or early twenties, then my life could have been very different.

In the Methodist Church in which I was socialized and became a Christian when I was 14 years old, there were no Black role models, no Black professionals and certainly no Black people who wrote books. I knew from a very early age that I wanted to write – comedy until the age of 30, until I realized I could be an academic British, Black theologian – still something of a novelty in the UK. When I was growing up in Bradford, I never imagined I would find my identity morphing into that of a recognized Black theologian. Encountering James Cone gave me an emotional and intellectual platform which enabled me to locate myself within a wider religious tradition. Once I discovered James Cone and Black theology, and undertook my doctoral studies, the appeals of comedy scriptwriting disappeared completely and have never returned.

Staying true to the cause

Perhaps the biggest joy I felt in reading *Said I Wasn't Gonna Tell Nobody* was the confirmation that the man I had met on many occasions at the American Academy of Religion remained as pugnacious and strident in old age as he been in his youth. Clearly, I didn't know James Cone when he was in his thirties, but from what I could discern from reading *Black Theology and Black Power* for the first time, he had not changed appreciably. His final book shows the extent to which, although there were developments in his thought, the centrality of Martin King and Malcolm X remained, as did the centrality of Black experience and the belief that God is revealed through Blackness. Added to these two titans of Black liberation, Cone appraises the significance of James Baldwin to his intellectual development.[19] Baldwin did not feature alongside Martin and Malcolm in the book discussed in Chapter 8. The significance of Baldwin appears to have grown since the early 1990s.

Baldwin is the poet for the Black liberation movement. His lyrical genius not only inspires Cone's attempts to write lucidly about his passionate commitment to Black theology, but his determination to tell the truth no matter how unpalatable is what marks him out as the crucial link between Martin and Malcolm. Interest in James Baldwin has increased in the past few years since the broadcast of the documentary *I am Not Your Negro*.[20] The list of pithy aphorisms coined by Baldwin has also increased over the past few years.[21]

Despite Baldwin's literary genius, his death in 1987 was not followed by an avalanche of news comment. James Cone, although greatly celebrated within certain academic circles, was nonetheless not a household name among many ordinary churchgoers and certainly was no media celebrity or popular public intellectual in the US when compared to other more contemporary Black scholarly thinkers. Yet Cone never sacrificed his commitment to the cause.[22] The importance of *Said I Wasn't Gonna Tell Nobody*, for me, lies in the fact that Cone did not care whether Black theology was in vogue or viewed as irrelevant by younger, less church-oriented Black activists. He certainly did not care what the White academic theological mainstream made of his work.

This fact has been the reason that I have reread the book several times since it was published. When I first attended the national Black Theology forum in the Selly Oak colleges[23] in Birmingham in 1994, I remember being giddy with the excitement of sitting alongside nearly 40 people in the room. This was the early flourishing of Black theology in Britain as a fledgling academic discipline. As a recent convert to Black theology, I believed in the very depth of my soul that this meeting heralded a new adventure in my life. Gone was any conviction that my future might lie in comedy scriptwriting. I believed that my future lay in seeking to participate in the development a Black British version of Black theology, especially one that could relate to and be a source of conscientization for ordinary Black people, in predominantly inner city areas in Britain. I knew that my life had changed and that my faith commitments would forever be informed by Black theology.

Said I Wasn't Gonna Tell Nobody distils the genius that was James Cone and provides the final curtain call on one of the most outstanding theologians of the twentieth and early twenty-first centuries and the greatest of all Black theologians. At the 2021 Society for the Study of Theology conference for postgraduate students, at Cambridge University, I found myself in deep conversation with a prospective Black doctoral theology student who wanted to pick my brains regarding his own future studies. One of the questions asked of me was how I had kept the fire going, as one of only a few academic Black theologians in the UK. My honest response was that I could not do anything else. Black theology is simply what I do. I love researching, writing and teaching Black theology.

So whereas the majority of the people in that room back in 1994 seem to have abandoned Black theology in Britain, I am still trying to write about and refine my commitment to this movement that has inspired my adult life since the early 1990s. I have never been an evangelical. Were it not for the presence of Black theology I doubt I would have remained in the church or been involved in Christian ministry. And central to that continued commitment and passionate desire to keep going, has been James Hal Cone. As I state at the beginning of this book, James Cone is my all-time academic and scholarly hero. I would not be a scholar and writer were it not for Cone's inspiration. I am sure I'm not alone in giving God thanks that when inspiration first hit the young James Hal Cone, like the famous gospel hymn after which his final book is named, he 'Couldn't keep it to myself.'[24]

Conclusion

I have chosen to conclude this introduction to James Cone by reflecting on the significance of his final book, not because it is his best work, but precisely because it is his final public work. Cone speaks personally, giving a window into the heart and mind of one of the greatest theologians ever to draw breath.

In some respects, I am not the ideal person to write a book introducing Cone to those unfamiliar with his brilliance. I was not one of his famed doctoral students; no doubt Cone would have wanted one of them to write about him and not a funny sounding Brit, whose work is an homage to the great man, but nevertheless, has adopted very different methodological choices in how Black theology is undertaken. I cannot claim any special friendship with James Cone. I have few very stories to share compared to many of my African American friends and colleagues. We were not friends, more acquaintances. I was pleased that he recognized me and deigned to endorse one of my early books. This was a very unequal scholarly acquaintance. I was a big fan of his. I think he respected my work.

I have written the only book I can about James Cone. I have offered my personal perspectives on him and his legacy. Others, especially his former students, may have written this text in a very different manner to that which I have produced. Cone was no saint. My reflections in the opening chapter are a reminder that his irascible persona was part and parcel of his scholarly means of engagement. He did not suffer fools gladly and I have been privy to many stories of students who found him more intimidating than inspirational.

Yet, without him, I wouldn't have written *any theological work*. I am a Cone-head. I recently found myself in an acrimonious argument with a leading Black evangelical church leader, as this person had the temerity to critique Cone's understanding of 'race' (when this person had singularly failed to speak out on the subject when he was in office for several years, prior to this conversation) and his Black theology work. My desire to defend Cone wasn't due to the belief that he is without fault. Cone never thought that about himself. My irritation lay in the fact that, while Cone had spoken out consistently against racism, earning much criticism for doing so, this individual had said next to nothing prior to the murder of George Floyd.

I hope that my book is not just hagiography. I have tried to be critical in my assessment of his work and legacy. But in the end, I loved his work, and I loved the man. He was my hero, and we will never see his like again. I trust my book has done him justice. I hope you have enjoyed reading it and most importantly of all, that it has encouraged you to go and read his challenging words and ideas for yourself.

Notes

1 James H. Cone, *Said I Wasn't Gonna Tell Nobody* (Maryknoll, NY: Orbis Books, 2018), pp. 78–81.

2 Some of the key theological texts in this emerging discourse are: James W. Perkinson, *White Theology: Outing Supremacy in Modernity* (New York: Palgrave Macmillan, 2004); James W. Perkinson, *Shamanism, Racism and Hip Hop Culture: Essays on White Supremacy and Black Subversion* (New York: Palgrave Macmillan, 2005); Laurie M. Cassidy and Alex Mikulich (eds), *Interrupting White Privilege: Catholic Theologians Break the Silence* (Maryknoll, NY: Orbis Books, 2007); Jennifer Harvey, Karin A. Case and Robin Hawley Gorsline (eds), *Disrupting White Supremacy from Within: White People on What We Need*

to Do (Cleveland, OH: Pilgrim, 2004); Jennifer Harvey, *Whiteness and Morality: Pursuing Racial Justice Through Reparations and Sovereignty* (New York: Palgrave Macmillan, 2007); Jennifer Harvey, *Dear White Christians: For Those Still Longing for Racial Reconciliation* (Grand Rapids, MI: Wm B. Eerdmans, 2014); Tom Beaudoin and Katherine Turpin, 'White Practical Theology' in Kathleen A. Cahalan and Gordon S. Mikoski (eds), *Opening the Field of Practical Theology* (Lanham, MD: Rowan and Littlefield, 2014), pp. 251–69; Sarah Azaransky, 'Citizenship in Jesus and the Disinherited: From Black Internationalism to Whiteness on the Contemporary Border', in *Black Theology: An International Journal*, vol. 11, no. 3, 2013, pp. 281–304; Edward J. Blum and Paul Harvey, *The Color of Christ: The Son of God and the Saga of Race in America* (Chapel Hill, NC: University of North Carolina Press, 2012).

3 Willie James Jennings, *After Whiteness: An Education in Belonging* (Grand Rapids, MI: Wm B. Eerdmans, 2020).

4 In using the term 'theological education', I am speaking to the process of teaching and learning for persons undertaking a mode of formation in which they are inducted into the charisms of the church in order that they make take on leadership roles, most usually public, authorized forms of ordained ministry. This mode of theological enquiry and learning is often adjacent to but not the same as more professional or objective forms of theology that are undertaken in public research universities. For a detailed articulation of theological education, see Dietrich Werner, Namsoon Kang, David Esterline and Joshva Raja (eds), *Handbook of Theological Education in World Christianity: Theological Perspectives – Regional Surveys – Ecumenical Trends* (Oxford: Regnum, 2010).

5 Willie James Jennings, *After Whiteness*, pp. 23–156.

6 See James H. Cone, 'Theology's Great Sin: Silence in the Face of White Supremacy', *Black Theology: An International Journal*, vol. 2, no. 2, 2002, pp. 139–52.

7 A text that predates the current intellectual focus on Whiteness is Robert E. Hood, *Must God Remain Greek? Afro Cultures and God-Talk* (Minneapolis, MN: Fortress Press, 1990).

8 John Wesley's progressive and enlightened social ethics in comparison to his contemporaries can be found in his publication *Thoughts Upon Slavery*, which for its time was remarkably prescient. See John Wesley, *Thoughts Upon Slavery* (London: Racial Justice Office, The Methodist Church, 2006, first published 1774).

9 Cone, *Said I Wasn't Gonna Tell Nobody*, pp. 22–8.

10 Cone, *Said I Wasn't Gonna Tell Nobody*, p. 37.

11 See Anthony G. Reddie, *Growing into Hope* (Peterborough:

Methodist Publishing House, 1998). This curriculum is published in two volumes. Volume one is subtitled *Believing and Expecting*. Volume two is entitled *Liberation and Change*.

12 Reddie, *Growing into Hope*, vol. 1, pp. 118–19.

13 Reddie, *Growing into Hope*, vol. 1, p. 72.

14 See Reddie, *Growing into Hope*, vol. 1, p. 76.

15 See Anthony G. Reddie, *Faith, Stories and the Experience of Black Elders: Singing the Lord's Song in a Strange Land* (London: Jessica Kingsley, 2001), pp. 65–72.

16 See Riggins R. Earl Jr, *Dark Salutations* (Harrisburg, PA: Trinity Press International, 2001).

17 See Reddie, *Growing into Hope*, vol. 1, section entitled 'Heroes', pp. 59–78. See also Anne S. Wimberly, *Soul Stories: African American Christian Education* (Nashville, TN: Abingdon Press, 1996). Wimberly's concept of 'Story linking' involves (African American) learners combining their personal narratives with heroic people of faith. The latter are historic and contemporary people who have been inspired by God to achieve major accomplishments for themselves and for others.

18 See Robert E. Hood, *Must God Remain Greek?: God Talk and Afro-cultures* (Minneapolis, MN: Fortress Press, 1990).

19 Cone, *Said I Wasn't Gonna Tell Nobody*, pp. 144–74.

20 For details of the film, see, 'I Am Not Your Negro', *Wikipedia*, https://en.wikipedia.org/wiki/I_Am_Not_Your_Negro (accessed 23.11.2021).

21 A list of quotations by James Baldwin can be found here: 'James Baldwin > Quotes', *Goodreads*, www.goodreads.com/author/quotes/10427.James_Baldwin (accessed 23.11.2021).

22 Cone, *Said I Wasn't Gonna Tell Nobody*, pp. 170–4.

23 Details on the Selly Oak Colleges can be found here: 'Selly Oak Colleges', *Wikipedia*, https://en.wikipedia.org/wiki/Selly_Oak_Colleges (accessed 30.11.2021).

24 Cone, *Said I Wasn't Gonna Tell Nobody*, p. vi.

Index of Names and Subjects

Abelard, Peter 22
abolition 85, 110
African diaspora 59, 98, 105, 110–11, 132, 158, 199
All Lives Matter 32, 99
Allen, Richard 127
alpha male 172, 186
Alt-Right 144
American Academy of Religion 23, 26, 203
'American Dream' 158, 166
American South 4, 18, 29, 66, 160, 198
Anansi 106
Angiolini, Elish 74, 79n49
  'Report of the Independent Review of Deaths and Serious Incidents in Police Custody' 73–4, 78n49
Anselm, Saint 22, 23, 38
anti-Christ 24, 66, 147
anti-intellectualism 36, 87
anti-racism 63, 77n20, 144, 164
anti-Semitism 32, 122
apartheid 42
Aquinas, Thomas of 22, 23
Arnold, Selwyn 31

Badenoch, Kemi 144
Baker, Moses 151
Baldwin, James 9, 102, 176, 203
BAME communities 73–4
Barth, Karl 41, 59, 104, 130, 131, 179, 183, 193–5
Beckford, Robert 17, 33n13, 89, 106, 109, 149, 187
Birmingham University Methodist Society 130

Black Christian Studies 17
Black experience 57, 76, 86, 87, 97, 101, 103, 104–6, 113, 121, 128, 171, 200–1, 203
  and the Bible 107–9
Black Lives Matter movement 66, 78n28, 87–8, 99, 122–5, 170–1
Black messiah 66, 186
Black nationalism 66, 100, 157, 169
Black Pentecostalism 4, 30, 107, 108
Black Power (movement) 29–30, 41, 44, 66, 100, 103, 109, 165, 189
  see also Civil Rights movement statement 86 see also National Committee of Negro Churchmen
Black power 24, 97, 99–100, 101, 123–7, 128
Black psyche 67, 71, 148
Black suffering and oppression 22, 26, 29, 37, 38, 46, 58–9, 62, 64, 68, 71–2, 101, 110, 121, 127, 135, 149, 164, 168, 176–9, 183–5, 193
Black Theology (journal) 34n14, 79n50, 84
Black Theology and Black Power (James Cone) 3, 6, 8–9, 15, 26, 47, 57, 99, 102, 121–8, 140, 184, 195, 199
Black Theology in Britain conference 79n50
Black Theology in Britain Forum 26, 33–4n13
A Black Theology of Liberation (James Cone) 3, 8, 29, 36, 41, 66, 82, 104, 121–36, 140
Black working class 38, 105, 110

INTRODUCING JAMES H. CONE

blues (music) 105–6, 139
Boateng, Lord Paul 180
Bonhoeffer, Dietrich 51–2, 100–1, 143, 184
Brexit 124
Britain First 75
Britishness 25

Calloway, Jamall 38–9
cancel culture 123, 143
Christianity 32, 50, 57–8, 63, 91, 102, 123, 125, 129, 131, 133, 135, 142–6, 147, 152, 157, 159, 167, 168, 170, 179, 182, 185, 187, 189, 200
   African, Afrocentric 110, 113, 169
   American 4, 46, 57, 61, 84, 147, 163
   Black 8, 51, 58–9, 68, 83, 87–8, 90–2, 107, 141, 172
   British 61, 90, 93
   corruption of 2, 68, 86
   Mission, missionary 25, 89, 91, 148
   White 24, 42, 44, 45, 47, 57, 59, 61, 69, 71, 83, 90, 148, 180, 182
   World 113, 170
Christology 7, 39, 41–2, 57, 59, 60, 74, 183 see also Jesus Christ
church 5, 8, 21, 25, 27, 29, 30, 47, 51, 73, 80–3, 84–6, 88–9, 90–2, 106, 108, 111, 130, 133, 134, 135, 148, 160, 166, 167, 168, 170, 183
   African Methodist Episcopal (AME) 4, 37, 48, 57, 86, 88, 148
   African Methodist Episcopal Zion (AMEZ) 148
   Black 4, 6, 8, 30, 37, 52, 57, 58, 59, 65, 81, 86–8, 91, 100, 127, 132, 147, 148, 151, 152, 153, 167, 187, 201
   Christian Methodist Episcopal (CME) 148
   divine calling of 81
   as gift of God 81
   Methodist Church 5, 27, 34n14, 46, 85, 133, 148, 150, 179–80, 202
   St George's, Philadelphia 127
   Trinity United, Chicago 147 see also Obama, Barack
   White 30, 47, 65, 68, 81–2, 85, 88
Church of England 40, 42, 69, 91, 133
Civil Rights movement 44, 78n28, 87, 88, 103, 160, 162, 165 see also Black Power
Claiming The Inheritance (group) 5
class analysis 32
Cleage, Revd Albert 2–3, 53, 66, 103, 121, 169
   Black Messiah 2
Cleophat, Nixon 169
colonialism, colonization 42, 47, 62, 67, 70, 75, 109, 110, 126, 134, 135, 138n20, 144, 146, 148, 177, 184, 196, 197
colorism 67
'colour-blind' approaches 102–3, 113, 133
Commission on Racial Justice (Church of England) 91
Copping, Harold 77n17
   'The Healer' (painting) 62
Council for World Mission 50
   'Legacies of Slavery' project 61, 62
   'Unmasking Empire' strategy 50
Covid-19 64, 77n24, 89, 111–12, 153 see also vaccine, vaccination provision
The Critic (magazine) 136n4
Critical Race Theory (CRT) 7, 40, 42
cross 10, 17–18, 31, 44, 51, 69, 75, 83, 143–4, 180–6
   connection with Black bodies 17, 176–7, 181, 183
   mystery of 72
The Cross and the Lynching Tree (James Cone) 9, 17, 51, 65, 70, 100, 175–89
Cruchley, Peter 61, 62
crucifixion 10, 18, 60, 70–1, 126, 175
culture wars 69

dialectical spirituality 106, 107
disability 32
discipleship 44, 51, 52, 83, 129, 185, 199

INDEX OF NAMES AND SUBJECTS

disenfranchisement 42, 58, 62, 105, 136
Douglas, Kelly Brown 67, 87, 175

Eadie, Revd Donald 180
Ecumenical Association of Third World Theologians (EATWOT) 89
empire 20, 25, 47, 61, 67, 68, 91, 92, 109, 123, 125, 126, 134, 144, 148, 168, 184 *see also* colonialism, imperialism
Erskine, Noel 9, 169
European expansion 45, 146, 197
Evangelical Christians for Racial Justice 5
Exodus 41, 45
Eze, Emmanuel 19, 110

faith 3, 8, 15, 25, 28, 29, 37, 38, 39, 46–7, 57, 59, 68, 72, 74, 83, 86, 87, 90, 97, 109, 122, 127, 130, 134, 136, 139, 141–3, 147–8, 153, 159, 168, 182, 188–9, 198, 202
  Christ of 8, 62, 66, 67
Fisher, Earle 53, 159
Floyd, George 26, 48, 50, 60, 63, 73, 114n3, 125, 145, 149, 164, 180, 206
For My People (James Cone) 192
formation 2, 4, 37, 57–9, 86, 134, 150, 153–4, 160, 177, 199, 207n4
freedom 65, 76, 81, 82, 86, 89, 100, 103, 107, 108, 142, 159, 163, 168, 171, 172, 186
  in Christ 144
Freire, Paulo 142
  Pedagogy of the Oppressed 155n6
'From Lament to Action' (Racism Task Force report) 40
fundamentalism 108

Garlington, Tee 167
Garrett Evangelical Theological Seminary 59
Garvey, Marcus 48–9, 64, 100, 169
genocide 25, 42, 45, 64
global North 85, 89, 153, 176
global South 45, 48, 86, 88, 89, 153

God
  of the Bible 37, 40, 41, 45, 129, 176
  is Black 41, 48, 50–2
  of Black theology 36–53
  doctrine of 7, 8, 38, 40–2, 43, 47–8, 49, 52, 64, 131, 183
  existence of 37–8, 40, 61, 141
  of history 37
  image of 49, 98, 168
  of the oppressed 32, 38, 43, 139, 193
  righteousness of 7, 27, 44, 63, 66, 80, 102, 124–5, 145
  Western constructions of 38
God of the Oppressed (James Cone) 9, 40, 47, 63, 122, 129, 139–54, 182
grace 46, 51, 185
  'cheap' 83, 143, 184, 188
Grant, Jacquelyn 33n8, 42, 59, 76, 136
  White Women's Christ and Black Women's Jesus 42
Great Commission (Matthew 28) 45
Gutiérrez, Gustavo 29
  A Theology of Liberation 29, 128

Hall, Delroy 110
Haslam, Revd David 180
hermeneutics 3, 41, 58, 70, 102, 104, 107, 108, 121, 127, 169
  'nitty-gritty' 71
heteronormativity 6, 92
Holy Spirit 38, 80–1, 132, 182, 200
homophobia 6
Hopkins, Dwight 5, 12n12, 30, 87
hypocrisy 30, 57, 58, 61, 125, 136, 143, 168

imperialism 48, 125, 126, 127, 149, 184 *see also* empire
Inclusive Church movement 5, 12n11
intellectual development 23, 203
inter-faith dialogue 32
Isiorho, David 75, 79n50

Jagessar, Michael N. 106, 133
Jennings, Willie James 20, 137n18, 163, 196–8
  After Whiteness 20, 196

Jesus Christ 7, 18, 25, 30, 38, 40, 41, 43, 44, 46, 47, 51, 58, 59, 74, 75, 80, 81-2, 85, 97, 102, 108, 125, 126, 129-32, 135, 142, 147, 153, 157, 170, 175-6, 181, 182, 200 *see also* Christology
Blackness of 62-7, 69-70
gospel of 3, 29, 52, 84, 103, 108, 109, 123, 124, 125, 128, 136, 143, 144
of history 42, 58, 60, 62-3, 66, 67, 69
life, death and resurrection of 8, 39, 45, 57, 59, 72, 141
'one of us' 62, 70, 81
was a Jew 58, 60, 61
White 26, 62, 67, 69
Jewish people 51
Jim, Jane Crow (era, laws) 4, 42, 44, 65, 100
John, Gus 133
Johnson, Andre 28, 30
Johnson, Boris 63
Johnson, Cedric 110
Jones, Absalom 127
Jones, William R. 38-9, 71
Is God A White Racist? 38
Joseph, Celucien 169
Judea 18, 60
Judeo-Christian tradition 45, 106, 129, 139, 142, 159, 169, 183
justice 27, 28, 30, 32, 44, 47, 52, 88, 92, 100, 103, 113, 123, 136-7n4, 142, 151, 152, 164, 165, 168, 171, 178, 186
racial 5, 7, 42, 52, 69, 73, 162, 166, 167, 180, 184

Kant, Emmanuel 110
Kierkegaard, Søren 184
King Jr, Martin Luther (MLK) 4, 9, 100, 102, 128, 157, 159-62, 184, 186
Ku Klux Klan 63, 75

Lartey, Emmanuel 33n13
Lee, James Michael 150-1
'Legacies of Slavery' project 61 *see also* Council for World Mission
liberation 27, 29, 30, 36, 37, 40, 43, 47, 52, 65, 81, 87, 88, 90, 92, 104, 113, 127, 128-30, 131, 139, 142-4, 146, 150, 153, 162, 179, 183, 184, 186, 193
Liele, George 151
Long, Charles 132
lynching 10, 18, 59, 68, 70-1, 72, 83, 92, 176

Maafa 110
Malcolm X 9, 100, 127, 157-9, 160-1, 163-4, 166, 168-9, 171-2, 203
marginalization 60, 69, 70, 148, 181, 185
Marley, Bob 106
Martin & Malcolm & America (James Cone) 9, 122, 140, 157-72
Marxism 7, 89
Mays, Benjamin E. 3, 127
McCarran-Walter Act 1952 158
McCurbin, Clinton, death of 72-3
McDonald, Chine 48
God is not a White Man 48
McKenzie, Dulcie Dixon 33-4n13
media 40, 69, 73, 92, 101, 147
Methodist Conference 90, 180
Mohammed, Elijah 160
Montgomery Bus boycott (1955) 160
Moore, Captain Tom 68
Moore, David 133
moral relativism 63
Mulrain, George 33n13
My Soul Looks Back (James Cone) 10, 28, 39, 45, 86, 192

Nanny of the Maroons 199
National Committee of Negro Churchmen 87 *see also* Black Power
Nation of Islam 160, 168, 169
neo-conservatism 87
neoliberal 111, 112
neo-Pentecostalism 88, 108, 185
Niebuhr, Reinhold 101, 178-9, 190n9

Obama, Barack 146-7, 178, 190n9
Oglesby, Enoch 167
Oluwale, David, death of 72

INDEX OF NAMES AND SUBJECTS

oppression 16, 37, 38, 59–60, 124, 126, 142, 147–8, 176, 177, 181, 184–5
Oxford Institute for Methodist Theological Studies 85, 94n16

Palestine 58, 63, 67
pardna 186, 190n18
pastoral ministry 53, 110
Patel, Priti 144
patriarchy 33n8, 114, 135, 196
Pentecost 80
Perkinson, James 42, 148
Pinn, Anthony 71–2, 132
  Why Lord? 71
  Varieties of African American Religious Experience 132
  Terror and Triumph 71, 132
police 63, 72, 99, 114–15n3
  custody, deaths in 50, 73–4
  Independent Police Complaints Commission (IPCC) 73
Pontius Pilate 60–1, 62, 69, 74, 125
post-colonial 89, 91, 110, 127, 135, 179
postmodern 124, 144
Program to Combat Racism 179 *see also* World Council of Churches
prosperity gospel 88, 185–8

Queen's Foundation for Ecumenical Theological Education (was Queen's College) 10, 17, 26, 33–4n13, 34n14, 79n50, 89, 101, 133, 175, 200, 202

Raboteau, Albert 68, 105
  Slave Religion 68
race 28, 31–2, 48, 64, 90, 102, 108, 109, 145–6, 149, 162, 163, 166, 179, 206
racism 2, 4, 16, 26, 31–2, 47–9, 63, 65, 67, 70, 73–5, 86, 88, 90, 92, 99–101, 108–10, 112, 125, 127–8, 135, 136, 143–6, 149, 153, 160, 163–4, 166–8, 179, 180, 186, 193, 206
Rastafari 169
reconciliation 101–3
Reform (magazine) 147

Reid-Salmon, Delroy 186
respectability politics 25, 87, 88
Roberts, J. Deotis 30
Robinson-Brown, Jarel 6, 68–9, 92
Roman imperialism 125, 126
Roman occupation 75, 125

safe space 86, 151
Said I Wasn't Gonna Tell Nobody (James Cone) 1, 7, 23–4, 58, 97, 103, 140, 192–206
salvation 46–7, 50, 51, 82, 83, 125–6, 143, 153, 178
segregation 2, 42, 65, 68, 100, 162
self-determination 19, 49, 98, 100, 101, 103, 109, 113, 114, 124, 134, 157, 162, 163, 168, 170, 172, 198
Sewell, Tony 101
sexism 32, 33n8, 135
Scripture 37, 40, 52, 65, 80, 81, 104, 108, 126, 129, 135, 165, 183, 200
Sharpe, Sam 186
sin 2, 18, 25, 31, 75, 98, 144, 167, 168
'Theology's Great Sin: Silence in the Face of White Supremacy' 123
slavery 4, 16, 28, 30, 42, 48, 65, 67–8, 71, 84–6, 91, 99, 109, 110, 135, 144, 146, 147, 169, 176–7, 186
  modern 32
slave ship *Jesus* 68
social media 40, 92
  Twitter 95n43
Society for the Study of Theology conference 204
'Speak Black truth to White power' 28, 31, 126
Speaking the Truth (James Cone) 45, 84, 89, 90
The Spirituals and the Blues (James Cone) 10, 104–5, 139, 157
spirituals (music) 30, 105–6, 139–40
SS *Empire Windrush* 90, 152, 155n18
Stone, Selina 91–2
Student Christian Movement 130
suffering 8, 22, 23, 26, 29, 37–40, 42, 44, 46–7, 51, 58–60, 62–4, 67–8, 71, 72, 75, 82, 101, 105,

110, 114, 121, 123, 127–8, 135, 149, 164, 168, 175–7, 178–9, 181, 183–5, 187, 193

theology 2, 6, 7, 21, 22, 25, 27, 31–2, 38, 42, 43, 50, 59, 69, 80, 82, 84, 97, 98, 122, 123–4, 128, 129, 130, 131, 133, 146, 147, 167, 175, 179, 183, 184, 194, 198, 201–2, 207n4
African 59, 114, 127
Black liberation 2–5, 7–8, 15–17, 30, 39, 41, 43, 49, 53, 57–9, 62, 67, 80, 86–8, 97, 99, 102, 104–9, 113–14, 124, 125–8, 131–6, 140–2, 146, 152–4, 157, 159, 163, 164–6, 169–71, 175, 176, 184, 185, 189, 193–4, 195, 199, 200, 201, 202, 204–5
Caribbean 31, 59, 127
Catholic 84
colour-blind 108, 162
contextual 5–6, 146, 194
feminist 5
Latin American 31, 59
liberal 36
liberation 6, 30, 135
practical 15, 114n1, 195
'Public' 113
systematic 52, 97, 131, 194
Trinitarian 7, 42, 57
White 21, 42–3, 46, 165, 195, 196
'woke' 40
womanist 33n8, 59, 135, 199
Thurman, Howard 3–4, 58, 127
Tillich, Paul 104, 130
Trump, Donald 63, 124, 146, 148
Tubman, Harriet 199
Turner, Henry McNeal 48, 127

Union Theological Seminary 22, 42, 51, 53, 83
University of Birmingham 17, 21, 34, 73, 182

vaccine, vaccination provision 64, 89, 112, 153 see also Covid-19

Vodou 169

Waller, Fats 98
  'Black and Blue' 98
Ware, Frederick 170
Wesley, John 31, 85, 92, 134, 197
White
  entitlement and privilege 63, 75, 76, 82, 103, 123, 143, 145, 146, 180, 189, 201
  microaggression 144, 149
  missionaries 25, 62, 144
  normality, normativity 19, 25, 42, 58, 145
  supremacy 2, 6, 16, 17, 18, 24–5, 28, 29, 30, 31–2, 41, 42, 44, 47–8, 49, 58, 59, 61, 62–4, 67, 68, 69, 75, 76, 79n52, 82, 84–6, 98, 99, 100, 101, 103, 107, 112, 113, 123, 124, 126, 135, 141–5, 148, 152, 153, 165, 168, 169, 171, 184, 193, 197
  theological scholarship 18
Whiteness 20, 21, 24, 25, 32, 42, 48, 62, 64, 69, 85–6, 91, 92, 93, 103, 110, 115n22, 123, 124, 134, 145, 146, 147, 163, 166, 170, 178–9, 194, 195, 196–8, 201
Williams, Delores 136, 176
Williams, Reggie 51, 101
  Bonhoeffer's Black Jesus 51
Wilmore, Gayraud 86, 87
  Black Religion and Black Radicalism 86
Windrush generation 38, 91, 145, 151
witch hunt 68
woke 63, 122, 143, 144
World Council of Churches (WCC) 179
World War One 100
World War Two 38, 91, 151
Wright Jr, Revd Dr Jeremiah 147

Young, Josiah 83

www.ingramcontent.com/pod-product-compliance
Lightning Source LLC
Chambersburg PA
CBHW022054290426
44109CB00014B/1091